Programming in Haskell

Second Edition

Haskell is a purely functional language that allows programmers to rapidly develop clear, concise and correct software. The language has grown in popularity in recent years, both in teaching and in industry. This book is based on the author's experience of teaching Haskell for more than 20 years. All concepts are explained from first principles and no programming experience is required, making this book accessible to a broad spectrum of readers. While Part I focuses on basic concepts, Part II introduces the reader to more advanced topics.

This new edition has been extensively updated and expanded to include recent and more advanced features of Haskell, new examples and exercises, selected solutions, and freely downloadable lecture slides and code. The presentation is clean and simple, while also being fully compliant with the latest version of the language, including recent changes concerning applicative, monadic, foldable and traversable types.

Graham Hutton is Professor of Computer Science at the University of Nottingham. He has taught Haskell to thousands of students and received numerous best lecturer awards. Hutton has served as an editor of the *Journal of Functional Programming*, chair of the Haskell Symposium and the International Conference on Functional Programming, vice-chair of the ACM Special Interest Group on Programming Languages, and he is an ACM Distinguished Scientist.

Programming in Haskell

Second Edition

GRAHAM HUTTON

University of Nottingham

CAMBRIDGE
UNIVERSITY PRESS

CAMBRIDGE
UNIVERSITY PRESS

University Printing House, Cambridge CB2 8BS, United Kingdom

One Liberty Plaza, 20th Floor, New York, NY 10006, USA

477 Williamstown Road, Port Melbourne, VIC 3207, Australia

4843/24, 2nd Floor, Ansari Road, Daryaganj, Delhi - 110002, India

79 Anson Road, #06-04/06, Singapore 079906

Cambridge University Press is part of the University of Cambridge.

It furthers the University's mission by disseminating knowledge in the pursuit of education, learning, and research at the highest international levels of excellence.

www.cambridge.org
Information on this title: www.cambridge.org/9781316626221
10.1017/9781316784099

First published 2007
Second edition 2016

Printed in the United Statesiof America by Sheridan Books, Inc.

A catalogue record for this publication is available from the British Library

ISBN 978-1-316-62622-1 Paperback

For Annette, Callum and Tom

Contents

Foreword

It is nearly a century ago that Alonzo Church introduced the lambda calculus, and over half a century ago that John McCarthy introduced Lisp, the world's second oldest programming language and the first functional language based on the lambda calculus. By now, every major programming language including JavaScript, C++, Swift, Python, PHP, Visual Basic, Java, ... has support for lambda expressions or anonymous higher-order functions.

As with any idea that becomes mainstream, inevitably the underlying foundations and principles get watered down or forgotten. Lisp allowed mutation, yet today many confuse functions as first-class citizens with immutability. At the same time, other effects such as exceptions, reflection, communication with the outside world, and concurrency go unmentioned. Adding recursion in the form of feedback-loops to pure combinational circuits lets us implement mutable state via flip-flops. Similarly, using one effect such as concurrency or input/output we can simulate other effects such as mutability. John Hughes famously stated in his classic paper *Why Functional Programming Matters* that we cannot make a language more powerful by eliminating features. To that, we add that often we cannot even make a language less powerful by removing features. In this book, Graham demonstrates convincingly that the true value of functional programming lies in leveraging first-class functions to achieve compositionality and equational reasoning. Or in Graham's own words, "functional programming can be viewed as a style of programming in which the basic method of computation is the application of functions to arguments". These functions do not necessarily have to be pure or statically typed in order to realise the simplicity, elegance, and conciseness of expression that we get from the functional style.

While you can code like a functional hacker in a plethora of languages, a semantically pure and lazy, and syntactically lean and terse language such as Haskell is still the best way to learn how to think like a fundamentalist. Based upon decades of teaching experience, and backed by an impressive stream of research papers, in this book Graham gently guides us through the whole gambit of key functional programming concepts such as higher-order functions, recursion, list comprehensions, algebraic datatypes and pattern matching. The book does not shy away from more advanced concepts. If you are still confused by the n-th blog post that attempts to explain monads, you are in the right place. Gently starting with the IO monad, Graham progresses from functors to applicatives using many concrete examples. By the time he arrives at monads, every reader will feel that they themselves could have come up with the concept of a monad as a generic pattern for composing functions with effects. The chapter on monadic parsers brings everything together in a compelling use-case of parsing arithmetic expressions in the implementation of a simple calculator.

This new edition not only adds many more concrete examples of concepts introduced throughout the book, it also introduces the novel Haskell concepts of foldable and traversable types. Readers familiar with object-oriented languages routinely use iterables and visitors to enumerate over all values in a container, or respectively to traverse complex data structures. Haskell's higher-kinded type classes allow for a very concise and abstract treatment of these concepts by means of the Foldable and Traversable classes. Last but not least, the final chapters of the book give an in-depth overview of lazy evaluation and equational reasoning to prove and derive programs. The capstone chapter on calculating compilers especially appeals to me because it touches a topic that has had my keen interest for many decades, ever since my own PhD thesis on the same topic.

While there are plenty of alternative textbooks on Haskell in particular and functional programming in general, Graham's book is unique amongst all of these in that it uses Haskell simply as a tool for thought, and never attempts to sell Haskell or functional programming as a silver bullet that magically solves all programming problems. It focuses on elegant and concise expression of intent and thus makes a strong case of how pure and lazy functional programming is an intelligible medium for efficiently reasoning about algorithms at a high level of abstraction. The skills you acquire by studying this book will make you a much better programmer no matter what language you use to actually program in. In the past decade, using the first edition of this book I have taught many tens of thousands of students how to juggle with code. With this new edition, I am looking forward to extending this streak for at least another 10 years.

Erik Meijer

Preface

What is this book?

Haskell is a purely functional language that allows programmers to rapidly develop software that is clear, concise and correct. The book is aimed at a broad spectrum of readers who are interested in learning the language, including professional programmers, university students and high-school students. However, no programming experience is required or assumed, and all concepts are explained from first principles with the aid of carefully chosen examples and exercises. Most of the material in the book should be accessible to anyone over the age of around sixteen with a reasonable aptitude for scientific ideas.

How is it structured?

The book is divided into two parts. Part I introduces the basic concepts of pure programming in Haskell and is structured around the core features of the language, such as types, functions, list comprehensions, recursion and higher-order functions. Part II covers impure programming and a range of more advanced topics, such as monads, parsing, foldable types, lazy evaluation and reasoning about programs. The book contains many extended programming examples, and each chapter includes suggestions for further reading and a series of exercises. The appendices provide solutions to selected exercises, and a summary of some of the most commonly used definitions from the Haskell standard prelude.

What is its approach?

The book aims to teach the key concepts of Haskell in a clean and simple manner. As this is a textbook rather than a reference manual we do not attempt to cover all aspects of the language and its libraries, and we sometimes choose to define functions from first principles rather than using library functions. As the book progresses the level of generality that is used is gradually increased. For example, in the beginning most of the functions that are used are specialised to simple types, and later on we see how many functions can be generalised to larger classes of types by exploiting particular features of Haskell.

How should it be read?

The basic material in part I can potentially be worked through fairly quickly, particularly for those with some prior programming experience, but additional time and effort may be required to absorb some of material in part II. Readers are recommended to work through all the material in part I, and then select appropriate material from part II depending on their own interests. It is vital to write Haskell code for yourself as you go along, as you can't learn to program just by reading. Try out the examples from each chapter as you proceed, and solve the exercises for each chapter before checking the solutions.

What's new in this edition?

The book is an extensively revised and expanded version of the first edition. It has been extended with new chapters that cover more advanced aspects of Haskell, new examples and exercises to further reinforce the concepts being introduced, and solutions to selected exercises. The remaining material has been completely reworked in response to changes in the language and feedback from readers. The new edition uses the Glasgow Haskell Compiler (GHC), and is fully compatible with the latest version of the language, including recent changes concerning applicative, monadic, foldable and traversable types.

How can it be used for teaching?

An introductory course might cover all of part I and a few selected topics from part II; my first-year course covers chapters 1–9, 10 and 15. An advanced course might start with a refresher of part I, and cover a selection of more advanced topics from part II; my second-year course focuses on chapters 12 and 16, and is taught interactively on the board. The website for the book provides a range of supporting materials, including PowerPoint slides and Haskell code for the extended examples. Instructors can obtain a large collection of exams and solutions based on material in the book from `solutions@cambridge.org`.

Acknowledgements

I am grateful to the University of Nottingham for providing a sabbatical to produce this new edition; Thorsten Altenkirch, Venanzio Capretta, Henrik Nilsson and other members of the FP lab for our many enjoyable discussions; Iván Pérez Domínguez for useful comments on a number of chapters; the students and tutors on all of my Haskell courses for their feedback; Clare Dennison, David Tranah and Abigail Walkington at CUP for their editorial work; the GHC team for producing such a great compiler; and finally, Catherine and Ian Hutton for getting me started in computing all those years ago.

Many thanks also to Ki Yung Ahn, Bob Davison, Philip Hölzenspies and Neil Mitchell for providing detailed comments on the first edition, and to the following for pointing our errors and typos: Paul Brown, Sergio Queiroz de Medeiros, David Duke, Robert Fabian, Ben Fleis, Robert Furber, Andrew Kish, Tomoyas Kobayashi, Florian Larysch, Carlos Oroz, Douglas Philips, Bruce Turner, Gregor Ulm, Marco Valtorta and Kazu Yamamoto. All of these comments have been taken into account when preparing the new edition.

Graham Hutton

Part I

Basic Concepts

1   Introduction

In this chapter we set the stage for the rest of the book. We start by reviewing the notion of a function, then introduce the concept of functional programming, summarise the main features of Haskell and its historical background, and conclude with three small examples that give a taste of Haskell.

1.1   Functions

In Haskell, a *function* is a mapping that takes one or more arguments and produces a single result, and is defined using an equation that gives a name for the function, a name for each of its arguments, and a body that specifies how the result can be calculated in terms of the arguments.

For example, a function `double` that takes a number x as its argument, and produces the result x + x, can be defined by the following equation:

```
double x = x + x
```

When a function is applied to actual arguments, the result is obtained by substituting these arguments into the body of the function in place of the argument names. This process may immediately produce a result that cannot be further simplified, such as a number. More commonly, however, the result will be an expression containing other function applications, which must then be processed in the same way to produce the final result.

For example, the result of the application `double 3` of the function `double` to the number 3 can be determined by the following calculation, in which each step is explained by a short comment in curly parentheses:

```
    double 3
=       { applying double }
    3 + 3
=       { applying + }
    6
```

Similarly, the result of the nested application `double (double 2)` in which the function `double` is applied twice can be calculated as follows:

```
    double (double 2)
```

```
=        { applying the inner double }
double (2 + 2)
=        { applying + }
double 4
=        { applying double }
4 + 4
=        { applying + }
8
```

Alternatively, the same result can also be calculated by starting with the outer application of the function double rather than the inner:

```
double (double 2)
=        { applying the outer double }
double 2 + double 2
=        { applying the first double }
(2 + 2) + double 2
=        { applying the first + }
4 + double 2
=        { applying double }
4 + (2 + 2)
=        { applying the second + }
4 + 4
=        { applying + }
8
```

However, this approach requires two more steps than our original version, because the expression double 2 is duplicated in the first step and hence simplified twice. In general, the order in which functions are applied in a calculation does not affect the value of the final result, but it may affect the number of steps required, and whether the calculation process terminates. These issues are explored in more detail when we consider how expressions are evaluated in chapter 15.

1.2   Functional programming

What is functional programming? Opinions differ, and it is difficult to give a precise definition. Generally speaking, however, functional programming can be viewed as a *style* of programming in which the basic method of computation is the application of functions to arguments. In turn, a functional programming language is one that *supports* and *encourages* the functional style.

To illustrate these ideas, let us consider the task of computing the sum of the integers (whole numbers) between one and some larger number n. In many current programming languages, this would normally be achieved using two integer variables whose values can be changed over time by means of the assignment operator =, with one such variable used to accumulate the total, and the other used to count from 1 to n. For example, in Java the following program computes the required sum using this approach:

```
int total = 0;
for (int count = 1; count <= n; count++)
    total = total + count;
```

That is, we first initialise an integer variable total to zero, and then enter a loop that ranges an integer variable count from 1 to n, adding the current value of the counter to the total each time round the loop.

In the above program, the basic method of computation is *changing stored values*, in the sense that executing the program results in a sequence of assignments. For example, the case of n = 5 gives the following sequence, in which the final value assigned to the variable total is the required sum:

```
total = 0;
count = 1;
total = 1;
count = 2;
total = 3;
count = 3;
total = 6;
count = 4;
total = 10;
count = 5;
total = 15;
```

In general, programming languages such as Java in which the basic method of computation is changing stored values are called *imperative* languages, because programs in such languages are constructed from imperative instructions that specify precisely how the computation should proceed.

Now let us consider computing the sum of the numbers between one and n using Haskell. This would normally be achieved using two library functions, one called [..] that is used to produce the list of numbers between 1 and n, and the other called sum that is used to produce the sum of this list:

```
sum [1..n]
```

In this program, the basic method of computation is *applying functions to arguments*, in the sense that executing the program results in a sequence of applications. For example, the case of n = 5 gives the following sequence, in which the final value in the sequence is the required sum:

```
    sum [1..5]
=       { applying [..] }
    sum [1,2,3,4,5]
```

$$= \quad \{ \text{ applying } \texttt{sum} \}$$
$$1 + 2 + 3 + 4 + 5$$
$$= \quad \{ \text{ applying } \texttt{+} \}$$
$$15$$

Most imperative languages provide some form of support for programming with functions, so the Haskell program `sum [1..n]` could be translated into such languages. However, many imperative languages do not *encourage* programming in the functional style. For example, many such languages discourage or prohibit functions from being stored in data structures such as lists, from constructing intermediate structures such as the list of numbers in the above example, from taking functions as arguments or producing functions as results, or from being defined in terms of themselves. In contrast, Haskell imposes no such restrictions on how functions can be used, and provides a range of features to make programming with functions both simple and powerful.

1.3   Features of Haskell

For reference, the main features of Haskell are listed below, along with particular chapters of this book that give further details.

- **Concise programs** (chapters 2 and 4)

  Due to the high-level nature of the functional style, programs written in Haskell are often much more *concise* than programs written in other languages, as illustrated by the example in the previous section. Moreover, the syntax of Haskell has been designed with concise programs in mind, in particular by having few keywords, and by allowing indentation to be used to indicate the structure of programs. Although it is difficult to make an objective comparison, Haskell programs are often between two and ten times shorter than programs written in other languages.

- **Powerful type system** (chapters 3 and 8)

  Most modern programming languages include some form of *type system* to detect incompatibility errors, such as erroneously attempting to add a number and a character. Haskell has a type system that usually requires little type information from the programmer, but allows a large class of incompatibility errors in programs to be automatically detected prior to their execution, using a sophisticated process called type inference. The Haskell type system is also more powerful than most languages, supporting very general forms of *polymorphism* and *overloading*, and providing a wide range of special purpose features concerning types.

- **List comprehensions** (chapter 5)

  One of the most common ways to structure and manipulate data in computing is using lists of values. To this end, Haskell provides lists as a basic concept in the language, together with a simple but powerful *comprehension* notation that constructs new lists by selecting and filtering elements from one or more existing lists. Using the comprehension notation allows many common functions on lists to be defined in a clear and concise manner, without the need for explicit recursion.

- **Recursive functions** (chapter 6)

  Most programs involve some form of looping. In Haskell, the basic mechanism by which looping is achieved is through *recursive* functions that are defined in terms of themselves. It can take some time to get used to recursion, particularly for those with experience of programming in other styles. But as we shall see, many computations have a simple and natural definition in terms of recursive functions, especially when *pattern matching* and *guards* are used to separate different cases into different equations.

- **Higher-order functions** (chapter 7)

  Haskell is a *higher-order* functional language, which means that functions can freely take functions as arguments and produce functions as results. Using higher-order functions allows common programming patterns, such as composing two functions, to be defined as functions within the language itself. More generally, higher-order functions can be used to define *domain-specific languages* within Haskell itself, such as for list processing, interactive programming, and parsing.

- **Effectful functions** (chapters 10 and 12)

  Functions in Haskell are pure functions that take all their inputs as arguments and produce all their outputs as results. However, many programs require some form of *side effect* that would appear to be at odds with purity, such as reading input from the keyboard, or writing output to the screen, while the program is running. Haskell provides a uniform framework for programming with effects, without compromising the purity of functions, based upon the use of *monads* and *applicatives*.

- **Generic functions** (chapters 12 and 14)

  Most languages allow functions to be defined that are *generic* over a range of simple types, such as different forms of numbers. However, the Haskell type system also supports functions that are generic over much richer kinds of structures. For example, the language provides a range of library functions that can be used with any type that is *functorial*, *applicative*, *monadic*, *foldable*, or *traversable*, and moreover, allows new structures and generic functions over them to be defined.

- **Lazy evaluation** (chapter 15)

  Haskell programs are executed using a technique called *lazy evaluation*, which is based upon the idea that no computation should be performed until its result is actually required. As well as avoiding unnecessary computation, lazy evaluation ensures that programs terminate whenever possible, encourages programming in a modular style using intermediate data structures, and even allows programming with infinite structures.

- **Equational reasoning** (chapters 16 and 17)

  Because programs in Haskell are pure functions, simple *equational reasoning* techniques can be used to execute programs, to transform programs, to prove properties of programs, and even to calculate programs directly from specifications of their intended behaviour. Equational reasoning is particularly powerful when combined with the use of *induction* to reason about functions that are defined using recursion.

1.4   Historical background

Many of the features of Haskell are not new, but were first introduced by other languages. To help place Haskell in context, some of the key historical developments related to the language are briefly summarised below:

- In the 1930s, Alonzo Church developed the lambda calculus, a simple but powerful mathematical theory of functions.

- In the 1950s, John McCarthy developed Lisp ("LISt Processor"), generally regarded as being the first functional programming language. Lisp had some influences from the lambda calculus, but still retained the concept of variable assignment as a central feature of the language.

- In the 1960s, Peter Landin developed ISWIM ("If you See What I Mean"), the first pure functional programming language, based strongly on the lambda calculus and having no variable assignments.

- In the 1970s, John Backus developed FP ("Functional Programming"), a functional programming language that particularly emphasised the idea of higher-order functions and reasoning about programs.

- Also in the 1970s, Robin Milner and others developed ML ("Meta-Language"), the first of the modern functional programming languages, which introduced the idea of polymorphic types and type inference.

- In the 1970s and 1980s, David Turner developed a number of lazy functional programming languages, culminating in the commercially produced language Miranda (meaning "admirable").

- In 1987, an international committee of programming language researchers initiated the development of Haskell (named after the logician Haskell Curry), a standard lazy functional programming language.

- In the 1990s, Philip Wadler and others developed the concept of type classes to support overloading, and the use of monads to handle effects, two of the main innovative features of Haskell.

- In 2003, the Haskell committee published the Haskell Report, which defined a long-awaited stable version of the language.

- In 2010, a revised and updated of the Haskell Report was published. Since then the language has continued to evolve, in response to both new foundational developments and new practical experience.

It is worthy of note that three of the above individuals — McCarthy, Backus, and Milner — have each received the ACM Turing Award, which is generally regarded as being the computing equivalent of a Nobel prize.

1.5   A taste of Haskell

We conclude this chapter with three small examples that give a taste of programming in Haskell. The examples involve processing lists of values of different types, and illustrate different features of the language.

Summing numbers

Recall the function **sum** used earlier in this chapter, which produces the sum of a list of numbers. In Haskell, **sum** can be defined using two equations:

```
sum []     = 0
sum (n:ns) = n + sum ns
```

The first equation states that the sum of the empty list is zero, while the second states that the sum of any non-empty list comprising a first number **n** and a remaining list of numbers **ns** is given by adding **n** and the sum of **ns**. For example, the result of **sum [1,2,3]** can be calculated as follows:

```
    sum [1,2,3]
=       { applying sum }
    1 + sum [2,3]
=       { applying sum }
    1 + (2 + sum [3])
=       { applying sum }
    1 + (2 + (3 + sum []))
=       { applying sum }
    1 + (2 + (3 + 0))
=       { applying + }
    6
```

Note that even though the function sum is defined in terms of itself and is hence *recursive*, it does not loop forever. In particular, each application of sum reduces the length of the argument list by one, until the list eventually becomes empty, at which point the recursion stops and the additions are performed. Returning zero as the sum of the empty list is appropriate because zero is the *identity* for addition. That is, $0 + x = x$ and $x + 0 = x$ for any number x.

In Haskell, every function has a *type* that specifies the nature of its arguments and results, which is automatically inferred from the definition of the function. For example, the function sum defined above has the following type:

```
Num a => [a] -> a
```

This type states that for any type a of numbers, sum is a function that maps a list of such numbers to a single such number. Haskell supports many different types of numbers, including integers such as 123, and floating-point numbers such as 3.14159. Hence, for example, sum could be applied to a list of integers, as in the calculation above, or to a list of floating-point numbers.

Types provide useful information about the nature of functions, but, more importantly, their use allows many errors in programs to be automatically detected prior to executing the programs themselves. In particular, for every occurrence of function application in a program, a check is made that the type of the actual arguments is compatible with the type of the function itself. For example, attempting to apply the function sum to a list of characters would be reported as an error, because characters are not a type of numbers.

Sorting values

Now let us consider a more sophisticated function concerning lists, which illustrates a number of other aspects of Haskell. Suppose that we define a function called qsort by the following two equations:

```
qsort []     = []
qsort (x:xs) = qsort smaller ++ [x] ++ qsort larger
               where
                   smaller = [a | a <- xs, a <= x]
                   larger  = [b | b <- xs, b > x]
```

In this definition, ++ is an operator that appends two lists together; for example, [1,2,3] ++ [4,5] = [1,2,3,4,5]. In turn, where is a keyword that introduces local definitions, in this case a list smaller comprising all elements a from the list xs that are less than or equal to x, together with a list larger comprising all elements b from xs that are greater than x. For example, if x = 3 and xs = [5,1,4,2], then smaller = [1,2] and larger = [5,4].

What does qsort actually do? First of all, we note that it has no effect on lists with a single element, in the sense that qsort [x] = [x] for any x. It is easy to verify this property using a simple calculation:

```
    qsort [x]
=       { applying qsort }
    qsort [] ++ [x] ++ qsort []
=       { applying qsort }
    [] ++ [x] ++ []
=       { applying ++ }
    [x]
```

In turn, we now work through the application of qsort to an example list, using the above property to simplify the calculation:

```
    qsort [3,5,1,4,2]
=       { applying qsort }
    qsort [1,2] ++ [3] ++ qsort [5,4]
=       { applying qsort }
    (qsort [] ++ [1] ++ qsort [2]) ++ [3]
      ++ (qsort [4] ++ [5] ++ qsort [])
=       { applying qsort, above property }
    ([] ++ [1] ++ [2]) ++ [3] ++ ([4] ++ [5] ++ [])
=       { applying ++ }
    [1,2] ++ [3] ++ [4,5]
=       { applying ++ }
    [1,2,3,4,5]
```

In summary, qsort has sorted the example list into numerical order. More generally, this function produces a sorted version of any list of numbers. The first equation for qsort states that the empty list is already sorted, while the second states that any non-empty list can be sorted by inserting the first number between the two lists that result from sorting the remaining numbers that are smaller and larger than this number. This method of sorting is called *quicksort*, and is one of the best such methods known.

The above implementation of quicksort is an excellent example of the power of Haskell, being both clear and concise. Moreover, the function qsort is also more general than might be expected, being applicable not just with numbers, but with any type of ordered values. More precisely, the type

```
    qsort :: Ord a => [a] -> [a]
```

states that, for any type a of ordered values, qsort is a function that maps between lists of such values. Haskell supports many different types of ordered values, including numbers, single characters such as 'a', and strings of characters such as "abcde". Hence, for example, the function qsort could also be used to sort a list of characters, or a list of strings.

Sequencing actions

Our third and final example further emphasises the level of precision and generality that can be achieved in Haskell. Consider a function called seqn that takes a list of input/output actions, such as reading or writing a single character, performs each of these actions in sequence, and returns a list of resulting values. In Haskell, this function can be defined as follows:

```
seqn []         = return []
seqn (act:acts) = do x  <- act
                     xs <- seqn acts
                     return (x:xs)
```

These two equations state that if the list of actions is empty we return the empty list of results, otherwise we perform the first action in the list, then perform the remaining actions, and finally return the list of results that were produced. For example, the expression seqn [getChar,getChar,getChar] reads three characters from the keyboard using the action getChar that reads a single character, and returns a list containing the three characters.

The interesting aspect of the function seqn is its type. One possible type that can inferred from the above definition is the following:

```
seqn :: [IO a] -> IO [a]
```

This type states that seqn maps a list of IO (input/output) actions that produce results of some type a to a single IO action that produces a list of such results, which captures the high-level behaviour of seqn in a clear and concise manner. More importantly, however, the type also makes explicit that the function seqn involves the *side effect* of performing input/output actions. Using types in this manner to keep a clear distinction between functions that are pure and those that involve side effects is a central aspect of Haskell, and brings important benefits in terms of both programming and reasoning.

In fact, the function seqn is more general than it may initially appear. In particular, the manner in which the function is defined is not specific to the case of input/output actions, but is equally valid for other forms of effects too. For example, it can also be used to sequence actions that may change stored values, fail to succeed, write to a log file, and so on. This flexibility is captured in Haskell by means of the following more general type:

```
seqn :: Monad m => [m a] -> m [a]
```

That is, for any *monadic* type m, of which IO is just one example, seqn maps a list of actions of type m a into a single action that returns a list of values of type a. Being able to define generic functions such as seqn that can be used with different kinds of effects is a key feature of Haskell.

1.6   Chapter remarks

The Haskell Report is freely available from `http://www.haskell.org`. More detailed historical accounts of the development of functional languages in general, and Haskell in particular, are given in [1] and [2].

1.7   Exercises

1. Give another possible calculation for the result of `double (double 2)`.

2. Show that `sum [x] = x` for any number x.

3. Define a function `product` that produces the product of a list of numbers, and show using your definition that `product [2,3,4] = 24`.

4. How should the definition of the function `qsort` be modified so that it produces a *reverse* sorted version of a list?

5. What would be the effect of replacing `<=` by `<` in the original definition of `qsort`? Hint: consider the example `qsort [2,2,3,1,1]`.

Solutions to exercises 1–3 are given in appendix A.

2 First steps

In this chapter we take our first proper steps with Haskell. We start by introducing the GHC system and the standard prelude, then explain the notation for function application, develop our first Haskell script, and conclude by discussing a number of syntactic conventions concerning scripts.

2.1 Glasgow Haskell Compiler

As we saw in the previous chapter, small Haskell programs can be executed by hand. In practice, however, we usually require a system that can execute programs automatically. In this book we use the *Glasgow Haskell Compiler*, a state-of-the-art, open source implementation of Haskell.

The system has two main components: a batch compiler called GHC, and an interactive interpreter called GHCi. We will primarily use the interpreter in this book, as its interactive nature makes it well suited for teaching and prototyping purposes, and its performance is sufficient for most of our applications. However, if greater performance or a stand-alone executable version of a Haskell program is required, the compiler itself can be used. For example, we will use the compiler in extended programming examples in chapters 9 and 11.

2.2 Installing and starting

The Glasgow Haskell Compiler is freely available for a range of operating systems from the Haskell home page, `http://www.haskell.org`. For first time users we recommend downloading the *Haskell Platform*, which provides a convenient means to install the system and a collection of commonly used libraries. More advanced users may prefer to install the system and libraries manually.

Once installed, the interactive GHCi system can be started from the terminal command prompt, such as $, by simply typing `ghci`:

```
$ ghci
```

All being well, a welcome message will then be displayed:

```
GHCi, version A.B.C: http://www.haskell.org/ghc/  :? for help
Prelude>
```

The GHCi prompt > indicates that the system is now waiting for the user to enter an expression to be evaluated. For example, it can be used as a calculator to evaluate simple numeric expressions:

```
> 2+3*4
14

> (2+3)*4
20

> sqrt (3^2 + 4^2)
5.0
```

Following normal mathematical convention, in Haskell exponentiation is assumed to have higher priority than multiplication and division, which in turn have higher priority than addition and subtraction. For example, 2*3^4 means 2*(3^4), while 2+3*4 means 2+(3*4). Moreover, exponentiation associates (or brackets) to the right, while the other four main arithmetic operators associate to the left. For example, 2^3^4 means 2^(3^4), while 2-3+4 means (2-3)+4. In practice, however, it is often clearer to use explicit parentheses in such expressions, rather than relying on the above rules.

2.3   Standard prelude

Haskell comes with a large number of built-in functions, which are defined in a library file called the *standard prelude*. In addition to familiar numeric functions such as + and *, the prelude also provides a range of useful functions that operate on lists. In Haskell, the elements of a list are enclosed in square parentheses and are separated by commas, as in [1,2,3,4,5]. Some of the most commonly used library functions on lists are illustrated below.

- Select the first element of a non-empty list:

  ```
  > head [1,2,3,4,5]
  1
  ```

- Remove the first element from a non-empty list:

  ```
  > tail [1,2,3,4,5]
  [2,3,4,5]
  ```

- Select the nth element of list (counting from zero):

```
> [1,2,3,4,5] !! 2
3
```

- Select the first n elements of a list:

```
> take 3 [1,2,3,4,5]
[1,2,3]
```

- Remove the first n elements from a list:

```
> drop 3 [1,2,3,4,5]
[4,5]
```

- Calculate the length of a list:

```
> length [1,2,3,4,5]
5
```

- Calculate the sum of a list of numbers:

```
> sum [1,2,3,4,5]
15
```

- Calculate the product of a list of numbers:

```
> product [1,2,3,4,5]
120
```

- Append two lists:

```
> [1,2,3] ++ [4,5]
[1,2,3,4,5]
```

- Reverse a list:

```
> reverse [1,2,3,4,5]
[5,4,3,2,1]
```

As a useful reference guide, appendix B presents some of the most commonly used definitions from the standard prelude.

2.4   Function application

In mathematics, the application of a function to its arguments is usually denoted by enclosing the arguments in parentheses, while the multiplication of two values is often denoted silently, by writing the two values next to one another. For example, in mathematics the expression

$$f(a, b) + c\, d$$

means apply the function f to two arguments a and b, and add the result to the product of c and d. Reflecting its central status in the language, function application in Haskell is denoted silently using spacing, while the multiplication of two values is denoted explicitly using the operator *. For example, the expression above would be written in Haskell as follows:

```
f a b + c*d
```

Moreover, function application has higher priority than all other operators in the language. For example, f a + b means (f a) + b rather than f (a + b). The following table gives a few further examples to illustrate the differences between function application in mathematics and in Haskell:

Mathematics	Haskell
$f(x)$	f x
$f(x, y)$	f x y
$f(g(x))$	f (g x)
$f(x, g(y))$	f x (g y)
$f(x) g(y)$	f x * g y

Note that parentheses are still required in the Haskell expression f (g x) above, because f g x on its own would be interpreted as the application of the function f to two arguments g and x, whereas the intention is that f is applied to one argument, namely the result of applying the function g to an argument x. A similar remark holds for the expression f x (g y).

2.5   Haskell scripts

As well as the functions provided in the standard prelude, it is also possible to define new functions. New functions are defined in a *script*, a text file comprising a sequence of definitions. By convention, Haskell scripts usually have a .hs suffix on their filename to differentiate them from other kinds of files. This is not mandatory, but is useful for identification purposes.

My first script

When developing a Haskell script, it is useful to keep two windows open, one running an editor for the script, and the other running GHCi. As an example, suppose that we start a text editor and type in the following two function definitions, and save the script to a file called test.hs:

```
double x = x + x

quadruple x = double (double x)
```

In turn, suppose that we leave the editor open, and in another window start up the GHCi system and instruct it to load the new script:

```
$ ghci test.hs
```

Now both the standard prelude and the script `test.hs` are loaded, and functions from both can be freely used. For example:

```
> quadruple 10
40

> take (double 2) [1,2,3,4,5]
[1,2,3,4]
```

Now suppose that we leave GHCi open, return to the editor, add the following two function definitions to those already typed in, and resave the file:

```
factorial n = product [1..n]

average ns = sum ns 'div' length ns
```

We could also have defined `average ns = div (sum ns) (length ns)`, but writing `div` between its two arguments is more natural. In general, any function with two arguments can be written between its arguments by enclosing the name of the function in single back quotes ' '.

GHCi does not automatically reload scripts when they are modified, so a reload command must be executed before the new definitions can be used:

```
> :reload

> factorial 10
3628800

> average [1,2,3,4,5]
3
```

For reference, the table in figure 2.1 summarises the meaning of some of the most commonly used GHCi commands. Note that any command can be abbreviated by its first character. For example, `:load` can be abbreviated by `:l`. The command `:set editor` is used to set the text editor that is used by the system. For example, if you wish to use `vim` you would enter `:set editor vim`. The command `:type` is explained in more detail in the next chapter.

Naming requirements

When defining a new function, the names of the function and its arguments must begin with a lower-case letter, but can then be followed by zero or more letters

Command	Meaning
:load name	load script name
:reload	reload current script
:set editor name	set editor to name
:edit name	edit script name
:edit	edit current script
:type expr	show type of expr
:?	show all commands
:quit	quit GHCi

Figure 2.1 Useful GHCi commands

(both lower- and upper-case), digits, underscores, and forward single quotes. For example, the following are all valid names:

$$myFun \quad fun1 \quad arg\_2 \quad x'$$

The following list of *keywords* have a special meaning in the language, and cannot be used as the names of functions or their arguments:

```
case    class   data    default   deriving
    do    else   foreign   if    import   in
  infix   infixl   infixr   instance   let
module   newtype   of    then   type   where
```

By convention, list arguments in Haskell usually have the suffix s on their name to indicate that they may contain multiple values. For example, a list of numbers might be named ns, a list of arbitrary values might be named xs, and a list of lists of characters might be named css.

The layout rule

Within a script, each definition at the same level must begin in precisely the same column. This *layout rule* makes it possible to determine the grouping of definitions from their indentation. For example, in the script

```
a = b + c
    where
        b = 1
        c = 2
d = a * 2
```

it is clear from the indentation that b and c are local definitions for use within the body of a. If desired, such grouping can be made explicit by enclosing a sequence of definitions in curly parentheses and separating each definition by a semi-colon. For example, the above script could also be written as

```
a = b + c
    where
        {b = 1;
         c = 2};
d = a * 2
```

or even be combined into a single line:

```
a = b + c where {b = 1; c = 2}; d = a * 2
```

In general, however, it is usually preferable to rely on the layout rule to determine the grouping of definitions, rather than using explicit syntax.

Tabs

Tab characters can cause problems in scripts, because layout is significant but different text editors interpret tabs in different ways. For this reason, it is recommended to avoid using tabs when indenting definitions, and the GHC system issues a warning message if they are used. If you do wish to use tabs in your scripts, it is best to configure your editor to automatically convert them to spaces. Haskell assumes that tab stops are 8 characters wide.

Comments

In addition to new definitions, scripts can also contain comments that will be ignored by the compiler. Haskell supports two kinds of comments, called *ordinary* and *nested*. Ordinary comments begin with the symbol -- and extend to the end of the current line, as in the following examples:

```
-- Factorial of a positive integer:
factorial n = product [1..n]

-- Average of a list of integers:
average ns = sum ns 'div' length ns
```

Nested comments begin and end with the symbols {- and -}, may span multiple lines, and may be nested in the sense that comments can contain other comments. Nested comments are particularly useful for temporarily removing sections of definitions from a script, as in the following example:

```
{-
double x = x + x

quadruple x = double (double x)
-}
```

2.6   Chapter remarks

In addition to the GHC system, http://www.haskell.org contains a wide range of other useful resources concerning Haskell, including community activities, language documentation, and news items.

2.7   Exercises

1. Work through the examples from this chapter using GHCi.

2. Parenthesise the following numeric expressions:

   2^3*4

   2*3+4*5

   2+3*4^5

3. The script below contains three syntactic errors. Correct these errors and then check that your script works properly using GHCi.

   ```
   N =  a 'div' length xs
        where
             a = 10
             xs = [1,2,3,4,5]
   ```

4. The library function `last` selects the last element of a non-empty list; for example, `last [1,2,3,4,5]` = 5. Show how the function `last` could be defined in terms of the other library functions introduced in this chapter. Can you think of another possible definition?

5. The library function `init` removes the last element from a non-empty list; for example, `init [1,2,3,4,5]` = `[1,2,3,4]`. Show how `init` could similarly be defined in two different ways.

Solutions to exercises 2–4 are given in appendix A.

3 Types and classes

In this chapter we introduce types and classes, two of the most fundamental concepts in Haskell. We start by explaining what types are and how they are used in Haskell, then present a number of basic types and ways to build larger types by combining smaller types, discuss function types in more detail, and conclude with the concepts of polymorphic types and type classes.

3.1 Basic concepts

A *type* is a collection of related values. For example, the type `Bool` contains the two logical values `False` and `True`, while the type `Bool -> Bool` contains all functions that map arguments from `Bool` to results from `Bool`, such as the logical negation function `not`. We use the notation v :: T to mean that v is a value in the type T, and say that v *has type* T. For example:

```
False :: Bool

True :: Bool

not :: Bool -> Bool
```

More generally, the symbol :: can also be used with expressions that have not yet been evaluated, in which case the notation e :: T means that evaluation of the expression e will produce a value of type T. For example:

```
not False :: Bool

not True :: Bool

not (not False) :: Bool
```

In Haskell, every expression must have a type, which is calculated prior to evaluating the expression by a process called *type inference*. The key to this process is the following simple typing rule for function application, which states that if f is a function that maps arguments of type A to results of type B, and e is an expression of type A, then the application f e has type B:

$$\frac{\texttt{f :: A -> B} \qquad \texttt{e :: A}}{\texttt{f e :: B}}$$

For example, the typing `not False :: Bool` can be inferred from this rule using the fact that `not :: Bool -> Bool` and `False :: Bool`. On the other hand, the expression `not 3` does not have a type under the above rule, because this would require that `3 :: Bool`, which is not valid because 3 is not a logical value. Expressions such as `not 3` that do not have a type are said to contain a *type error*, and are deemed to be invalid expressions.

Because type inference precedes evaluation, Haskell programs are *type safe*, in the sense that type errors can never occur during evaluation. In practice, type inference detects a very large class of program errors, and is one of the most useful features of Haskell. Note, however, that the use of type inference does not eliminate the possibility that other kinds of error may occur during evaluation. For example, the expression 1 `div` 0 is well-typed, but produces an error when evaluated because the result of division by zero is undefined.

The downside of type safety is that some expressions that evaluate successfully will be rejected on type grounds. For example, the conditional expression `if True then 1 else False` evaluates to the number 1, but contains a type error and is hence deemed invalid. In particular, the typing rule for a conditional expression requires that both possible results have the same type, whereas in this case the first such result, 1, is a number and the second, `False`, is a logical value. In practice, however, programmers quickly learn how to work within the limits of the type system and avoid such problems.

In GHCi, the type of any expression can be displayed by preceding the expression by the command `:type`. For example:

```
> :type not
not :: Bool -> Bool

> :type False
False :: Bool

> :type not False
not False :: Bool
```

3.2   Basic types

Haskell provides a number of basic types that are built-in to the language, of which the most commonly used are described below.

Bool – logical values

This type contains the two logical values `False` and `True`.

Char – single characters

This type contains all single characters in the Unicode system, the international standard for representing text-based information. For example, it contains all characters on a normal English keyboard, such as `'a'`, `'A'`, `'3'` and `'_'`, as well as a number of control characters that have a special effect, such as `'\n'` (move to a new line) and `'\t'` (move to the next tab stop). As in most programming languages, single characters must be enclosed in single forward quotes `' '`.

String – strings of characters

This type contains all sequences of characters, such as `"abc"`, `"1+2=3"`, and the empty string `""`. Again, as is standard in most programming languages, strings of characters must be enclosed in double quotes `" "`.

Int – fixed-precision integers

This type contains integers such as `-100`, `0`, and `999`, with a fixed amount of memory being used for their storage. For example, the GHC system has values of type `Int` in the range -2^{63} to $2^{63} - 1$. Going outside this range can give unexpected results. For example, evaluating `2^63 :: Int` gives a negative number as the result, which is incorrect. (The use of `::` in this example forces the result to be an `Int` rather than some other numeric type.)

Integer – arbitrary-precision integers

This type contains all integers, with as much memory as necessary being used for their storage, thus avoiding the imposition of lower and upper limits on the range of numbers. For example, evaluating `2^63 :: Integer` using any Haskell system will produce the correct result.

   Apart from the different memory requirements and precision for numbers of type `Int` and `Integer`, the choice between these two types is also one of performance. In particular, most computers have built-in hardware for fixed-precision integers, whereas arbitrary-precision integers are usually processed using the slower medium of software, as sequences of digits.

Float – single-precision floating-point numbers

This type contains numbers with a decimal point, such as `-12.34`, `1.0`, and `3.1415927`, with a fixed amount of memory being used for their storage. The term *floating-point* comes from the fact that the number of digits permitted after the decimal point depends upon the size of the number. For example, evaluating `sqrt 2 :: Float` using GHCi gives the result `1.4142135` (the library function `sqrt` calculates the square root of a floating-point number), which has seven digits after the decimal point, whereas `sqrt 99999 :: Float` gives `316.2262`, which only has four digits after the point.

Double – double-precision floating-point numbers

This type is similar to `Float`, except that twice as much memory is used for storage of these numbers to increase their precision. For example, evaluating `sqrt 2 :: Double` gives `1.4142135623730951`. Using floating-point numbers is a specialist topic that requires a careful treatment of rounding errors, and we don't often use such numbers in this book.

We conclude this section by noting that a single number may have more than one numeric type. For example, the number 3 could have type `Int`, `Integer`, `Float` or `Double`. This raises the interesting question of what type such numbers should be assigned during the process of type inference, which will be answered later in this chapter when we consider type classes.

3.3   List types

A *list* is a sequence of *elements* of the same type, with the elements being enclosed in square parentheses and separated by commas. We write `[T]` for the type of all lists whose elements have type `T`. For example:

```
[False,True,False] :: [Bool]
```

```
['a','b','c','d'] :: [Char]
```

```
["One","Two","Three"] :: [String]
```

The number of elements in a list is called its *length*. The list `[]` of length zero is called the empty list, while lists of length one, such as `[False]`, `['a']`, and `[[]]` are called singleton lists. Note that `[[]]` and `[]` are different lists, the former being a singleton list comprising the empty list as its only element, and the latter being simply the empty list that has no elements.

There are three further points to note about list types. First of all, the type of a list conveys no information about its length. For example, the lists `[False,True]` and `[False,True,False]` both have type `[Bool]`, even though they have different lengths. Secondly, there are no restrictions on the type of the elements of a list. At present we are limited in the range of examples that we can give because the only non-basic type that we have introduced at this point is list types, but we can have lists of lists, such as:

```
[['a','b'],['c','d','e']] :: [[Char]]
```

Finally, there is no restriction that a list must have a finite length. In particular, due to the use of lazy evaluation in Haskell, lists with an infinite length are both natural and practical, as we shall see in chapter 15.

3.4   Tuple types

A *tuple* is a finite sequence of *components* of possibly different types, with the components being enclosed in round parentheses and separated by commas. We write (T1,T2,...,Tn) for the type of all tuples whose ith components have type Ti for any i in the range 1 to n. For example:

```
(False,True) :: (Bool,Bool)

(False,'a',True) :: (Bool,Char,Bool)

("Yes",True,'a') :: (String,Bool,Char)
```

The number of components in a tuple is called its *arity*. The tuple () of arity zero is called the empty tuple, tuples of arity two are called pairs, tuples of arity three are called triples, and so on. Tuples of arity one, such as (False), are not permitted because they would conflict with the use of parentheses to make the evaluation order explicit, such as in (1+2)*3.

In a similar manner to list types, there are three further points to note about tuple types. First of all, the type of a tuple conveys its arity. For example, the type (Bool,Char) contains all pairs comprising a first component of type Bool and a second component of type Char. Secondly, there are no restrictions on the types of the components of a tuple. For example, we can now have tuples of tuples, tuples of lists, and lists of tuples:

```
('a',(False,'b')) :: (Char,(Bool,Char))

(['a','b'],[False,True]) :: ([Char],[Bool])

[('a',False),('b',True)] :: [(Char,Bool)]
```

Finally, note that tuples must have a finite arity, in order to ensure that tuple types can always be inferred prior to evaluation.

3.5   Function types

A *function* is a mapping from arguments of one type to results of another type. We write T1 -> T2 for the type of all functions that map arguments of type T1 to results of type T2. For example, we have:

```
not :: Bool -> Bool
```

```
even :: Int -> Bool
```

(The library function **even** decides if an integer is even.) Because there are no restrictions on the types of the arguments and results of a function, the simple notion of a function with a single argument and a single result is already sufficient to handle the case of multiple arguments and results, by packaging multiple values using lists or tuples. For example, we can define a function **add** that calculates the sum of a pair of integers, and a function **zeroto** that returns the list of integers from zero to a given limit, as follows:

```
add :: (Int,Int) -> Int
add (x,y) = x+y
```

```
zeroto :: Int -> [Int]
zeroto n = [0..n]
```

In these examples we have followed the Haskell convention of preceding function definitions by their types, which serves as useful documentation. Any such types provided manually by the user are checked for consistency with the types calculated automatically using type inference.

Note that there is no restriction that functions must be *total* on their argument type, in the sense that there may be some arguments for which the result is not defined. For example, the result of the library function **head** that selects the first element of a list is undefined if the list is empty:

```
> head []
*** Exception: Prelude.head: empty list
```

3.6   Curried functions

Functions with multiple arguments can also be handled in another, perhaps less obvious way, by exploiting the fact that functions are free to return functions as results. For example, consider the following definition:

```
add' :: Int -> (Int -> Int)
add' x y = x+y
```

The type states that `add'` is a function that takes an argument of type `Int`, and returns a result that is a function of type `Int -> Int`. The definition itself states that `add'` takes an integer x followed by an integer y, and returns the result x+y. More precisely, `add'` takes an integer x and returns a function, which in turn takes an integer y and returns the result x+y.

Note that the function `add'` produces the same final result as the function `add` from the previous section, but whereas `add` takes its two arguments at the same time packaged as a pair, `add'` takes its two arguments one at a time, as reflected in the different types of the two functions:

```
add :: (Int,Int) -> Int
```

```
add' :: Int -> (Int -> Int)
```

Functions with more than two arguments can also be handled using the same technique, by returning functions that return functions, and so on. For example, a function `mult` that takes three integers x, y and z, one at a time, and returns their product, can be defined as follows:

```
mult :: Int -> (Int -> (Int -> Int))
mult x y z = x*y*z
```

This definition states that `mult` takes an integer x and returns a function, which in turn takes an integer y and returns another function, which finally takes an integer z and returns the result x*y*z.

Functions such as `add'` and `mult` that take their arguments one at a time are called *curried functions*. As well as being interesting in their own right, curried functions are also more flexible than functions on tuples, because useful functions can often be made by partially applying a curried function with less than its full complement of arguments. For example, a function that increments an integer can be given by the partial application `add' 1 :: Int -> Int` of the curried function `add'` with only one of its two arguments.

To avoid excess parentheses when working with curried functions, two simple conventions are adopted. First of all, the function arrow `->` in types is assumed to associate to the right. For example, the type

```
Int -> Int -> Int -> Int
```

means

```
Int -> (Int -> (Int -> Int))
```

Consequently, function application, which is denoted silently using spacing, is assumed to associate to the left. For example, the application

```
mult x y z
```

means

```
((mult x) y) z
```

Unless tupling is explicitly required, all functions in Haskell with multiple arguments are normally defined as curried functions, and the two conventions above are used to reduce the number of parentheses that are required. In chapter 4 we will see how the meaning of curried function definitions can be formalised in a simple manner using the notion of lambda expressions.

3.7   Polymorphic types

The library function `length` calculates the length of any list, irrespective of the type of the elements of the list. For example, it can be used to calculate the length of a list of integers, a list of strings, or even a list of functions:

```
> length [1,3,5,7]
4

> length ["Yes","No"]
2

> length [sin,cos,tan]
3
```

The idea that `length` can be applied to lists whose elements have any type is made precise in its type by the inclusion of a *type variable*. Type variables must begin with a lower-case letter, and are usually simply named a, b, c, and so on. For example, the type of `length` is as follows:

```
length :: [a] -> Int
```

That is, for any type a, the function `length` has type `[a] -> Int`. A type that contains one or more type variables is called *polymorphic* ("of many forms"), as is an expression with such a type. Hence, `[a] -> Int` is a polymorphic type and `length` is a polymorphic function. More generally, many of the functions provided in the standard prelude are polymorphic. For example:

```
fst :: (a,b) -> a

head :: [a] -> a

take :: Int -> [a] -> [a]

zip :: [a] -> [b] -> [(a,b)]

id :: a -> a
```

The type of a polymorphic function often gives a strong indication about the function's behaviour. For example, from the type `[a] -> [b] -> [(a,b)]` we can conclude that `zip` pairs up elements from two lists, although the type on its own doesn't capture the precise manner in which this is done.

3.8   Overloaded types

The arithmetic operator + calculates the sum of any two numbers of the same numeric type. For example, it can be used to calculate the sum of two integers, or the sum of two floating-point numbers:

```
> 1 + 2
3

> 1.0 + 2.0
3.0
```

The idea that + can be applied to numbers of any numeric type is made precise in its type by the inclusion of a *class constraint*. Class constraints are written in the form `C a`, where `C` is the name of a class and `a` is a type variable. For example, the type of the addition operator + is as follows:

```
(+) :: Num a => a -> a -> a
```

That is, for any type `a` that is an *instance* of the class `Num` of numeric types, the function (+) has type `a -> a -> a`. (Parenthesising an operator converts it into a curried function, as we shall see in chapter 4.)

A type that contains one or more class constraints is called *overloaded*, as is an expression with such a type. Hence, `Num a => a -> a -> a` is an overloaded type and (+) is an overloaded function. More generally, most of the numeric functions provided in the prelude are overloaded. For example:

```
(*) :: Num a => a -> a -> a

negate :: Num a => a -> a

abs :: Num a => a -> a
```

Numbers themselves are also overloaded. For example, `3 :: Num a => a` means that for any numeric type `a`, the value `3` has type `a`. In this manner, the value `3` could be an integer, a floating-point number, or more generally a value of any numeric type, depending on the context in which it is used.

3.9   Basic classes

Recall that a type is a collection of related values. Building upon this notion, a *class* is a collection of types that support certain overloaded operations called *methods*. Haskell provides a number of basic classes that are built-in to the language, of which the most commonly used are described below. (More advanced built-in classes are considered in part II of the book.)

Eq – equality types

This class contains types whose values can be compared for equality and inequality using the following two methods:

```
(==) :: a -> a -> Bool
```

```
(/=) :: a -> a -> Bool
```

All the basic types `Bool`, `Char`, `String`, `Int`, `Integer`, `Float`, and `Double` are instances of the `Eq` class, as are list and tuple types, provided that their element and component types are instances. For example:

```
> False == False
True

> 'a' == 'b'
False

> "abc" == "abc"
True

> [1,2] == [1,2,3]
False

> ('a',False) == ('a',False)
True
```

Note that function types are not in general instances of the `Eq` class, because it is not feasible in general to compare two functions for equality.

Ord – ordered types

This class contains types that are instances of the equality class `Eq`, but in addition whose values are totally (linearly) ordered, and as such can be compared and processed using the following six methods:

```
(<) :: a -> a -> Bool
```

```
(<=) :: a -> a -> Bool

(>) :: a -> a -> Bool

(>=) :: a -> a -> Bool

min :: a -> a -> a

max :: a -> a -> a
```

All the basic types `Bool`, `Char`, `String`, `Int`, `Integer`, `Float`, and `Double` are instances of the `Ord` class, as are list types and tuple types, provided that their element and component types are instances. For example:

```
> False < True
True

> min 'a' 'b'
'a'

> "elegant" < "elephant"
True

> [1,2,3] < [1,2]
False

> ('a',2) < ('b',1)
True

> ('a',2) < ('a',1)
False
```

Note that strings, lists and tuples are ordered *lexicographically*; that is, in the same way as words in a dictionary. For example, two pairs of the same type are in order if their first components are in order, in which case their second components are not considered, or if their first components are equal, in which case their second components must be in order.

Show – showable types

This class contains types whose values can be converted into strings of characters using the following method:

```
show :: a -> String
```

All the basic types `Bool`, `Char`, `String`, `Int`, `Integer`, `Float`, and `Double` are instances of the `Show` class, as are list types and tuple types, provided that their element and component types are instances. For example:

```
> show False
"False"

> show 'a'
"'a'"

> show 123
"123"

> show [1,2,3]
"[1,2,3]"

> show ('a',False)
"('a',False)"
```

Read – readable types

This class is dual to `Show`, and contains types whose values can be converted from strings of characters using the following method:

```
read :: String -> a
```

All the basic types `Bool`, `Char`, `String`, `Int`, `Integer`, `Float`, and `Double` are instances of the `Read` class, as are list types and tuple types, provided that their element and component types are instances. For example:

```
> read "False" :: Bool
False

> read "'a'" :: Char
'a'

> read "123" :: Int
123

> read "[1,2,3]" :: [Int]
[1,2,3]

> read "('a',False)" :: (Char,Bool)
('a',False)
```

The use of :: in these examples resolves the type of the result, which would otherwise not be able to be inferred by GHCi. In practice, however, the necessary type information can usually be inferred automatically from the context. For example, the expression not (read "False") requires no explicit type information, because the application of the logical negation function not implies that read "False" must have type Bool.

Note that the result of read is undefined if its argument is not syntactically valid. For example, the expression not (read "abc") produces an error when evaluated, because "abc" cannot be read as a logical value:

```
> not (read "abc")
*** Exception: Prelude.read: no parse
```

Num – numeric types

This class contains types whose values are numeric, and as such can be processed using the following six methods:

```
(+) :: a -> a -> a

(-) :: a -> a -> a

(*) :: a -> a -> a

negate :: a -> a

abs :: a -> a

signum :: a -> a
```

(The method negate returns the negation of a number, abs returns the absolute value, while signum returns the sign.) The basic types Int, Integer, Float, and Double are instances of the Num class. For example:

```
> 1 + 2
3

> 1.0 + 2.0
3.0

> negate 3.0
-3.0

> abs (-3)
3
```

```
> signum (-3)
-1
```

As illustrated above, negative numbers must be parenthesised when used as arguments to functions, to ensure the correct interpretation of the minus sign. For example, `abs -3` without parentheses means `abs - 3`, which is both the incorrect meaning here and an ill-typed expression.

Note that the `Num` class does not provide a division method, but as we shall now see, division is handled separately using two special classes, one for integral numbers and one for fractional numbers.

Integral — integral types

This class contains types that are instances of the numeric class `Num`, but in addition whose values are integers, and as such support the methods of integer division and integer remainder:

```
div :: a -> a -> a

mod :: a -> a -> a
```

In practice, these two methods are often written between their two arguments by enclosing their names in single back quotes. The basic types `Int` and `Integer` are instances of the `Integral` class. For example:

```
> 7 'div' 2
3

> 7 'mod' 2
1
```

For efficiency reasons, a number of prelude functions that involve both lists and integers (such as `take` and `drop`) are restricted to the type `Int` of finite-precision integers, rather than being applicable to any instance of the `Integral` class. If required, however, such generic versions of these functions are provided as part of an additional library file called `Data.List`.

Fractional — fractional types

This class contains types that are instances of the numeric class `Num`, but in addition whose values are non-integral, and as such support the methods of fractional division and fractional reciprocation:

```
(/) :: a -> a -> a

recip :: a -> a
```

The basic types `Float` and `Double` are instances. For example:

```
> 7.0 / 2.0
3.5

> recip 2.0
0.5
```

3.10   Chapter remarks

The term `Bool` for the type of logical values celebrates the pioneering work of George Boole on symbolic logic, while the term *curried* for functions that take their arguments one at a time celebrates the work of Haskell Curry (after whom the language Haskell itself is named) on such functions. The relationship between the type of a polymorphic function and its behaviour is formalised in [3]. A more detailed account of the type system is given in the Haskell Report [4], and a formal description of the type system can be found in [5].

3.11   Exercises

1. What are the types of the following values?

    ```
    ['a','b','c']

    ('a','b','c')

    [(False,'0'),(True,'1')]

    ([False,True],['0','1'])

    [tail, init, reverse]
    ```

2. Write down definitions that have the following types; it does not matter what the definitions actually do as long as they are type correct.

    ```
    bools :: [Bool]

    nums :: [[Int]]

    add :: Int -> Int -> Int -> Int

    copy :: a -> (a,a)
    ```

```
apply :: (a -> b) -> a -> b
```

3. What are the types of the following functions?

```
second xs = head (tail xs)
```

```
swap (x,y) = (y,x)
```

```
pair x y = (x,y)
```

```
double x = x*2
```

```
palindrome xs = reverse xs == xs
```

```
twice f x = f (f x)
```

Hint: take care to include the necessary class constraints in the types if the functions are defined using overloaded operators.

4. Check your answers to the preceding three questions using GHCi.

5. Why is it not feasible in general for function types to be instances of the Eq class? When is it feasible? Hint: two functions of the same type are equal if they always return equal results for equal arguments.

Solutions to exercises 1 and 2 are given in appendix A.

4 Defining functions

In this chapter we introduce a range of mechanisms for defining functions in Haskell. We start with conditional expressions and guarded equations, then introduce the simple but powerful idea of pattern matching, and conclude with the concepts of lambda expressions and operator sections.

4.1 New from old

Perhaps the most straightforward way to define new functions is simply by combining one or more existing functions. For example, a few library functions that can be defined in this way are shown below.

- Decide if an integer is even:

```
even :: Integral a => a -> Bool
even n = n 'mod' 2 == 0
```

- Split a list at the nth element:

```
splitAt :: Int -> [a] -> ([a],[a])
splitAt n xs = (take n xs, drop n xs)
```

- Reciprocation:

```
recip :: Fractional a => a -> a
recip n = 1/n
```

Note the use of the class constraints in the types for `even` and `recip` above, which make precise the idea that these functions can be applied to numbers of any integral and fractional types, respectively.

4.2 Conditional expressions

Haskell provides a range of different ways to define functions that choose between a number of possible results. The simplest are *conditional expressions*, which use a logical expression called a *condition* to choose between two results of the same type. If the condition is `True`, then the first result is chosen, and if it is `False`, then the second result is chosen. For example, the library function `abs` that returns the absolute value of an integer can be defined as follows:

```
abs :: Int -> Int
abs n = if n >= 0 then n else -n
```

Conditional expressions may be nested, in the sense that they can contain other conditional expressions. For example, the library function `signum` that returns the sign of an integer can be defined as follows:

```
signum :: Int -> Int
signum n = if n < 0 then -1 else
              if n == 0 then 0 else 1
```

Note that unlike in some programming languages, conditional expressions in Haskell must always have an `else` branch, which avoids the well-known *dangling else* problem. For example, if `else` branches were optional, then the expression `if True then if False then 1 else 2` could either return the result 2 or produce an error, depending upon whether the single `else` branch was assumed to be part of the inner or outer conditional expression.

4.3   Guarded equations

As an alternative to using conditional expressions, functions can also be defined using *guarded equations*, in which a sequence of logical expressions called *guards* is used to choose between a sequence of results of the same type. If the first guard is `True`, then the first result is chosen; otherwise, if the second is `True`, then the second result is chosen, and so on. For example, the library function `abs` can also be defined using guarded equations as follows:

```
abs n | n >= 0    = n
      | otherwise = -n
```

The symbol | is read as *such that*, and the guard `otherwise` is defined in the standard prelude simply by `otherwise = True`. Ending a sequence of guards with `otherwise` is not necessary, but provides a convenient way of handling all other cases, as well as avoiding the possibility that none of the guards in the sequence is `True`, which would otherwise result in an error.

The main benefit of guarded equations over conditional expressions is that definitions with multiple guards are easier to read. For example, the library function `signum` is easier to understand when defined as follows:

```
signum n | n < 0     = -1
         | n == 0    = 0
         | otherwise = 1
```

4.4   Pattern matching

Many functions have a simple and intuitive definition using *pattern matching*, in which a sequence of syntactic expressions called *patterns* is used to choose between a sequence of results of the same type. If the first pattern is *matched*, then the first result is chosen; otherwise, if the second is matched, then the second result is chosen, and so on. For example, the library function `not` that returns the negation of a logical value can be defined as follows:

```
not :: Bool -> Bool
not False = True
not True  = False
```

Functions with more than one argument can also be defined using pattern matching, in which case the patterns for each argument are matched in order within each equation. For example, the library operator `&&` that returns the conjunction of two logical values can be defined as follows:

```
(&&) :: Bool -> Bool -> Bool
True && True   = True
True && False  = False
False && True  = False
False && False = False
```

However, this definition can be simplified by combining the last three equations into a single equation that returns `False` independent of the values of the two arguments, using the *wildcard pattern* _ that matches any value:

```
True && True = True
_    && _    = False
```

This version also has the benefit that, under lazy evaluation as discussed in chapter 15, if the first argument is `False`, then the result `False` is returned without the need to evaluate the second argument. In practice, the prelude defines `&&` using equations that have this same property, but make the choice about which equation applies using the value of the first argument only:

```
True  && b = b
False && _ = False
```

That is, if the first argument is `True`, then the result is the value of the second argument, and, if the first argument is `False`, then the result is `False`.

Note that Haskell does not permit the same name to be used for more than one argument in a single equation. For example, the following definition for the operator `&&` is based upon the observation that, if the two logical arguments are equal, then the result is the same value, otherwise the result is `False`, but is invalid because of the above naming requirement:

```
b && b = b
_ && _ = False
```

If desired, however, a valid version of this definition can be obtained by using a guard to decide if the two arguments are equal:

```
b && c | b == c   = b
       | otherwise = False
```

So far, we have only considered basic patterns that are either values, variables, or the wildcard pattern. In the remainder of this section we introduce two useful ways to build larger patterns by combining smaller patterns.

Tuple patterns

A tuple of patterns is itself a pattern, which matches any tuple of the same arity whose components all match the corresponding patterns in order. For example, the library functions fst and snd that respectively select the first and second components of a pair are defined as follows:

```
fst :: (a,b) -> a
fst (x,_) = x

snd :: (a,b) -> b
snd (_,y) = y
```

List patterns

Similarly, a list of patterns is itself a pattern, which matches any list of the same length whose elements all match the corresponding patterns in order. For example, a function test that decides if a list contains precisely three characters beginning with the letter 'a' can be defined as follows:

```
test :: [Char] -> Bool
test ['a',_,_] = True
test _         = False
```

Up to this point, we have viewed lists as a primitive notion in Haskell. In fact they are not primitive as such, but are constructed one element at a time starting from the empty list [] using an operator : called *cons* that *cons*tructs a new list by prepending a new element to the start of an existing list. For example, the list [1,2,3] can be decomposed as follows:

```
    [1,2,3]
=       { list notation }
    1 : [2,3]
=       { list notation }
```

$$1 : (2 : [3])$$
$$= \quad \{ \text{ list notation } \}$$
$$1 : (2 : (3 : []))$$

That is, `[1,2,3]` is just an abbreviation for `1:(2:(3:[]))`. To avoid excess parentheses when working with such lists, the cons operator is assumed to associate to the right. For example, `1:2:3:[]` means `1:(2:(3:[]))`.

As well as being used to construct lists, the cons operator can also be used to construct patterns, which match any non-empty list whose first and remaining elements match the corresponding patterns in order. For example, we can now define a more general version of the function `test` that decides if a list containing any number of characters begins with the letter `'a'`:

```
test :: [Char] -> Bool
test ('a':_) = True
test _       = False
```

Similarly, the library functions `head` and `tail` that respectively select and remove the first element of a non-empty list are defined as follows:

```
head :: [a] -> a
head (x:_) = x

tail :: [a] -> [a]
tail (_:xs) = xs
```

Note that cons patterns must be parenthesised, because function application has higher priority than all other operators in the language. For example, the definition `head x:_ = x` without parentheses means `(head x):_ = x`, which is both the incorrect meaning and an invalid definition.

4.5   Lambda expressions

As an alternative to defining functions using equations, functions can also be constructed using *lambda expressions*, which comprise a pattern for each of the arguments, a body that specifies how the result can be calculated in terms of the arguments, but do not give a name for the function itself. In other words, lambda expressions are nameless functions.

For example, the nameless function that takes a single number `x` as its argument, and produces the result `x + x`, can be constructed as follows:

```
\x -> x + x
```

The symbol `\` represents the Greek letter *lambda*, written as λ. Despite the fact that they have no names, functions constructed using lambda expressions can be used in the same way as any other functions. For example:

```
> (\x -> x + x) 2
4
```

As well as being interesting in their own right, lambda expressions have a number of practical applications. First of all, they can be used to formalise the meaning of curried function definitions. For example, the definition

```
add :: Int -> Int -> Int
add x y = x + y
```

can be understood as meaning

```
add :: Int -> (Int -> Int)
add = \x -> (\y -> x + y)
```

which makes precise that `add` is a function that takes an integer `x` and returns a function, which in turn takes another integer `y` and returns the result `x + y`. Moreover, rewriting the original definition in this manner also has the benefit that the type for the function and the manner in which it is defined now have the same syntactic form, namely `? -> (? -> ?)`.

Secondly, lambda expressions are also useful when defining functions that return functions as results by their very nature, rather than as a consequence of currying. For example, the library function `const` that returns a constant function that always produces a given value can be defined as follows:

```
const :: a -> b -> a
const x _ = x
```

However, it is more appealing to define `const` in a way that makes explicit that it returns a function as its result, by including parentheses in the type and using a lambda expression in the definition itself:

```
const :: a -> (b -> a)
const x = \_ -> x
```

Finally, lambda expressions can be used to avoid having to name a function that is only referenced once in a program. For example, a function `odds` that returns the first n odd integers can be defined as follows:

```
odds :: Int -> [Int]
odds n = map f [0..n-1]
         where f x = x*2 + 1
```

(The library function `map` applies a function to all elements of a list.) However, because the locally defined function `f` is only referenced once, the definition for `odds` can be simplified by using a lambda expression:

```
odds :: Int -> [Int]
odds n = map (\x -> x*2 + 1) [0..n-1]
```

4.6   Operator sections

Functions such as + that are written between their two arguments are called
operators. As we have already seen, any function with two arguments can be
converted into an operator by enclosing the name of the function in single back
quotes, as in 7 ‘div‘ 2. However, the converse is also possible. In particular,
any operator can be converted into a curried function that is written before its
arguments by enclosing the name of the operator in parentheses, as in (+) 1 2.
Moreover, this convention also allows one of the arguments to be included in the
parentheses if desired, as in (1+) 2 and (+2) 1.

In general, if # is an operator, then expressions of the form (#), (x #), and
(# y) for arguments x and y are called *sections*, whose meaning as functions
can be formalised using lambda expressions as follows:

```
(#)   = \x -> (\y -> x # y)
```

```
(x #)  = \y -> x # y
```

```
(# y)  = \x -> x # y
```

Sections have three primary applications. First of all, they can be used to
construct a number of simple but useful functions in a particularly compact way,
as shown in the following examples:

(+) is the addition function \x -> (\y -> x+y)

(1+) is the successor function \y -> 1+y

(1/) is the reciprocation function \y -> 1/y

(*2) is the doubling function \x -> x*2

(/2) is the halving function \x -> x/2

Secondly, sections are necessary when stating the type of operators, because
an operator itself is not a valid expression in Haskell. For example, the type of
the addition operator + for integers is stated as follows:

```
(+) :: Int -> Int -> Int
```

Finally, sections are also necessary when using operators as arguments to other
functions. For example, the library function sum that calculates the sum of a list
of integers can be defined by using the operator + as an argument to the library
function foldl, which is itself discussed in chapter 7:

```
sum :: [Int] -> Int
sum = foldl (+) 0
```

4.7   Chapter remarks

A formal meaning for pattern matching by translation using more primitive features of the language is given in the Haskell Report [4]. The Greek letter λ used when defining nameless functions comes from the *lambda calculus* [6], the mathematical theory of functions upon which Haskell is founded.

4.8   Exercises

1. Using library functions, define a function `halve :: [a] -> ([a],[a])` that splits an even-lengthed list into two halves. For example:

   ```
   > halve [1,2,3,4,5,6]
   ([1,2,3],[4,5,6])
   ```

2. Define a function `third :: [a] -> a` that returns the third element in a list that contains at least this many elements using:

   a. `head` and `tail`;

   b. list indexing `!!`;

   c. pattern matching.

3. Consider a function `safetail :: [a] -> [a]` that behaves in the same way as `tail` except that it maps the empty list to itself rather than producing an error. Using `tail` and the function `null :: [a] -> Bool` that decides if a list is empty or not, define `safetail` using:

   a. a conditional expression;

   b. guarded equations;

   c. pattern matching.

4. In a similar way to `&&` in section 4.4, show how the disjunction operator `||` can be defined in four different ways using pattern matching.

5. Without using any other library functions or operators, show how the meaning of the following pattern matching definition for logical conjunction `&&` can be formalised using conditional expressions:

   ```
   True && True = True
   _    && _    = False
   ```

   Hint: use two nested conditional expressions.

6. Do the same for the following alternative definition, and note the difference in the number of conditional expressions that are required:

```
True  && b = b
False && _ = False
```

7. Show how the meaning of the following curried function definition can be formalised in terms of lambda expressions:

```
mult :: Int -> Int -> Int -> Int
mult x y z = x*y*z
```

8. The *Luhn algorithm* is used to check bank card numbers for simple errors such as mistyping a digit, and proceeds as follows:

   - consider each digit as a separate number;
   - moving left, double every other number from the second last;
   - subtract 9 from each number that is now greater than 9;
   - add all the resulting numbers together;
   - if the total is divisible by 10, the card number is valid.

   Define a function `luhnDouble :: Int -> Int` that doubles a digit and subtracts 9 if the result is greater than 9. For example:

   ```
   > luhnDouble 3
   6

   > luhnDouble 6
   3
   ```

   Using `luhnDouble` and the integer remainder function `mod`, define a function `luhn :: Int -> Int -> Int -> Int -> Bool` that decides if a four-digit bank card number is valid. For example:

   ```
   > luhn 1 7 8 4
   True

   > luhn 4 7 8 3
   False
   ```

   In the exercises for chapter 7 we will consider a more general version of this function that accepts card numbers of any length.

Solutions to exercises 1–4 are given in appendix A.

5 List comprehensions

In this chapter we introduce list comprehensions, which allow many functions on lists to be defined in simple manner. We start by explaining generators and guards, then introduce the function `zip` and the idea of string comprehensions, and conclude by developing a program to crack the Caesar cipher.

5.1 Basic concepts

In mathematics, the *comprehension* notation can be used to construct new sets from existing sets. For example, the comprehension $\{x^2 \mid x \in \{1..5\}\}$ produces the set $\{1, 4, 9, 16, 25\}$ of all numbers x^2 such that x is an element of the set $\{1..5\}$. In Haskell, a similar comprehension notation can be used to construct new lists from existing lists. For example:

```
> [x^2 | x <- [1..5]]
[1,4,9,16,25]
```

The symbol | is read as *such that*, <- is read as *is drawn from*, and the expression x <- [1..5] is called a *generator*. A list comprehension can have more than one generator, with successive generators being separated by commas. For example, the list of all possible pairings of an element from the list [1,2,3] with an element from the list [4,5] can be produced as follows:

```
> [(x,y) | x <- [1,2,3], y <- [4,5]]
[(1,4),(1,5),(2,4),(2,5),(3,4),(3,5)]
```

Changing the order of the two generators in this example produces the same set of pairs, but arranged in a different order:

```
> [(x,y) | y <- [4,5], x <- [1,2,3]]
[(1,4),(2,4),(3,4),(1,5),(2,5),(3,5)]
```

In particular, whereas in this case the x components of the pairs change more frequently than the y components (1,2,3,1,2,3 versus 4,4,4,5,5,5), in the previous case the y components change more frequently than the x components (4,5,4,5,4,5 versus 1,1,2,2,3,3). These behaviours can be understood by thinking of later generators as being more deeply nested, and hence changing the values of their variables more frequently than earlier generators.

Later generators can also depend upon the values of variables from earlier generators. For example, the list of all possible ordered pairings of elements from the list [1..3] can be produced as follows:

```
> [(x,y) | x <- [1..3], y <- [x..3]]
[(1,1),(1,2),(1,3),(2,2),(2,3),(3,3)]
```

As a more practical example of this idea, the library function concat that concatenates a list of lists can be defined by using one generator to select each list in turn, and another to select each element from each list:

```
concat :: [[a]] -> [a]
concat xss = [x | xs <- xss, x <- xs]
```

The wildcard pattern _ is sometimes useful in generators to discard certain elements from a list. For example, a function that selects all the first components from a list of pairs can be defined as follows:

```
firsts :: [(a,b)] -> [a]
firsts ps = [x | (x,_) <- ps]
```

Similarly, the library function that calculates the length of a list can be defined by replacing each element by one and summing the resulting list:

```
length :: [a] -> Int
length xs = sum [1 | _ <- xs]
```

In this case, the generator _ <- xs simply serves as a counter to govern the production of the appropriate number of ones.

5.2   Guards

List comprehensions can also use logical expressions called *guards* to filter the values produced by earlier generators. If a guard is True, then the current values are retained; if it is False, then they are discarded. For example, the comprehension [x | x <- [1..10], even x] produces the list [2,4,6,8,10] of all even numbers from the list [1..10]. Similarly, a function that maps a positive integer to its list of positive factors can be defined by:

```
factors :: Int -> [Int]
factors n = [x | x <- [1..n], n `mod` x == 0]
```

For example:

```
> factors 15
[1,3,5,15]

> factors 7
[1,7]
```

Recall that an integer greater than one is *prime* if its only positive factors are one and the number itself. Hence, by using `factors`, a simple function that decides if an integer is prime can be defined as follows:

```
prime :: Int -> Bool
prime n = factors n == [1,n]
```

For example:

```
> prime 15
False

> prime 7
True
```

Note that deciding that a number such as 15 is not prime does not require the function `prime` to produce all of its factors, because under lazy evaluation the result `False` is returned as soon as any factor other than one or the number itself is produced, which for this example is given by the factor 3.

Returning to list comprehensions, using `prime` we can now define a function that produces the list of all prime numbers up to a given limit:

```
primes :: Int -> [Int]
primes n = [x | x <- [2..n], prime x]
```

For example:

```
> primes 40
[2,3,5,7,11,13,17,19,23,29,31,37]
```

In chapter 15 we will present a more efficient program to generate prime numbers using the famous *sieve of Eratosthenes*, which has a particularly clear and concise implementation in Haskell using the idea of lazy evaluation.

As a final example concerning guards, suppose that we represent a lookup table by a list of pairs of keys and values. Then for any type of keys that supports equality, a function `find` that returns the list of all values that are associated with a given key in a table can be defined as follows:

```
find :: Eq a => a -> [(a,b)] -> [b]
find k t = [v | (k',v) <- t, k == k']
```

For example:

```
> find 'b' [('a',1),('b',2),('c',3),('b',4)]
[2,4]
```

5.3   The zip function

The library function `zip` produces a new list by pairing successive elements from two existing lists until either or both lists are exhausted. For example:

```
> zip ['a','b','c'] [1,2,3,4]
[('a',1),('b',2),('c',3)]
```

The function `zip` is often useful when programming with list comprehensions. For example, suppose that we define a function that returns the list of all pairs of adjacent elements from a list as follows:

```
pairs   :: [a] -> [(a,a)]
pairs xs = zip xs (tail xs)
```

For example:

```
> pairs [1,2,3,4]
[(1,2),(2,3),(3,4)]
```

Then using `pairs` we can now define a function that decides if a list of elements of any ordered type is sorted by simply checking that all pairs of adjacent elements from the list are in the correct order:

```
sorted :: Ord a => [a] -> Bool
sorted xs = and [x <= y | (x,y) <- pairs xs]
```

For example:

```
> sorted [1,2,3,4]
True

> sorted [1,3,2,4]
False
```

Similarly to the function `prime`, deciding that a list such as [1,3,2,4] is not sorted may not require the function `sorted` to produce all pairs of adjacent elements, because the result `False` is returned as soon as any non-ordered pair is produced, which in this example is given by the pair (3,2).

Using `zip` we can also define a function that returns the list of all positions at which a value occurs in a list, by pairing each element with its position, and selecting those positions at which the desired value occurs:

```
positions :: Eq a => a -> [a] -> [Int]
positions x xs = [i | (x',i) <- zip xs [0..], x == x']
```

For example:

```
> positions False [True, False, True, False]
[1,3]
```

Within the definition for `positions`, the expression `[0..]` produces the list of indices `[0,1,2,3,...]`. This list is notionally *infinite*, but under lazy evaluation only as many elements of the list as required by the context in which it is used, in this case zipping with the input list `xs`, will actually be produced. Exploiting lazy evaluation in this manner avoids the need to explicitly produce a list of indices of the same length as the input list.

5.4 String comprehensions

Up to this point we have viewed strings as a primitive notion in Haskell. In fact they are not primitive, but are constructed as lists of characters. For example, the string `"abc"` :: `String` is just an abbreviation for the list of characters `['a','b','c']` :: `[Char]`. Because strings are lists, any polymorphic function on lists can also be used with strings. For example:

```
> "abcde" !! 2
'c'

> take 3 "abcde"
"abc"

> length "abcde"
5

> zip "abc" [1,2,3,4]
[('a',1),('b',2),('c',3)]
```

For the same reason, list comprehensions can also be used to define functions on strings, such as functions that return the number of lower-case letters and particular characters that occur in a string, respectively:

```
lowers :: String -> Int
lowers xs = length [x | x <- xs, x >= 'a' && x <= 'z']

count :: Char -> String -> Int
count x xs = length [x' | x' <- xs, x == x']
```

For example:

```
> lowers "Haskell"
6

> count 's' "Mississippi"
4
```

5.5   The Caesar cipher

We conclude this chapter with an extended programming example. Consider the problem of encoding a string in order to disguise its contents. A well-known encoding method is the *Caesar cipher*, named after its use by Julius Caesar more than 2,000 years ago. To encode a string, Caesar simply replaced each letter in the string by the letter three places further down in the alphabet, wrapping around at the end of the alphabet. For example, the string

```
"haskell is fun"
```

would be encoded as

```
"kdvnhoo lv ixq"
```

More generally, the specific shift factor of three used by Caesar can be replaced by any integer between one and twenty-five, thereby giving twenty-five different ways of encoding a string. For example, with a shift factor of ten, the original string above would be encoded as follows:

```
"rkcuovv sc pex"
```

In the remainder of this section we show how Haskell can be used to implement the Caesar cipher, and how the cipher itself can easily be cracked by exploiting information about letter frequencies in English text.

Encoding and decoding

We will use a number of standard functions on characters that are provided in a library called **Data.Char**, which can be loaded into a Haskell script by including the following declaration at the start of the script:

```
import Data.Char
```

For simplicity, we will only encode the lower-case letters within a string, leaving other characters such as upper-case letters and punctuation unchanged. We begin by defining a function **let2int** that converts a lower-case letter between 'a' and 'z' into the corresponding integer between 0 and 25, together with a function **int2let** that performs the opposite conversion:

```
let2int :: Char -> Int
let2int c = ord c - ord 'a'

int2let :: Int -> Char
int2let n = chr (ord 'a' + n)
```

(The library functions ord :: Char -> Int and chr :: Int -> Char convert between characters and their Unicode numbers.) For example:

```
> let2int 'a'
0

> int2let 0
'a'
```

Using these two functions, we can define a function shift that applies a shift factor to a lower-case letter by converting the letter into the corresponding integer, adding on the shift factor and taking the remainder when divided by twenty-six (thereby wrapping around at the end of the alphabet), and converting the resulting integer back into a lower-case letter:

```
shift :: Int -> Char -> Char
shift n c | isLower c = int2let ((let2int c + n) `mod` 26)
          | otherwise = c
```

(The library function isLower :: Char -> Bool decides if a character is a lower-case letter.) Note that this function accepts both positive and negative shift factors, and that only lower-case letters are changed. For example:

```
> shift 3 'a'
'd'

> shift 3 'z'
'c'

> shift (-3) 'c'
'z'

> shift 3 ' '
' '
```

Using shift within a list comprehension, it is now easy to define a function that encodes a string using a given shift factor:

```
encode :: Int -> String -> String
encode n xs = [shift n x | x <- xs]
```

A separate function to decode a string is not required, because this can be achieved by simply using a negative shift factor. For example:

```
> encode 3 "haskell is fun"
"kdvnhoo lv ixq"

> encode (-3) "kdvnhoo lv ixq"
"haskell is fun"
```

Frequency tables

The key to cracking the Caesar cipher is the observation that some letters are used more frequently than others in English text. By analysing a large volume of such text, one can derive the following table of approximate percentage frequencies of the twenty-six letters of alphabet:

```
table :: [Float]
table = [8.1, 1.5, 2.8, 4.2, 12.7, 2.2, 2.0, 6.1, 7.0,
         0.2, 0.8, 4.0, 2.4, 6.7, 7.5, 1.9, 0.1, 6.0,
         6.3, 9.0, 2.8, 1.0, 2.4, 0.2, 2.0, 0.1]
```

For example, the letter 'e' occurs most often, with a frequency of 12.7%, while 'q' and 'z' occur least often, with a frequency of just 0.1%. It is also useful to produce frequency tables for individual strings. To this end, we first define a function that calculates the percentage of one integer with respect to another, returning the result as a floating-point number:

```
percent :: Int -> Int -> Float
percent n m = (fromIntegral n / fromIntegral m) * 100
```

(The library function `fromIntegral :: Int -> Float` converts an integer into a floating-point number.) For example:

```
> percent 5 15
33.333336
```

Using `percent` within a list comprehension, together with the functions `lowers` and `count` from the previous section, we can now define a function that returns a frequency table for any given string:

```
freqs :: String -> [Float]
freqs xs = [percent (count x xs) n | x <- ['a'..'z']]
           where n = lowers xs
```

For example:

```
> freqs "abbcccddddeeeee"
[6.666667, 13.333334, 20.0, 26.666668, ..., 0.0]
```

That is, the letter 'a' occurs with a frequency of approximately 6.6%, the letter 'b' with a frequency of 13.3%, and so on. The use of the local definition n = lowers xs within freqs ensures that the number of lower-case letters in the argument string is calculated once, rather than each of the twenty-six times that this number is used within the list comprehension.

Cracking the cipher

A standard method for comparing a list of observed frequencies *os* with a list of expected frequencies *es* is the *chi-square statistic*, defined by the following summation in which n denotes the length of the two lists, and xs_i denotes the ith element of a list xs counting from zero:

$$\sum_{i=0}^{n-1} \frac{(os_i - es_i)^2}{es_i}$$

The details of the chi-square statistic need not concern us here, only the fact that the smaller the value it produces the better the match between the two frequency lists. Using the library function zip and a list comprehension, it is easy to translate the above formula into a function definition:

```
chisqr :: [Float] -> [Float] -> Float
chisqr os es = sum [((o-e)^2)/e | (o,e) <- zip os es]
```

In turn, we define a function that rotates the elements of a list n places to the left, wrapping around at the start of the list, and assuming that the integer argument n is between zero and the length of the list:

```
rotate :: Int -> [a] -> [a]
rotate n xs = drop n xs ++ take n xs
```

For example:

```
> rotate 3 [1,2,3,4,5]
[4,5,1,2,3]
```

Now suppose that we are given an encoded string, but not the shift factor that was used to encode it, and wish to determine this number in order that we can decode the string. This can usually be achieved by producing the frequency table of the encoded string, calculating the chi-square statistic for each possible rotation of this table with respect to the table of expected frequencies, and using the position of the minimum chi-square value as the shift factor. For example, if we let table' = freqs "kdvnhoo lv ixq", then

```
[chisqr (rotate n table') table | n <- [0..25]]
```

gives the result

[1408.8524, 640.0218, 612.3969, 202.42024, ..., 626.4024]

in which the minimum value, 202.42024, appears at position three in this list. Hence, we conclude that three is the most likely shift factor that was used to encode the string. Using the function `positions` from earlier in this chapter, this procedure can be implemented as follows:

```
crack :: String -> String
crack xs = encode (-factor) xs
  where
     factor = head (positions (minimum chitab) chitab)
     chitab = [chisqr (rotate n table') table | n <- [0..25]]
     table' = freqs xs
```

For example:

```
> crack "kdvnhoo lv ixq"
"haskell is fun"

> crack "vscd mywzboroxcsyxc kbo ecopev"
"list comprehensions are useful"
```

More generally, the `crack` function can decode most strings produced using the Caesar cipher. Note, however, that it may not be successful if the string is short or has an unusual distribution of letters. For example:

```
> crack (encode 3 "haskell")
"piasmtt"

> crack (encode 3 "boxing wizards jump quickly")
"wjsdib rduvmyn ephk lpdxfgt"
```

5.6   Chapter remarks

The term *comprehension* comes from the *axiom of comprehension* in set theory, which makes precise the idea of constructing a set by selecting all values that satisfy a particular property. A formal meaning for list comprehensions by translation using more primitive features of the language is given in the Haskell Report [4]. A popular account of the Caesar cipher, and many other famous cryptographic methods, is given in *The Code Book* [7].

5.7   Exercises

1. Using a list comprehension, give an expression that calculates the sum $1^2 + 2^2 + \ldots 100^2$ of the first one hundred integer squares.

2. Suppose that a *coordinate grid* of size $m \times n$ is given by the list of all pairs (x, y) of integers such that $0 \leqslant x \leqslant m$ and $0 \leqslant y \leqslant n$. Using a list comprehension, define a function `grid :: Int -> Int -> [(Int,Int)]` that returns a coordinate grid of a given size. For example:

   ```
   > grid 1 2
   [(0,0),(0,1),(0,2),(1,0),(1,1),(1,2)]
   ```

3. Using a list comprehension and the function `grid` above, define a function `square :: Int -> [(Int,Int)]` that returns a coordinate square of size n, excluding the diagonal from $(0,0)$ to (n, n). For example:

   ```
   > square 2
   [(0,1),(0,2),(1,0),(1,2),(2,0),(2,1)]
   ```

4. In a similar way to the function `length`, show how the library function `replicate :: Int -> a -> [a]` that produces a list of identical elements can be defined using a list comprehension. For example:

   ```
   > replicate 3 True
   [True,True,True]
   ```

5. A triple (x, y, z) of positive integers is *Pythagorean* if it satisfies the equation $x^2 + y^2 = z^2$. Using a list comprehension with three generators, define a function `pyths :: Int -> [(Int,Int,Int)]` that returns the list of all such triples whose components are at most a given limit. For example:

   ```
   > pyths 10
   [(3,4,5),(4,3,5),(6,8,10),(8,6,10)]
   ```

6. A positive integer is *perfect* if it equals the sum of all of its factors, excluding the number itself. Using a list comprehension and the function `factors`, define a function `perfects :: Int -> [Int]` that returns the list of all perfect numbers up to a given limit. For example:

   ```
   > perfects 500
   [6,28,496]
   ```

7. Show how the list comprehension `[(x,y) | x <- [1,2], y <- [3,4]]` with

two generators can be re-expressed using two comprehensions with single generators. Hint: nest one comprehension within the other and make use of the library function `concat :: [[a]] -> [a]`.

8. Redefine the function `positions` using the function `find`.

9. The *scalar product* of two lists of integers xs and ys of length n is given by the sum of the products of corresponding integers:

$$\sum_{i=0}^{n-1} (xs_i * ys_i)$$

In a similar manner to `chisqr`, show how a list comprehension can be used to define a function `scalarproduct :: [Int] -> [Int] -> Int` that returns the scalar product of two lists. For example:

```
> scalarproduct [1,2,3] [4,5,6]
32
```

10. Modify the Caesar cipher program to also handle upper-case letters.

Solutions to exercises 1–5 are given in appendix A.

6 Recursive functions

In this chapter we introduce recursion, the basic mechanism for looping in Haskell. We start with recursion on integers, then extend the idea to recursion on lists, consider multiple arguments, multiple recursion, and mutual recursion, and conclude with some advice on defining recursive functions.

6.1 Basic concepts

As we have seen in previous chapters, many functions can naturally be defined in terms of other functions. For example, a function that returns the *factorial* of a non-negative integer can be defined by using library functions to calculate the product of the integers between one and the given number:

```
fac :: Int -> Int
fac n = product [1..n]
```

In Haskell, it is also permissible to define functions in terms of themselves, in which case the functions are called *recursive*. For example, the factorial function can be defined in this manner as follows:

```
fac :: Int -> Int
fac 0 = 1
fac n = n * fac (n-1)
```

The first equation states that the factorial of zero is one, and is called a *base case*. The second equation states that the factorial of any other number is given by the product of that number and the factorial of its predecessor, and is called a *recursive case*. For example, the following calculation shows how the factorial of three can be computed using this definition:

```
    fac 3
=       { applying fac }
    3 * fac 2
=       { applying fac }
    3 * (2 * fac 1)
=       { applying fac }
    3 * (2 * (1 * fac 0))
```

```
=       { applying fac }
    3 * (2 * (1 * 1))
=       { applying * }
    6
```

Note that even though the `fac` function is defined in terms of itself it does not loop forever. In particular, each application of `fac` decreases the (non-negative) integer argument by one, until it eventually reaches zero at which point the recursion stops and the multiplications are performed. Returning one as the factorial of zero is appropriate because one is the identity for multiplication. That is, `1 * x = x` and `x * 1 = x` for any integer `x`.

For the case of the factorial function, the original definition using library functions is simpler than the definition using recursion. However, as we shall see in the remainder of this book, many functions have a simple and natural definition using recursion. For example, many of the library functions in Haskell are defined in this way. Moreover, as we shall see in chapter 16, defining functions using recursion also allows properties of those functions to be proved using the simple but powerful technique of induction.

As another example of recursion on integers, consider the multiplication operator `*` used above. For efficiency reasons, this operator is provided as a primitive in Haskell. However, for non-negative integers it can also be defined using recursion on either of its two arguments, such as the second:

```
(*) :: Int -> Int -> Int
m * 0 = 0
m * n = m + (m * (n-1))
```

For example:

```
    4 * 3
=       { applying * }
    4 + (4 * 2)
=       { applying * }
    4 + (4 + (4 * 1))
=       { applying * }
    4 + (4 + (4 + (4 * 0)))
=       { applying * }
    4 + (4 + (4 + 0))
=       { applying + }
    12
```

That is, the recursive definition for the `*` operator formalises the idea that multiplication can be reduced to repeated addition.

6.2   Recursion on lists

Recursion is not restricted to functions on integers, but can also be used to define functions on lists. For example, the library function product used in the preceding section can be defined as follows:

```
product :: Num a => [a] -> a
product []     = 1
product (n:ns) = n * product ns
```

The first equation states that the product of the empty list of numbers is one, which is appropriate because one is the identity for multiplication. The second equation states that the product of any non-empty list is given by multiplying the first number and the product of the remaining list. For example:

```
    product [2,3,4]
=       { applying product }
    2 * product [3,4]
=       { applying product }
    2 * (3 * product [4])
=       { applying product }
    2 * (3 * (4 * product []))
=       { applying product }
    2 * (3 * (4 * 1))
=       { applying * }
    24
```

Recall that lists in Haskell are actually constructed one element at a time using the cons operator. Hence, [2,3,4] is just an abbreviation for 2:(3:(4:[])). As another simple example of recursion on lists, the library function length can be defined using the same pattern of recursion as product:

```
length :: [a] -> Int
length []     = 0
length (_:xs) = 1 + length xs
```

That is, the length of the empty list is zero, and the length of any non-empty list is the successor of the length of its tail. Note the use of the wildcard pattern _ in the recursive case, which reflects the fact that calculating the length of a list does not depend upon the values of its elements.

Now let us consider the library function that reverses a list. This function can be defined using recursion as follows:

```
reverse :: [a] -> [a]
reverse []     = []
reverse (x:xs) = reverse xs ++ [x]
```

That is, the reverse of the empty list is simply the empty list, and the reverse of any non-empty list is given by appending the reverse of its tail and a singleton list comprising the head of the list. For example:

```
      reverse [1,2,3]
=        { applying reverse }
      reverse [2,3] ++ [1]
=        { applying reverse }
      (reverse [3] ++ [2]) ++ [1]
=        { applying reverse }
      ((reverse [] ++ [3]) ++ [2]) ++ [1]
=        { applying reverse }
      (([] ++ [3]) ++ [2]) ++ [1]
=        { applying ++ }
      [3,2,1]
```

In turn, the append operator ++ used in the above definition of reverse can itself be defined using recursion on its first argument:

```
(++) :: [a] -> [a] -> [a]
[]       ++ ys = ys
(x:xs) ++ ys = x : (xs ++ ys)
```

For example:

```
      [1,2,3] ++ [4,5]
=        { applying ++ }
      1 : ([2,3] ++ [4,5])
=        { applying ++ }
      1 : (2 : ([3] ++ [4,5]))
=        { applying ++ }
      1 : (2 : (3 : ([] ++ [4,5])))
=        { applying ++ }
      1 : (2 : (3 : [4,5]))
=        { list notation }
      [1,2,3,4,5]
```

That is, the recursive definition for ++ formalises the idea that two lists can be appended by copying elements from the first list until it is exhausted, at which point the second list is joined on at the end.

We conclude this section with two examples of recursion on sorted lists. First of all, a function that inserts a new element of any ordered type into a sorted list to give another sorted list can be defined as follows:

```
insert :: Ord a => a -> [a] -> [a]
insert x []                    = [x]
insert x (y:ys) | x <= y     = x : y : ys
```

```
          | otherwise = y : insert x ys
```

That is, inserting a new element into an empty list gives a singleton list, while for a non-empty list the result depends upon the ordering of the new element `x` and the head of the list `y`. In particular, if `x <= y` then the new element `x` is simply prepended to the start of the list, otherwise the head `y` becomes the first element of the resulting list, and we then proceed to insert the new element into the tail of the given list. For example, we have:

```
      insert 3 [1,2,4,5]
=        { applying insert }
      1 : insert 3 [2,4,5]
=        { applying insert }
      1 : 2 : insert 3 [4,5]
=        { applying insert }
      1 : 2 : 3 : [4,5]
=        { list notation }
      [1,2,3,4,5]
```

Using `insert` we can now define a function that implements *insertion sort*, in which the empty list is already sorted, and any non-empty list is sorted by inserting its head into the list that results from sorting its tail:

```
isort :: Ord a => [a] -> [a]
isort []     = []
isort (x:xs) = insert x (isort xs)
```

For example:

```
      isort [3,2,1,4]
=        { applying isort }
      insert 3 (insert 2 (insert 1 (insert 4 [])))
=        { applying insert }
      insert 3 (insert 2 (insert 1 [4]))
=        { applying insert }
      insert 3 (insert 2 [1,4])
=        { applying insert }
      insert 3 [1,2,4]
=        { applying insert }
      [1,2,3,4]
```

6.3   Multiple arguments

Functions with multiple arguments can also be defined using recursion on more than one argument at the same time. For example, the library function `zip` that takes two lists and produces a list of pairs is defined as follows:

```
zip :: [a] -> [b] -> [(a,b)]
zip []    _    = []
zip _     []   = []
zip (x:xs) (y:ys) = (x,y) : zip xs ys
```

For example:

```
    zip ['a','b','c'] [1,2,3,4]
=      { applying zip }
    ('a',1) : zip ['b','c'] [2,3,4]
=      { applying zip }
    ('a',1) : ('b',2) : zip ['c'] [3,4]
=      { applying zip }
    ('a',1) : ('b',2) : ('c',3) : zip [] [4]
=      { applying zip }
    ('a',1) : ('b',2) : ('c',3) : []
=      { list notation }
    [('a',1), ('b',2), ('c',3)]
```

Note that two base cases are required in the definition of `zip`, because either of the two argument lists may be empty. As another example of recursion on multiple arguments, the library function `drop` that removes a given number of elements from the start of a list is defined as follows:

```
drop :: Int -> [a] -> [a]
drop 0 xs     = xs
drop _ []     = []
drop n (_:xs) = drop (n-1) xs
```

Again, two base cases are required, one for removing zero elements, and one for attempting to remove elements from the empty list.

6.4   Multiple recursion

Functions can also be defined using *multiple recursion*, in which a function is applied more than once in its own definition. For example, recall the Fibonacci sequence $0, 1, 1, 2, 3, 5, 8, 13, \ldots$, in which the first two numbers are 0 and 1, and each subsequent number is given by adding the preceding two numbers in the sequence. A function that calculates the nth Fibonacci number for any integer $n \geqslant 0$ can be defined using double recursion as follows:

```
fib :: Int -> Int
fib 0 = 0
fib 1 = 1
fib n = fib (n-2) + fib (n-1)
```

As another example, in chapter 1 we showed how to implement another well-known method of sorting a list, known as quicksort:

```
qsort :: Ord a => [a] -> [a]
qsort []     = []
qsort (x:xs) = qsort smaller ++ [x] ++ qsort larger
               where
                   smaller = [a | a <- xs, a <= x]
                   larger  = [b | b <- xs, b > x]
```

That is, the empty list is already sorted, and any non-empty list can be sorted by placing its head between the two lists that result from sorting those elements of its tail that are `smaller` and `larger` than the head.

6.5   Mutual recursion

Functions can also be defined using *mutual recursion*, in which two or more functions are all defined recursively in terms of each other. For example, consider the library functions **even** and **odd**. For efficiency, these functions are normally defined using the remainder after dividing by two. However, for non-negative integers they can also be defined using mutual recursion:

```
even:: Int -> Bool
even 0 = True
even n = odd (n-1)

odd :: Int -> Bool
odd 0 = False
odd n = even (n-1)
```

That is, zero is even but not odd, and any other number is even if its predecessor is odd, and odd if its predecessor is even. For example:

```
    even 4
=      { applying even }
    odd 3
=      { applying odd }
    even 2
=      { applying even }
    odd 1
=      { applying odd }
    even 0
=      { applying even }
    True
```

Similarly, functions that select the elements from a list at all even and odd positions (counting from zero) can be defined as follows:

```
evens :: [a] -> [a]
evens []     = []
evens (x:xs) = x : odds xs

odds :: [a] -> [a]
odds []     = []
odds (_:xs) = evens xs
```

For example:

```
    evens "abcde"
=       { applying evens }
    'a' : odds "bcde"
=       { applying odds }
    'a' : evens "cde"
=       { applying evens }
    'a' : 'c' : odds "de"
=       { applying odds }
    'a' : 'c' : evens "e"
=       { applying evens }
    'a' : 'c' : 'e' : odds []
=       { applying odds }
    'a' : 'c' : 'e' : []
=       { string notation }
    "ace"
```

Recall that strings in Haskell are actually constructed as lists of characters. Hence, "abcde" is just an abbreviation for ['a','b','c','d','e'].

6.6   Advice on recursion

Defining recursive functions is like riding a bicycle: it looks easy when someone else is doing it, may seem impossible when you first try to do it yourself, but becomes simple and natural with practice. In this section we offer some advice for defining functions in general, and recursive functions in particular, using a five-step process that we introduce by means of three examples.

Example – product

As a simple first example, we show how the definition given earlier in this chapter for the library function that calculates the **product** of a list of numbers can be systematically constructed in a stepwise manner.

Step 1: define the type

Thinking about types is very helpful when defining functions, so it is good practice to define the type of a function prior to starting to define the function itself. In this case, we begin with the type

```
product :: [Int] -> Int
```

that states that `product` takes a list of integers and produces a single integer. As in this example, it is often useful to begin with a simple type, which can be refined or generalised later on in the process.

Step 2: enumerate the cases

For most types of argument, there are a number of standard cases to consider. For lists, the standard cases are the empty list and non-empty lists, so we can write down the following skeleton definition using pattern matching:

```
product []     =
product (n:ns) =
```

For non-negative integers, the standard cases are 0 and `n`, for logical values they are `False` and `True`, and so on. As with the type, we may need to refine the cases later on, but it is useful to begin with the standard cases.

Step 3: define the simple cases

By definition, the product of zero integers is one, because one is the identity for multiplication. Hence it is straightforward to define the empty list case:

```
product []     = 1
product (n:ns) =
```

As in this example, the simple cases often become base cases.

Step 4: define the other cases

How can we calculate the product of a non-empty list of integers? For this step, it is useful to first consider the ingredients that can be used, such as the function itself (`product`), the arguments (`n` and `ns`), and library functions of relevant types (`+`, `-`, `*`, and so on.) In this case, we simply multiply the first integer and the product of the remaining list of integers:

```
product []     = 1
product (n:ns) = n * product ns
```

As in this example, the other cases often become recursive cases.

Step 5: generalise and simplify

Once a function has been defined using the above process, it often becomes clear that it can be generalised and simplified. For example, the function `product` does not depend on the precise kind of numbers to which it is applied, so its type can be generalised from integers to any numeric type:

```
product :: Num a => [a] -> a
```

In terms of simplification, we will see in chapter 7 that the pattern of recursion used in `product` is encapsulated by a library function called `foldr`, using which `product` can be redefined by a single equation:

```
product = foldr (*) 1
```

In conclusion, our final definition for `product` is as follows:

```
product :: Num a => [a] -> a
product = foldr (*) 1
```

This is precisely the definition for lists from the standard prelude in appendix B, except that for efficiency reasons the use of `foldr` is replaced by the related function `foldl`, which is also discussed in chapter 7.

Example – drop

As a more substantial example, we now show how the definition given earlier for the library function `drop` that removes a given number of elements from the start of a list can be constructed using the five-step process.

Step 1: define the type

Let us begin with a type that states that `drop` takes an integer and a list of values of some type `a`, and produces another list of such values:

```
drop :: Int -> [a] -> [a]
```

Note that we have already made four design decisions in defining this type: using integers rather than a more general numeric type, for simplicity; using currying rather than taking the arguments as a pair, for flexibility; supplying the integer argument before the list argument, for readability (an expression of the form `drop n xs` can be read as *drop* n *elements from* xs); and, finally, making the function polymorphic in the type of the list elements, for generality.

Step 2: enumerate the cases

As there are two standard cases for the integer argument (0 and n) and two for the list argument ([] and x:xs), writing down a skeleton definition for the function using pattern matching requires four cases in total:

```
drop 0 []     =
drop 0 (x:xs) =
drop n []     =
drop n (x:xs) =
```

Step 3: define the simple cases

By definition, removing zero elements from the start of any list gives the same list, so it is straightforward to define the first two cases:

```
drop 0 []     = []
drop 0 (x:xs) = x:xs
drop n []     =
drop n (x:xs) =
```

Attempting to remove one or more elements from the empty list is invalid, so the third case could be omitted, which would result in an error being produced if this situation arises. In practice, however, we choose to avoid the production of an error by returning the empty list in this case:

```
drop 0 []     = []
drop 0 (x:xs) = x:xs
drop n []     = []
drop n (x:xs) =
```

Step 4: define the other cases

How can we remove one or more elements from a non-empty list? By simply removing one fewer elements from the tail of the list:

```
drop 0 []     = []
drop 0 (x:xs) = x:xs
drop n []     = []
drop n (x:xs) = drop (n-1) xs
```

Step 5: generalise and simplify

Because the function `drop` does not depend on the precise kind of integers to which it is applied, its type could be generalised to any integral type, of which `Int` and `Integer` are the standard instances:

```
drop :: Integral b => b -> [a] -> [a]
```

For efficiency reasons, however, this generalisation is not in fact made in the standard prelude, as noted in section 3.9. In terms of simplification, the first two equations for `drop` can be combined into a single equation that states that removing zero elements from any list gives the same list:

```
drop 0 xs    = xs
drop n []    = []
drop n (x:xs) = drop (n-1) xs
```

Moreover, the variable n in the second equation and x in the third can be replaced by the wildcard pattern _, because these variables are not used in the bodies of their equations. In conclusion, our final definition for drop is as follows, which is precisely the definition from the standard prelude.

```
drop :: Int -> [a] -> [a]
drop 0 xs    = xs
drop _ []    = []
drop n (_:xs) = drop (n-1) xs
```

Example – init

As a final example, let us consider how the definition for library function init that removes the last element from a non-empty list can be constructed.

Step 1: define the type

We begin with a type that states that init takes a list of values of some type a, and produces another list of such values:

```
init :: [a] -> [a]
```

Step 2: enumerate the cases

As the empty list is not a valid argument for init, writing down a skeleton definition using pattern matching requires just one case:

```
init (x:xs) =
```

Step 3: define the simple cases

Whereas in the previous two examples defining the simple cases was straightforward, a little more thought is required for the function init. By definition, however, removing the last element from a list with one element gives the empty list, so we can introduce a guard to handle this simple case:

```
init (x:xs) | null xs   = []
            | otherwise =
```

(The library function null :: [a] -> Bool decides if a list is empty.)

Step 4: define the other cases

How can we remove the last element from a list with at least two elements? By simply retaining the head and removing the last element from the tail:

```
init (x:xs) | null xs   = []
            | otherwise = x : init xs
```

Step 5: generalise and simplify

The type for `init` is already as general as possible, but the definition itself can now be simplified by using pattern matching rather than guards, and by using a wildcard pattern in the first equation rather than a variable:

```
init :: [a] -> [a]
init [_]    = []
init (x:xs) = x : init xs
```

Again, this is precisely the definition from the standard prelude.

6.7   Chapter remarks

The recursive definitions presented in this chapter emphasise clarity, but many can be improved in terms of efficiency or generality, as we shall see later on in the book. The five-step process for defining functions is based on [8].

6.8   Exercises

1. How does the recursive version of the factorial function behave if applied to a negative argument, such as `(-1)`? Modify the definition to prohibit negative arguments by adding a guard to the recursive case.

2. Define a recursive function `sumdown :: Int -> Int` that returns the sum of the non-negative integers from a given value down to zero. For example, `sumdown 3` should return the result `3+2+1+0 = 6`.

3. Define the exponentiation operator `^` for non-negative integers using the same pattern of recursion as the multiplication operator `*`, and show how the expression `2 ^ 3` is evaluated using your definition.

4. Define a recursive function `euclid :: Int -> Int -> Int` that implements *Euclid's algorithm* for calculating the greatest common divisor of two non-negative integers: if the two numbers are equal, this number is the result; otherwise, the smaller number is subtracted from the larger, and the same process is then repeated. For example:

   ```
   > euclid 6 27
   3
   ```

5. Using the recursive definitions given in this chapter, show how `length [1,2,3]`, `drop 3 [1,2,3,4,5]`, and `init [1,2,3]` are evaluated.

6. Without looking at the definitions from the standard prelude, define the following library functions on lists using recursion.

   a. Decide if all logical values in a list are `True`:

      ```
      and :: [Bool] -> Bool
      ```

   b. Concatenate a list of lists:

      ```
      concat :: [[a]] -> [a]
      ```

   c. Produce a list with n identical elements:

      ```
      replicate :: Int -> a -> [a]
      ```

   d. Select the nth element of a list:

      ```
      (!!) :: [a] -> Int -> a
      ```

   e. Decide if a value is an element of a list:

      ```
      elem :: Eq a => a -> [a] -> Bool
      ```

   Note: most of these functions are defined in the prelude using other library functions rather than using explicit recursion, and are generic functions rather than being specific to the type of lists.

7. Define a recursive function `merge :: Ord a => [a] -> [a] -> [a]` that merges two sorted lists to give a single sorted list. For example:

   ```
   > merge [2,5,6] [1,3,4]
   [1,2,3,4,5,6]
   ```

   Note: your definition should not use other functions on sorted lists such as `insert` or `isort`, but should be defined using explicit recursion.

8. Using `merge`, define a function `msort :: Ord a => [a] -> [a]` that implements *merge sort*, in which the empty list and singleton lists are already sorted, and any other list is sorted by merging together the two lists that result from sorting the two halves of the list separately.

   Hint: first define a function `halve :: [a] -> ([a],[a])` that splits a list into two halves whose lengths differ by at most one.

9. Using the five-step process, construct the library functions that:

   a. calculate the `sum` of a list of numbers;
   b. `take` a given number of elements from the start of a list;
   c. select the `last` element of a non-empty list.

Solutions to exercises 1–4 are given in appendix A.

7 Higher-order functions

In this chapter we introduce higher-order functions, which allow common programming patterns to be encapsulated as functions. We start by explaining what higher-order functions are and why they are useful, then introduce a number of higher-order functions from the standard prelude, and conclude by implementing a binary string transmitter and two voting algorithms.

7.1 Basic concepts

As we have seen in previous chapters, functions with multiple arguments are usually defined in Haskell using the notion of currying. That is, the arguments are taken one at a time by exploiting the fact that functions can return functions as results. For example, the definition

```
add :: Int -> Int -> Int
add x y = x + y
```

means

```
add :: Int -> (Int -> Int)
add = \x -> (\y -> x + y)
```

and states that add is a function that takes an integer x and returns a function, which in turn takes another integer y and returns their sum x + y. In Haskell, it is also permissible to define functions that take functions as arguments. For example, a function that takes a function and a value, and returns the result of applying the function twice to the value, can be defined as follows:

```
twice :: (a -> a) -> a -> a
twice f x = f (f x)
```

For example:

```
> twice (*2) 3
12

> twice reverse [1,2,3]
[1,2,3]
```

Moreover, because `twice` is a curried function, it can be partially applied with just one argument to build other useful functions. For example, a function that quadruples a number is given by `twice (*2)`, and the fact that reversing a (finite) list twice has no effect i captured by the equation `twice reverse = id`, where `id` is the identity function defined by `id x = x`.

Formally speaking, a function that takes a function as an argument or returns a function as a result is called a *higher-order function*. In practice, however, because the term curried already exists for returning functions as results, the term higher-order is often just used for taking functions as arguments. It is this latter interpretation that is the subject of this chapter.

Using higher-order functions considerably increases the power of Haskell, by allowing common programming patterns to be encapsulated as functions within the language itself. More generally, higher-order functions can be used to define domain-specific languages within Haskell. For example, in this chapter we present a simple language for processing lists, and in part II of the book we will develop languages for a range of other domains, including interactive programming, effectful programming, and building parsers.

7.2   Processing lists

The standard prelude defines a number of useful higher-order functions for processing lists. Many of these are actually generic functions that can be used with a range of different types, but here we restrict our attention to lists. As our first example, the function `map` applies a function to all elements of a list, and can be defined using a list comprehension as follows:

```
map :: (a -> b) -> [a] -> [b]
map f xs = [f x | x <- xs]
```

That is, `map f xs` returns the list of all values `f x` such that `x` is an element of the argument list `xs`. For example, we have:

```
> map (+1) [1,3,5,7]
[2,4,6,8]

> map even [1,2,3,4]
[False,True,False,True]

> map reverse ["abc","def","ghi"]
["cba","fed","ihg"]
```

There are three further points to note about `map`. First of all, it is a polymorphic function that can be applied to lists of any type, as are most higher-order functions on lists. Secondly, it can be applied to itself to process nested lists. For example, the function map (map (+1)) increments each number in a list of lists of numbers, as shown in the following calculation:

```
    map (map (+1)) [[1,2,3],[4,5]]
=      { applying the outer map }
    [map (+1) [1,2,3], map (+1) [4,5]]
=      { applying the inner maps }
    [[2,3,4],[5,6]]
```

And, finally, the function map can also be defined using recursion:

```
map :: (a -> b) -> [a] -> [b]
map f []     = []
map f (x:xs) = f x : map f xs
```

That is, applying a function to all elements of the empty list gives the empty list, while for a non-empty list the function is simply applied to the head of the list, and we then proceed to apply the function to all elements of the tail. The original definition for map using a list comprehension is simpler, but the recursive definition is preferable for reasoning purposes (see chapter 16.)

Another useful higher-order library function is filter, which selects all elements of a list that satisfy a predicate, where a predicate (or property) is a function that returns a logical value. As with map, the function filter also has a simple definition using a list comprehension:

```
filter :: (a -> Bool) -> [a] -> [a]
filter p xs = [x | x <- xs, p x]
```

That is, filter p xs returns the list of all values x such that x is an element of the list xs and the value of p x is True. For example:

```
> filter even [1..10]
[2,4,6,8,10]

> filter (> 5) [1..10]
[6,7,8,9,10]

> filter (/= ' ') "abc def ghi"
"abcdefghi"
```

As with map, the function filter can be applied to lists of any type, and can be defined using recursion for the purposes of reasoning:

```
filter :: (a -> Bool) -> [a] -> [a]
filter p []                 = []
filter p (x:xs) | p x       = x : filter p xs
                | otherwise = filter p xs
```

That is, selecting all elements that satisfy a predicate from the empty list gives the empty list, while for a non-empty list the result depends upon whether the head satisfies the predicate. If it does then the head is retained and we then proceed to filter elements from the tail of the list, otherwise the head is discarded and we simply filter elements from the tail.

The functions `map` and `filter` are often used together in programs, with `filter` being used to select certain elements from a list, each of which is then transformed using `map`. For example, a function that returns the sum of the squares of the even integers from a list could be defined as follows:

```
sumsqreven :: [Int] -> Int
sumsqreven ns = sum (map (^2) (filter even ns))
```

We conclude this section by illustrating a number of other higher-order functions for processing lists that are defined in the standard prelude.

- Decide if all elements of a list satisfy a predicate:

  ```
  > all even [2,4,6,8]
  True
  ```

- Decide if any element of a list satisfies a predicate:

  ```
  > any odd [2,4,6,8]
  False
  ```

- Select elements from a list while they satisfy a predicate:

  ```
  > takeWhile even [2,4,6,7,8]
  [2,4,6]
  ```

- Remove elements from a list while they satisfy a predicate:

  ```
  > dropWhile odd [1,3,5,6,7]
  [6,7]
  ```

7.3 The `foldr` function

Many functions that take a list as their argument can be defined using the following simple pattern of recursion on lists:

```
f []     = v
f (x:xs) = x # f xs
```

That is, the function maps the empty list to a value v, and any non-empty list to an operator # applied to the head of the list and the result of recursively processing the tail. For example, a number of familiar library functions on lists can be defined using this pattern of recursion:

```
sum []     = 0
sum (x:xs) = x + sum xs

product []     = 1
product (x:xs) = x * product xs

or []     = False
or (x:xs) = x || or xs

and []     = True
and (x:xs) = x && and xs
```

The higher-order library function `foldr` (abbreviating *fold right*) encapsulates this pattern of recursion for defining functions on lists, with the operator # and the value v as arguments. For example, using `foldr` the four definitions above can be rewritten more compactly as follows:

```
sum :: Num a => [a] -> a
sum = foldr (+) 0

product :: Num a => [a] -> a
product = foldr (*) 1

or :: [Bool] -> Bool
or = foldr (||) False

and :: [Bool] -> Bool
and = foldr (&&) True
```

(Recall that operators must be parenthesised when used as arguments.) These new definitions could also include explicit list arguments, as in

```
sum xs = foldr (+) 0 xs
```

but we prefer the above definitions in which these arguments are made implicit using partial application because they are simpler.

The `foldr` function itself can be defined using recursion:

```
foldr :: (a -> b -> b) -> b -> [a] -> b
foldr f v []     = v
foldr f v (x:xs) = f x (foldr f v xs)
```

That is, the function `foldr f v` maps the empty list to the value v, and any non-empty list to the function f applied to the head of the list and the recursively processed tail. In practice, however, it is best to think of the behaviour of `foldr f v` in a non-recursive manner, as simply replacing each cons operator in a list by the function f, and the empty list at the end by the value v. For example, applying the function `foldr (+) 0` to the list

```
1 : (2 : (3 : []))
```

gives the result

```
1 + (2 + (3 + 0))
```

in which : and [] have been replaced by + and 0, respectively. Hence, the definition sum = foldr (+) 0 states that summing a list of numbers amounts to replacing each cons by addition and the empty list by zero.

Even though foldr encapsulates a simple pattern of recursion, it can be used to define many more functions than might first be expected. First of all, recall the following definition for the library function length:

```
length :: [a] -> Int
length []     = 0
length (_:xs) = 1 + length xs
```

For example, applying length to the list

```
1 : (2 : (3 : []))
```

gives the result

```
1 + (1 + (1 + 0))
```

That is, calculating the length of a list amounts to replacing each cons by the function that adds one to its second argument, and the empty list by zero. Hence, the definition for length can be rewritten using foldr:

```
length :: [a] -> Int
length = foldr (\_ n -> 1+n) 0
```

Now let us consider the library function that reverses a list, which can be defined in a simple manner using explicit recursion as follows:

```
reverse :: [a] -> [a]
reverse []     = []
reverse (x:xs) = reverse xs ++ [x]
```

For example, applying reverse to the list

```
1 : (2 : (3 : []))
```

gives the result

```
(([] ++ [3]) ++ [2]) ++ [1]
```

It is perhaps not clear from the definition, or the example, how reverse can be defined using foldr. However, if we define a function snoc x xs = xs ++ [x] that adds a new element at the end of a list rather than at the start (snoc is cons backwards), then reverse can be redefined as

```
reverse []     = []
reverse (x:xs) = snoc x (reverse xs)
```

from which a definition using `foldr` is then immediate:

```
reverse :: [a] -> [a]
reverse = foldr snoc []
```

We conclude this section by noting that the name *fold right* reflects the use of an operator that is assumed to associate to the right. For example, evaluating `foldr (+) 0 [1,2,3]` gives the result `1+(2+(3+0))`, in which the bracketing specifies that addition is assumed to associate to the right. More generally, the behaviour of `foldr` can be summarised as follows:

```
foldr (#) v [x0,x1,...,xn]  =  x0 # (x1 # (... (xn # v) ...))
```

7.4   The `foldl` function

It is also possible to define recursive functions on lists using an operator that is assumed to associate to the left. For example, the function `sum` can be redefined in this manner by using an auxiliary function `sum'` that takes an extra argument v that is used to accumulate the final result:

```
sum :: Num a => [a] -> a
sum = sum' 0
      where
         sum' v []     = v
         sum' v (x:xs) = sum' (v+x) xs
```

For example:

```
      sum [1,2,3]
=        { applying sum }
      sum' 0 [1,2,3]
=        { applying sum' }
      sum' (0+1) [2,3]
=        { applying sum' }
      sum' ((0+1)+2) [3]
=        { applying sum' }
      sum' (((0+1)+2)+3) []
=        { applying sum' }
      ((0+1)+2)+3
=        { applying + }
      6
```

The bracketing in this calculation specifies that addition is now assumed to associate to the left. In practice, however, the order of association does not affect the value of the result in this case, because addition is associative. That is, x+(y+z) = (x+y)+z for any numbers x, y, and z.

Generalising from the **sum** example, many functions on lists can be defined using the following simple pattern of recursion:

```
f v []     = v
f v (x:xs) = f (v # x) xs
```

That is, the function maps the empty list to the *accumulator* value v, and any non-empty list to the result of recursively processing the tail using a new accumulator value obtained by applying an operator # to the current value and the head of the list. The higher-order library function **foldl** (abbreviating *fold left*) encapsulates this pattern of recursion, with the operator # and the accumulator v as arguments. For example, using **foldl** the above definition for the function **sum** can be rewritten more compactly as follows:

```
sum :: Num a => [a] -> a
sum = foldl (+) 0
```

Similarly, we have:

```
product :: Num a => [a] -> a
product = foldl (*) 1

or :: [Bool] -> Bool
or = foldl (||) False

and :: [Bool] -> Bool
and = foldl (&&) True
```

The other **foldr** examples from the previous section can also be redefined using **foldl**, by supplying the appropriate operators:

```
length :: [a] -> Int
length = foldl (\n _ -> n+1) 0

reverse :: [a] -> [a]
reverse = foldl (\xs x -> x:xs) []
```

For example, with these new definitions,

```
length [1,2,3] = ((0 + 1) + 1) + 1 = 3

reverse [1,2,3] = 3 : (2 : (1 : [])) = [3,2,1]
```

When a function can be defined using both **foldr** and **foldl**, as in the above examples, the choice of which definition is preferable is usually made on grounds of efficiency and requires careful consideration of the evaluation mechanism underlying Haskell, which is discussed in chapter 15.

The `foldl` function itself can be defined using recursion:

```
foldl :: (a -> b -> a) -> a -> [b] -> a
foldl f v []    = v
foldl f v (x:xs) =  foldl f (f v x) xs
```

In practice, however, as with `foldr` it is best to think of the behaviour of `foldl` in a non-recursive manner, in terms of an operator `#` that is assumed to associate to the left, as summarised by the following equation:

```
foldl (#) v [x0,x1,...,xn]   =   (... ((v # x0) # x1) ...) # xn
```

7.5   The composition operator

The higher-order library operator `.` returns the composition of two functions as a single function, and can be defined as follows:

```
(.) :: (b -> c) -> (a -> b) -> (a -> c)
f . g = \x -> f (g x)
```

That is, `f . g`, which is read as f *composed with* g, is the function that takes an argument x, applies the function g to this argument, and applies the function f to the result. This operator could also be defined by `(f . g) x = f (g x)`. However, we prefer the above definition in which the x argument is shunted to the body of the definition using a lambda expression, because it makes explicit the idea that composition returns a function as its result.

Composition can be used to simplify nested function applications, by reducing parentheses and avoiding the need to explicitly refer to the initial argument. For example, using composition the definitions

```
odd n = not (even n)
```

```
twice f x = f (f x)
```

```
sumsqreven ns = sum (map (^2) (filter even ns))
```

can be rewritten more simply:

```
odd = not . even
```

```
twice f = f . f
```

```
sumsqreven = sum . map (^2) . filter even
```

The last definition exploits the fact that composition is associative. That is, `f . (g . h) = (f . g) . h` for any functions f, g, and h of the appropriate types. Hence, in a composition of three of more functions, as in `sumsqreven`, there is no need to include parentheses to indicate the order of association, because associativity ensures that this does not affect the result.

Composition also has an identity, given by the identity function:

```
id :: a -> a
id = \x -> x
```

That is, `id` is the function that simply returns its argument unchanged, and has the property that `id . f = f` and `f . id = f` for any function `f`. The identity function is often useful when reasoning about programs, and also provides a suitable starting point for a sequence of compositions. For example, the composition of a list of functions can be defined as follows:

```
compose :: [a -> a] -> (a -> a)
compose = foldr (.) id
```

7.6   Binary string transmitter

We conclude this chapter with two extended programming examples. First of all, we consider the problem of simulating the transmission of a string of characters in low-level form as a list of binary digits.

Binary numbers

As a consequence of having ten fingers, people normally find it most convenient to use numbers written in base-ten or *decimal* notation. A decimal number is sequence of digits in the range zero to nine, in which the rightmost digit has a weight of one, and successive digits as we move to the left in the number increase in weight by a factor of ten. For example, the decimal number 2345 can be understood in these terms as follows:

$$2345 \quad = \quad (1000 * 2) + (100 * 3) + (10 * 4) + (1 * 5)$$

That is, 2345 represents the sum of the products of the weights $1000, 100, 10, 1$ with the digits $2, 3, 4, 5$, which evaluates to the integer 2345.

In contrast, computers normally find it more convenient to use numbers written in the more primitive base-two or *binary* notation. A binary number is a sequence of zeros and ones, called binary digits or *bits*, in which successive bits as we move to the left increase in weight by a factor of two. For example, the binary number 1101 can be understood as follows:

$$1101 \quad = \quad (8 * 1) + (4 * 1) + (2 * 0) + (1 * 1)$$

That is, 1101 represents the sum of the products of the weights $8, 4, 2, 1$ with the bits $1, 1, 0, 1$, which evaluates to the integer 13.

To simplify the definition of certain functions, we assume for the remainder of this example that binary numbers are written in *reverse* order to normal. For example, 1101 would now be written as 1011, with successive bits as we move to the right increasing in weight by a factor of two:

$$1011 \quad = \quad (1 * 1) + (2 * 0) + (4 * 1) + (8 * 1)$$

Base conversion

We begin by importing the library of useful functions on characters:

```
import Data.Char
```

To make the types of the functions that we define more meaningful, we declare a type for bits as a synonym for the type of integers:

```
type Bit = Int
```

A binary number, represented as a list of bits, can be converted into an integer by simply evaluating the appropriate weighted sum:

```
bin2int :: [Bit] -> Int
bin2int bits = sum [w*b | (w,b) <- zip weights bits]
               where weights = iterate (*2) 1
```

The higher-order library function `iterate` produces an infinite list by applying a function an increasing number of times to a value:

```
iterate f x  =  [x, f x, f (f x), f (f (f x)), ...]
```

Hence the expression `iterate (*2) 1` in the definition of `bin2int` produces the list of weights `[1,2,4,8,...]`, which is then used to compute the weighted sum by means of a list comprehension. For example:

```
> bin2int [1,0,1,1]
13
```

There is, however, a simpler way to define `bin2int`, which can be revealed with the aid of some algebra. Consider an arbitrary four-bit binary number $[a, b, c, d]$. Applying `bin2int` to this list will produce the weighted sum

$$(1 * a) + (2 * b) + (4 * c) + (8 * d)$$

which can be restructured as follows:

$$
\begin{array}{ll}
& (1 * a) + (2 * b) + (4 * c) + (8 * d) \\
= & \quad \{ \text{ simplifying } 1 * a \} \\
& a + (2 * b) + (4 * c) + (8 * d) \\
= & \quad \{ \text{ factoring out } 2 * \} \\
& a + 2 * (b + (2 * c) + (4 * d)) \\
= & \quad \{ \text{ factoring out } 2 * \} \\
& a + 2 * (b + 2 * (c + (2 * d)))
\end{array}
$$

$$= \quad \{ \text{ complicating } d \}$$
$$a + 2 * (b + 2 * (c + 2 * (d + 2 * 0)))$$

The final result shows that converting a list of bits $[a, b, c, d]$ into an integer amounts to replacing each cons by the function that adds its first argument to twice its second argument, and replacing the empty list by zero. More generally, we conclude that `bin2int` can be rewritten using `foldr`:

```
bin2int :: [Bit] -> Int
bin2int = foldr (\x y -> x + 2*y) 0
```

Now let us consider the opposite conversion, from a non-negative integer into a binary number. This can be achieved by repeatedly dividing the integer by two and taking the remainder, until the integer becomes zero. For example, starting with the integer 13, we proceed as follows:

13	divided by	2	=	6	remainder	1
6	divided by	2	=	3	remainder	0
3	divided by	2	=	1	remainder	1
1	divided by	2	=	0	remainder	1

The sequence of remainders, 1011, provides the binary representation of the integer 13. It is easy to implement this procedure using recursion:

```
int2bin :: Int -> [Bit]
int2bin 0 = []
int2bin n = n 'mod' 2 : int2bin (n 'div' 2)
```

For example:

```
> int2bin 13
[1,0,1,1]
```

We will ensure that all our binary numbers have the same length, in this case eight bits, by using a function `make8` that truncates or extends a binary number as appropriate to make it precisely eight bits:

```
make8 :: [Bit] -> [Bit]
make8 bits = take 8 (bits ++ repeat 0)
```

The library function `repeat :: a -> [a]` produces an infinite list of copies of a value, but lazy evaluation ensures that only as many elements as required by the context will actually be produced. For example:

```
> make8 [1,0,1,1]
[1,0,1,1,0,0,0,0]
```

Transmission

We can now define a function that encodes a string of characters as a list of bits by converting each character into a Unicode number, converting each such number into an eight-bit binary number, and concatenating each of these numbers together to produce a list of bits. Using the higher-order functions `map` and composition, this conversion can be implemented as follows:

```
encode :: String -> [Bit]
encode = concat . map (make8 . int2bin . ord)
```

For example:

```
> encode "abc"
[1,0,0,0,0,1,1,0,0,1,0,0,0,1,1,0,1,1,0,0,0,1,1,0]
```

To decode a list of bits produced using `encode`, we first define a function `chop8` that chops such a list up into eight-bit binary numbers:

```
chop8 :: [Bit] -> [[Bit]]
chop8 []   = []
chop8 bits = take 8 bits : chop8 (drop 8 bits)
```

It is now easy to define a function that decodes a list of bits as a string of characters by chopping the list up, and converting each resulting binary number into a Unicode number and then a character:

```
decode :: [Bit] -> String
decode = map (chr . bin2int) . chop8
```

For example:

```
> decode [1,0,0,0,0,1,1,0,0,1,0,0,0,1,1,0,1,1,0,0,0,1,1,0]
"abc"
```

Finally, we define a function `transmit` that simulates the transmission of a string of characters as a list of bits, using a perfect communication channel that we model using the identity function:

```
transmit :: String -> String
transmit = decode . channel . encode

channel :: [Bit] -> [Bit]
channel = id
```

For example:

```
> transmit "higher-order functions are easy"
"higher-order functions are easy"
```

7.7   Voting algorithms

For our second extended programming example, we consider two different algorithms for deciding the winner in an election: the simple *first past the post* system, and the more refined *alternative vote* system.

First past the post

In this system, each person has one vote, and the candidate with the largest number of votes is declared the winner. For example, if we define

```
votes :: [String]
votes = ["Red", "Blue", "Green", "Blue", "Blue", "Red"]
```

then candidate "Green" has one vote, "Red" has two votes, while "Blue" has three votes and is hence the winner. Rather than making our implementation specific to candidate names represented as strings, we exploit the class system of Haskell to define our functions in a more general manner.

First of all, we define a function that counts the number of times that a given value occurs in a list, for any type whose values can be compared for equality. This function could be defined using recursion, but a simpler definition is possible using higher-order functions by selecting all elements from the list that are equal to the target value, and taking the length of the resulting list:

```
count :: Eq a => a -> [a] -> Int
count x = length . filter (== x)
```

For example:

```
> count "Red" votes
2
```

In turn, the higher-order function `filter` can also be used to define a function that removes duplicate values from a list:

```
rmdups :: Eq a => [a] -> [a]
rmdups []     = []
rmdups (x:xs) = x : filter (/= x) (rmdups xs)
```

For example:

```
> rmdups votes
["Red", "Blue", "Green"]
```

The functions `count` and `rmdups` can then be combined using a list comprehension to define a function that returns the result of a first-past-the-post election in increasing order of the number of votes received:

```
result :: Ord a => [a] -> [(Int,a)]
result vs = sort [(count v vs, v) | v <- rmdups vs]
```

For example:

```
> result votes
[(1,"Green"), (2,"Red"), (3,"Blue")]
```

The sorting function `sort :: Ord a => [a] -> [a]` used above is provided in the library `Data.List`. Note that because pairs are ordered lexicographically, candidates with the same number of votes are returned in order of the candidate name by `result`. Finally, the winner of an election can now be obtained simply by selecting the second component of the last result:

```
winner :: Ord a => [a] -> a
winner = snd . last . result
```

For example:

```
> winner votes
"Blue"
```

Alternative vote

In this voting system, each person can vote for as many or as few candidates as they wish, listing them in preference order on their ballot (1st choice, 2nd choice, and so on). To decide the winner, any empty ballots are first removed, then the candidate with the smallest number of 1st-choice votes is eliminated from the ballots, and same process is repeated until only one candidate remains, who is then declared the winner. For example, if we define

```
ballots :: [[String]]
ballots = [["Red", "Green"],
           ["Blue"],
           ["Green", "Red", "Blue"],
           ["Blue", "Green", "Red"],
           ["Green"]]
```

then the first ballot has `"Red"` as 1st choice and `"Green"` as 2nd, while the second has `"Blue"` as the only choice, and so on. Now let us consider how the winner is decided for this example. First of all, `"Red"` has the smallest number of 1st-choice votes (just one), and is therefore eliminated:

```
[["Green"],
 ["Blue"],
 ["Green", "Blue"],
 ["Blue", "Green"],
 ["Green"]]
```

Within these revised ballots, candidate `"Blue"` now has the smallest number of 1st-choice votes (just two), and is therefore also eliminated:

```
[["Green"],
 [],
 ["Green"],
 ["Green"],
 ["Green"]]
```

After removing the second ballot, which is now empty, `"Green"` is the only remaining candidate and is hence the winner.

Using `filter` and `map`, it is easy to define functions that remove empty ballots, and eliminate a given candidate from each ballot:

```
rmempty :: Eq a => [[a]] -> [[a]]
rmempty = filter (/= [])
```

```
elim :: Eq a => a -> [[a]] -> [[a]]
elim x = map (filter (/= x))
```

As before, we define such functions in a general manner rather than just for strings. In turn, using the function **result** from the previous section, we can define a function that ranks the 1st-choice candidates in each ballot in increasing order of the number of such votes that were received:

```
rank :: Ord a => [[a]] -> [a]
rank = map snd . result . map head
```

For example:

```
> rank ballots
["Red", "Blue", "Green"]
```

Finally, it is now straightforward to define a recursive function that implements the alternative vote algorithm, as follows:

```
winner' :: Ord a => [[a]] -> a
winner' bs = case rank (rmempty bs) of
                [c]    -> c
                (c:cs) -> winner' (elim c bs)
```

That is, we first remove empty ballots, then rank the remaining 1st-choice candidates in increasing order of votes. If only one such candidate remains, they are the winner, otherwise we eliminate the candidate with the smallest number of 1st-choice votes and repeat the process. For example:

```
> winner' ballots
"Green"
```

We conclude by noting that the **case** mechanism of Haskell that is used in the above definition allows pattern matching to be used in the body of a definition, and is sometimes useful for avoiding the need to introduce an extra function definition just for the purposes of performing pattern matching.

7.8   Chapter remarks

Further applications of higher-order functions, including the production of computer music, financial contracts, graphical images, hardware descriptions, logic programs, and pretty printers can be found in *The Fun of Programming* [9]. A more in-depth tutorial on `foldr` is given in [10].

7.9   Exercises

1. Show how the list comprehension [f x | x <- xs, p x] can be re-expressed using the higher-order functions `map` and `filter`.

2. Without looking at the definitions from the standard prelude, define the following higher-order library functions on lists.

   a. Decide if all elements of a list satisfy a predicate:

   ```
   all :: (a -> Bool) -> [Bool] -> Bool
   ```

   b. Decide if any element of a list satisfies a predicate:

   ```
   any :: (a -> Bool) -> [Bool] -> Bool
   ```

   c. Select elements from a list while they satisfy a predicate:

   ```
   takeWhile :: (a -> Bool) -> [a] -> [a]
   ```

   d. Remove elements from a list while they satisfy a predicate:

   ```
   dropWhile :: (a -> Bool) -> [a] -> [a]
   ```

   Note: in the prelude the first two of these functions are generic functions rather than being specific to the type of lists.

3. Redefine the functions `map f` and `filter p` using `foldr`.

4. Using `foldl`, define a function `dec2int :: [Int] -> Int` that converts a decimal number into an integer. For example:

   ```
   > dec2int [2,3,4,5]
   2345
   ```

5. Without looking at the definitions from the standard prelude, define the higher-order library function `curry` that converts a function on pairs into a curried function, and, conversely, the function `uncurry` that converts a curried function with two arguments into a function on pairs.

   Hint: first write down the types of the two functions.

6. A higher-order function `unfold` that encapsulates a simple pattern of recursion for producing a list can be defined as follows:

   ```
   unfold p h t x | p x       = []
                  | otherwise = h x : unfold p h t (t x)
   ```

   That is, the function `unfold p h t` produces the empty list if the predicate `p` is true of the argument value, and otherwise produces a non-empty list by applying the function `h` to this value to give the head, and the function `t` to generate another argument that is recursively processed in the same way to produce the tail of the list. For example, the function `int2bin` can be rewritten more compactly using `unfold` as follows:

   ```
   int2bin = unfold (== 0) ('mod' 2) ('div' 2)
   ```

   Redefine the functions `chop8`, `map f` and `iterate f` using `unfold`.

7. Modify the binary string transmitter example to detect simple transmission errors using the concept of parity bits. That is, each eight-bit binary number produced during encoding is extended with a parity bit, set to one if the number contains an odd number of ones, and to zero otherwise. In turn, each resulting nine-bit binary number consumed during decoding is checked to ensure that its parity bit is correct, with the parity bit being discarded if this is the case, and a parity error being reported otherwise.

   Hint: the library function `error :: String -> a` displays the given string as an error message and terminates the program; the polymorphic result type ensures that `error` can be used in any context.

8. Test your new string transmitter program from the previous exercise using a faulty communication channel that forgets the first bit, which can be modelled using the `tail` function on lists of bits.

9. Define a function `altMap :: (a -> b) -> (a -> b) -> [a] -> [b]` that alternately applies its two argument functions to successive elements in a list, in turn about order. For example:

   ```
   > altMap (+10) (+100) [0,1,2,3,4]
   [10,101,12,103,14]
   ```

10. Using `altMap`, define a function `luhn :: [Int] -> Bool` that implements the *Luhn algorithm* from the exercises in chapter 4 for bank card numbers of any length. Test your new function using your own bank card.

Solutions to exercises 1–5 are given in appendix A.

8 Declaring types and classes

In this chapter we introduce mechanisms for declaring new types and classes in Haskell. We start with three approaches to declaring types, then consider recursive types, show how to declare classes and their instances, and conclude by developing a tautology checker and an abstract machine.

8.1 Type declarations

The simplest way of declaring a new type is to introduce a new name for an existing type, using the **type** mechanism of Haskell. For example, the following declaration from the standard prelude states that the type **String** is just a synonym for the type **[Char]** of lists of characters:

```
type String = [Char]
```

As in this example, the name of a new type must begin with a capital letter. Type declarations can be nested, in the sense that one such type can be declared in terms of another. For example, if we were defining a number of functions that transform coordinate positions, we might declare a position as a pair of integers, and a transformation as a function on positions:

```
type Pos = (Int,Int)
```

```
type Trans = Pos -> Pos
```

However, type declarations cannot be recursive. For example, consider the following recursive declaration for a type of trees:

```
type Tree = (Int,[Tree])
```

That is, a tree is a pair comprising an integer and a list of subtrees. While this declaration is perfectly reasonable, with the empty list of subtrees forming the base case for the recursion, it is not permitted in Haskell because it is recursive. If required, recursive types can be declared using the more powerful **data** mechanism, which will be introduced in the next section.

Type declarations can also be parameterised by other types. For example, if we were defining a number of functions that manipulate pairs of values of the same type, we could declare a synonym for such pairs:

```
type Pair a = (a,a)
```

Finally, type declarations with more than one parameter are possible too. For example, a type of lookup tables that associate keys of one type to values of another type can be declared as a list of (key,value) pairs:

```
type Assoc k v = [(k,v)]
```

Using this type, a function that returns the first value that is associated with a given key in a table can then be defined as follows:

```
find :: Eq k => k -> Assoc k v -> v
find k t = head [v | (k',v) <- t, k == k']
```

8.2   Data declarations

A completely new type, as opposed to a synonym for an existing type, can be declared by specifying its values using the **data** mechanism of Haskell. For example, the following declaration from the standard prelude states that the type **Bool** comprises two new values, named **False** and **True**:

```
data Bool = False | True
```

In such declarations, the symbol | is read as *or*, and the new values of the type are called *constructors*. As with new types themselves, the names of new constructors must begin with a capital letter. Moreover, the same constructor name cannot be used in more than one type.

Note that the names given to new types and constructors have no inherent meaning to the Haskell system. For example, the above declaration could equally well be written as **data A = B | C**, because the precise details of the names are not relevant, other than the fact that they have not been used before. The meaning of names such as **Bool**, **False**, and **True** is assigned by the programmer, via the functions that they define on new types.

Values of new types in Haskell can be used in precisely the same way as those of built-in types. In particular, they can freely be passed as arguments to functions, returned as results from functions, stored in data structures, and used in patterns. For example, given the declaration

```
data Move = North | South | East | West
```

functions that apply a move to a position, apply a list of moves to a position, and reverse the direction of a move, can be defined as follows:

```
move :: Move -> Pos -> Pos
move North (x,y) = (x,y+1)
move South (x,y) = (x,y-1)
move East  (x,y) = (x+1,y)
```

```
move West  (x,y) = (x-1,y)

moves :: [Move] -> Pos -> Pos
moves []     p = p
moves (m:ms) p = moves ms (move m p)

rev :: Move -> Move
rev North = South
rev South = North
rev East  = West
rev West  = East
```

(If you wish to try out such examples in GHCi, the phrase `deriving Show` must be added to the end of the `data` declaration, to ensure the system can display values of the new type; the `deriving` mechanism itself will be covered in later on in this chapter when we consider type classes.)

The constructors in a data declaration can also have arguments. For example, a type of shapes that comprise circles with a given radius and rectangles with given dimensions can be declared by:

```
data Shape = Circle Float | Rect Float Float
```

That is, the type `Shape` has values of the form `Circle r`, where `r` is a floating-point number, and `Rect x y`, where `x` and `y` are floating-point numbers. These constructors can then be used to define functions on shapes, such as to produce a square of a given size, and to calculate the area of a shape:

```
square :: Float -> Shape
square n = Rect n n

area :: Shape -> Float
area (Circle r) = pi * r^2
area (Rect x y) = x * y
```

Because of their use of arguments, the constructors `Circle` and `Rect` are actually constructor *functions*, which produce results of type `Shape` from arguments of type `Float`, as can be demonstrated using GHCi:

```
> :type Circle
Circle :: Float -> Shape

> :type Rect
Rect :: Float -> Float -> Shape
```

The difference between normal functions and constructor functions is that the latter have no defining equations, and exist purely for the purposes of building pieces of data. For example, whereas the expression `negate 1.0` can be evaluated to -1.0 by applying the definition of **negate**, the expression **Circle 1.0** is already fully evaluated and cannot be further simplified, because there are no defining equations for **Circle**. Rather, the expression **Circle 1.0** is just a piece of data, in the same way that **1.0** itself is just data.

Not surprisingly, data declarations themselves can also be parameterised. For example, the standard prelude declares the following type:

```
data Maybe a = Nothing | Just a
```

That is, a value of type **Maybe a** is either **Nothing**, or of the form **Just x** for some value x of type **a**. We can think of values of type **Maybe a** as being values of type **a** that may either fail or succeed, with **Nothing** representing failure, and **Just** representing success. For example, using this type we can define safe versions of the library functions **div** and **head**, which return **Nothing** in the case of invalid arguments, rather than producing an error:

```
safediv :: Int -> Int -> Maybe Int
safediv _ 0 = Nothing
safediv m n = Just (m `div` n)

safehead :: [a] -> Maybe a
safehead [] = Nothing
safehead xs = Just (head xs)
```

8.3   Newtype declarations

If a new type has a single constructor with a single argument, then it can also be declared using the **newtype** mechanism. For example, a type of natural numbers (non-negative integers) could be declared as follows:

```
newtype Nat = N Int
```

In this case, the single constructor **N** takes a single argument of type **Int**, and it is then up to the programmer to ensure that this is always non-negative. Of course, it is natural to ask how the above declaration using **newtype** compares to the following alternative versions using **type** and **data**:

```
type Nat = Int

data Nat = N Int
```

First of all, using **newtype** rather than **type** means that **Nat** and **Int** are different types rather than synonyms, and hence the type system of Haskell ensures that they cannot accidentally be mixed up in our programs, for example by using an integer when we expect a natural number. And secondly, using **newtype** rather than **data** brings an efficiency benefit, because **newtype** constructors such as **N** do not incur any cost when programs are evaluated, as they are automatically removed by the compiler once type checking is completed. In summary, using `newtype` helps improve type safety, without affecting performance.

8.4 Recursive types

New types declared using the `data` and `newtype` mechanisms can also be recursive. As a simple first example, the type of natural numbers from the previous section can also be declared in a recursive manner:

```
data Nat = Zero | Succ Nat
```

That is, a value of type `Nat` is either `Zero`, or of the form `Succ n` for some value n of type `Nat`. Hence, this declaration gives rise to an infinite sequence of values, starting with the value `Zero`, and continuing by applying the constructor function `Succ` to the previous value in the sequence:

```
Zero
Succ Zero
Succ (Succ Zero)
Succ (Succ (Succ Zero))
 .
 .
 .
```

In this manner, values of type `Nat` correspond to natural numbers with `Zero` representing the number 0, and `Succ` representing the successor function $(1+)$. For example, `Succ (Succ (Succ Zero))` represents $1 + (1 + (1 + 0)) = 3$. More formally, we can define the following conversion functions:

```
nat2int :: Nat -> Int
nat2int Zero     = 0
nat2int (Succ n) = 1 + nat2int n

int2nat :: Int -> Nat
int2nat 0 = Zero
int2nat n = Succ (int2nat (n-1))
```

For example, using these functions, two natural numbers can be added together by first converting them into integers, adding these integers, and then converting the result back into a natural number:

```
add :: Nat -> Nat -> Nat
add m n = int2nat (nat2int m + nat2int n)
```

However, using recursion the function `add` can be redefined without the need for such conversions, and hence more efficiently:

```
add :: Nat -> Nat -> Nat
add Zero     n = n
add (Succ m) n = Succ (add m n)
```

This definition formalises the idea that two natural numbers can be added by copying Succ constructors from the first number until they are exhausted, at which point the Zero at the end is replaced by the second number. For example, showing that $2 + 1 = 3$ proceeds as follows:

```
    add (Succ (Succ Zero)) (Succ Zero)
=       { applying add }
    Succ (add (Succ Zero) (Succ Zero))
=       { applying add }
    Succ (Succ (add Zero (Succ Zero)))
=       { applying add }
    Succ (Succ (Succ Zero))
```

As another example, the data mechanism can be used to declare our own version of the built-in type of lists, parameterised by an arbitrary type:

```
data List a = Nil | Cons a (List a)
```

That is, a value of type List a is either Nil, representing the empty list, or of the form Cons x xs for some values x :: a and xs :: List a, representing a non-empty list. Using this type, we can then also define our own versions of library functions on lists, such as to calculate the length of a list:

```
len :: List a -> Int
len Nil          = 0
len (Cons _ xs) = 1 + len xs
```

While lists are one of the most commonly used data structure in computing, it is often useful to store data in a two-way branching structure, or *binary tree*, as depicted in the following example tree:

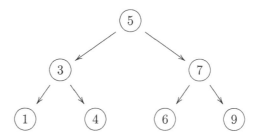

In this example, the numbers $1, 4, 6, 9$ appear at the external *leaves* of the tree, and the numbers $5, 3, 7$ appear at the internal *nodes*. Using recursion, a suitable type for representing such trees can be declared by

```
data Tree a = Leaf a | Node (Tree a) a (Tree a)
```

and the tree pictured above can then be represented as follows:

```
t :: Tree Int
t = Node (Node (Leaf 1) 3 (Leaf 4)) 5
         (Node (Leaf 6) 7 (Leaf 9))
```

We now consider a number of functions on such trees. First of all, we define a function that decides if a given value occurs in a tree:

```
occurs :: Eq a => a -> Tree a -> Bool
occurs x (Leaf y)     = x == y
occurs x (Node l y r) = x == y || occurs x l || occurs x r
```

That is, a value occurs in a leaf if it matches the value at the leaf, and occurs in a node if it either matches the value at the node, occurs in the left subtree, or occurs in the right subtree. Note that under lazy evaluation, if either of the first two conditions in the node case is True, then the result True is returned without the need to evaluate the remaining conditions.

In the worst case, however, the function occurs may still traverse the entire tree, in particular when the given value does not occur anywhere in the tree. Now consider a function that flattens a tree to a list:

```
flatten :: Tree a -> [a]
flatten (Leaf x)     = [x]
flatten (Node l x r) = flatten l ++ [x] ++ flatten r
```

If applying this function to a tree gives a sorted list, then the tree is called a *search tree*. For instance, our example tree is a search tree, because:

```
flatten t  =  [1,3,4,5,6,7,9]
```

Search trees have the important property that, when trying to decide if a given value occurs in a tree, which of the two subtrees of a node it may occur in can always be determined in advance. In particular, if the value is less than the value at the node, then it can only occur in the left subtree, and if it is greater than this value, it can only occur in the right subtree. Hence, for search trees the occurs function can be rewritten as follows:

```
occurs :: Ord a => a -> Tree a -> Bool
occurs x (Leaf y)                = x == y
occurs x (Node l y r) | x == y   = True
                      | x < y    = occurs x l
                      | otherwise = occurs x r
```

This definition is more efficient than the previous version, because it only traverses one path down the tree, rather than potentially the entire tree.

We conclude this section by noting that, as in nature, trees in computing come in many different forms. For example, we can declare types for trees that have data only in their leaves, data only in their nodes, data of different types in their leaves and nodes, or have a list of subtrees:

```
data Tree a = Leaf a | Node (Tree a) (Tree a)

data Tree a = Leaf | Node (Tree a) a (Tree a)

data Tree a b = Leaf a | Node (Tree a b) b (Tree a b)

data Tree a = Node a [Tree a]
```

Which form of tree is most appropriate depends upon the situation. Note that in the last example, there is no constructor for leaves, because a node with an empty list of subtrees can play the role of a leaf.

8.5 Class and instance declarations

We now turn our attention from types to classes. In Haskell, a new class can be declared using the class mechanism. For example, the class Eq of equality types is declared in the standard prelude as follows:

```
class Eq a where
    (==), (/=) :: a -> a -> Bool

    x /= y = not (x == y)
```

This declaration states that for a type a to be an instance of the class Eq, it must support equality and inequality operators of the specified types. In fact, because a *default definition* has already been included for the /= operator, declaring an instance only requires a definition for the == operator. For example, the type Bool can be made into an equality type as follows:

```
instance Eq Bool where
    False == False = True
    True  == True  = True
    _     == _     = False
```

Only types that are declared using the data and newtype mechanisms can be made into instances of classes. Note also that default definitions can be overridden in instance declarations if desired. For example, for some equality types there may be a more efficient or appropriate way to decide if two values are different than simply checking if they are not equal.

Classes can also be extended to form new classes. For example, the class Ord of types whose values are totally ordered is declared in the standard prelude as an extension of the class Eq as follows:

```
class Eq a => Ord a where
   (<), (<=), (>), (>=) :: a -> a -> Bool
   min, max             :: a -> a -> a

   min x y | x <= y     = x
           | otherwise = y

   max x y | x <= y     = y
           | otherwise = x
```

That is, for a type to be an instance of Ord it must be an instance of Eq, and support six additional operators. Because default definitions have already been included for min and max, declaring an equality type (such as Bool) as an ordered type only requires defining the four comparison operators:

```
instance Ord Bool where
   False < True = True
   _     < _     = False

   b <= c = (b < c) || (b == c)
   b >  c = c < b
   b >= c = c <= b
```

Derived instances

When new types are declared, it is usually appropriate to make them into instances of a number of built-in classes. Haskell provides a simple facility for automatically making new types into instances of the classes Eq, Ord, Show, and Read, in the form of the **deriving** mechanism. For example, the type Bool is actually declared in the standard prelude as follows:

```
data Bool = False | True
            deriving (Eq, Ord, Show, Read)
```

As a result, all the member functions from the four derived classes can then be used with logical values. For example:

```
> False == False
True

> False < True
True
```

```
> show False
"False"

> read "False" :: Bool
False
```

The use of :: in the last example is required to resolve the type of the result, which in this case cannot be inferred from the context in which the function is used. Note that for the purposes of deriving instances of the class Ord of ordered types, the ordering on the constructors of a type is determined by their position in its declaration. Hence, the above declaration for the type Bool, in which False appears before True, results in the ordering False < True.

In the case of constructors with arguments, the types of these arguments must also be instances of any derived classes. For example, recall the following two declarations from earlier in this chapter:

```
data Shape = Circle Float | Rect Float Float

data Maybe a = Nothing | Just a
```

To derive Shape as an equality type requires that the type Float is also an equality type, which is indeed the case. Similarly, to derive Maybe a as an equality type requires that the type a is also such a type, which then becomes a class constraint on this parameter. In the same manner as lists and tuples, values built using constructors with arguments are ordered lexicographically. For example, if Shape is also derived as an ordered type, then we have:

```
> Rect 1.0 4.0 < Rect 2.0 3.0
True

> Rect 1.0 4.0 < Rect 1.0 3.0
False
```

8.6   Tautology checker

We conclude this chapter with two extended programming examples. For our first example, we develop a function that decides if simple logical propositions are always true. Such propositions are called *tautologies*.

Consider a language of propositions built up from basic values (*False*, *True*) and variables ($A, B, \cdots, Z$) using negation ($\neg$), conjunction ($\wedge$), implication ($\Rightarrow$), and parentheses. For example, the following are all propositions:

$$A \wedge \neg A$$

$$(A \wedge B) \Rightarrow A$$

$$A \Rightarrow (A \wedge B)$$

$$(A \wedge (A \Rightarrow B)) \Rightarrow B$$

The meaning of the logical operators can be defined using *truth tables*, which give the resulting value for each combination of argument values:

A	$\neg A$
F	T
T	F

A	B	$A \wedge B$
F	F	F
F	T	F
T	F	F
T	T	T

A	B	$A \Rightarrow B$
F	F	T
F	T	T
T	F	F
T	T	T

(To save space in such tables, we abbreviate the basic values by F and T.) For example, the truth table for conjunction states that $A \wedge B$ returns *True* if both A and B are *True*, and *False* otherwise. Using these definitions, the truth table for any proposition can then be constructed. In the case of our four example propositions, the resulting tables are as follows:

A	$A \wedge \neg A$
F	F
T	F

A	B	$(A \wedge B) \Rightarrow A$
F	F	T
F	T	T
T	F	T
T	T	T

A	B	$A \Rightarrow (A \wedge B)$
F	F	T
F	T	T
T	F	F
T	T	T

A	B	$(A \wedge (A \Rightarrow B)) \Rightarrow B$
F	F	T
F	T	T
T	F	T
T	T	T

These tables show that the second and fourth propositions are tautologies, because their result value is always *True*, while the first and third are not tautologies, because their result is *False* in at least one case.

The first step towards defining a function that decides if a proposition is a tautology is to declare a type for propositions, with one constructor for each of the five possible forms that a proposition can have:

```
data Prop = Const Bool
          | Var Char
          | Not Prop
          | And Prop Prop
          | Imply Prop Prop
```

Note that an explicit constructor for parentheses is not required, as parentheses within Haskell itself can be used to indicate grouping. For example, the four propositions above can be represented as follows:

```
p1 :: Prop
p1 = And (Var 'A') (Not (Var 'A'))

p2 :: Prop
p2 = Imply (And (Var 'A') (Var 'B')) (Var 'A')

p3 :: Prop
p3 = Imply (Var 'A') (And (Var 'A') (Var 'B'))

p4 :: Prop
p4 = Imply (And (Var 'A') (Imply
        (Var 'A') (Var 'B'))) (Var 'B')
```

In order to evaluate a proposition to a logical value, we need to know the value of each of its variables. For this purpose, we declare a *substitution* as a lookup table that associates variable names to logical values, using the `Assoc` type that was introduced at the start of this chapter:

```
type Subst = Assoc Char Bool
```

For example, the substitution `[('A',False),('B',True)]` assigns the variable A to `False`, and B to `True`. A function that evaluates a proposition given a substitution for its variables can now be defined by pattern matching on the five possible forms that the proposition can have:

```
eval :: Subst -> Prop -> Bool
eval _ (Const b)   = b
eval s (Var x)     = find x s
eval s (Not p)     = not (eval s p)
eval s (And p q)   = eval s p && eval s q
eval s (Imply p q) = eval s p <= eval s q
```

For example, the value of a constant proposition is simply the constant itself, the value of a variable is obtained by looking up its value in the substitution, and the value of a conjunction is given by taking the conjunction of the values of the two argument propositions. Note that the logical implication operator ⇒ is implemented simply by the `<=` ordering on logical values.

To decide if a proposition is a tautology, we will consider all possible substitutions for the variables that it contains. First of all, we define a function that returns a list of all the variables in a proposition:

```
vars :: Prop -> [Char]
vars (Const _)   = []
```

```
vars (Var x)     = [x]
vars (Not p)     = vars p
vars (And p q)   = vars p ++ vars q
vars (Imply p q) = vars p ++ vars q
```

For example, vars p2 = ['A','B','A']. Note that this function does not remove duplicates, which will be done separately later on.

The key to generating substitutions is producing lists of logical values of a given length. Hence we seek to define a function bools :: Int -> [[Bool]] which, for example, will return all eight lists of three logical values:

```
> bools 3
[[False, False, False],
 [False, False, True],
 [False, True,  False],
 [False, True,  True],
 [True,  False, False],
 [True,  False, True],
 [True,  True,  False],
 [True,  True,  True]]
```

One way to achieve this behaviour is to observe that each component list corresponds to a binary number, by interpreting False and True as the binary digits 0 and 1. For example, the list [True,False,True] corresponds to the binary number 101. Given this interpretation, we can think of the function bools as simply counting in binary over the appropriate range of numbers.

This idea leads to the following definition for bools, in terms of the function int2bin :: Int -> [Bit] from chapter 7 that converts a non-negative integer into a binary number represented as a list of bits:

```
bools :: Int -> [[Bool]]
bools n = map (reverse . map conv . make n . int2bin) range
          where
                 range      = [0..(2^n)-1]
                 make n bs = take n (bs ++ repeat 0)
                 conv 0     = False
                 conv 1     = True
```

There is, however, a simpler way to define bools, which can be revealed by thinking about the structure of the resulting lists. For example, we can observe that bools 3 contains two copies of bools 2, the first preceded by False in each case, and the second preceded by True in each case:

False	False	False
False	False	True
False	True	False
False	True	True
True	False	False
True	False	True
True	True	False
True	True	True

This observation leads to a recursive definition for `bools`. In the base case, `bools 0`, we return all lists of zero logical values, of which the empty list is the only one. In the recursive case, `bools n`, we take two copies of the lists produced by `bools (n-1)`, place `False` in front of each list in the first copy, `True` in front of each list in the second, and append the results:

```
bools :: Int -> [[Bool]]
bools 0 = [[]]
bools n = map (False:) bss ++ map (True:) bss
          where bss = bools (n-1)
```

Using `bools`, it is now straightforward to define a function that generates all possible substitutions for a proposition by extracting its variables, removing duplicates from this list (using the function `rmdups` from chapter 7), generating all possible lists of logical values for this many variables, and then zipping the list of variables with each of the resulting lists:

```
substs :: Prop -> [Subst]
substs p = map (zip vs) (bools (length vs))
           where vs = rmdups (vars p)
```

For example:

```
> substs p2
[[('A',False),('B',False)],
 [('A',False),('B',True)],
 [('A',True),('B',False)],
 [('A',True),('B',True)]]
```

Finally, we define a function that decides if a proposition is a tautology, by simply checking if it evaluates to `True` for all possible substitutions:

```
isTaut :: Prop -> Bool
isTaut p = and [eval s p | s <- substs p]
```

For example:

```
> isTaut p1
False


> isTaut p2
True


> isTaut p3
False


> isTaut p4
True
```

8.7   Abstract machine

For our second extended example, consider a type of simple arithmetic expressions built up from integers using an addition operator, together with a function that evaluates such an expression to an integer value:

```
data Expr = Val Int | Add Expr Expr

value :: Expr -> Int
value (Val n)   = n
value (Add x y) = value x + value y
```

For example, the expression $(2 + 3) + 4$ is evaluated as follows:

$$
\begin{array}{cl}
& \texttt{value (Add (Add (Val 2) (Val 3)) (Val 4))} \\
= & \quad \{ \text{applying } \texttt{value} \} \\
& \texttt{value (Add (Val 2) (Val 3)) + value (Val 4)} \\
= & \quad \{ \text{applying the first } \texttt{value} \} \\
& \texttt{(value (Val 2) + value (Val 3)) + value (Val 4)} \\
= & \quad \{ \text{applying the first } \texttt{value} \} \\
& \texttt{(2 + value (Val 3)) + value (Val 4)} \\
= & \quad \{ \text{applying the first } \texttt{value} \} \\
& \texttt{(2 + 3) + value (Val 4)} \\
= & \quad \{ \text{applying the first } \texttt{+} \} \\
& \texttt{5 + value (Val 4)} \\
= & \quad \{ \text{applying } \texttt{value} \} \\
& \texttt{5 + 4} \\
= & \quad \{ \text{applying } \texttt{+} \} \\
& \texttt{9}
\end{array}
$$

Note that the definition of the `value` function does not specify that the left argument of an addition should be evaluated before the right, or, more generally, what the next step of evaluation should be at each point. Rather, the order of evaluation is determined by Haskell. If desired, however, such control information can be made explicit by defining an *abstract machine* for expressions, which specifies the step-by-step process of their evaluation.

To this end, we first declare a type of *control stacks* for the abstract machine, which comprise a list of operations to be performed by the machine after the current evaluation has been completed:

```
type Cont = [Op]

data Op = EVAL Expr | ADD Int
```

The meaning of the two operations will be explained shortly. We now define a function that evaluates an expression in the context of a control stack:

```
eval :: Expr -> Cont -> Int
eval (Val n)   c = exec c n
eval (Add x y) c = eval x (EVAL y : c)
```

That is, if the expression is an integer, it is already fully evaluated, and we begin executing the control stack. If the expression is an addition, we evaluate the first argument, x, placing the operation EVAL y on top of the control stack to indicate that the second argument, y, should be evaluated once evaluation of the first argument is completed. In turn, we define the function that executes a control stack in the context of an integer argument:

```
exec :: Cont -> Int -> Int
exec []          n = n
exec (EVAL y : c) n = eval y (ADD n : c)
exec (ADD n : c)  m = exec c (n+m)
```

That is, if the control stack is empty, we return the integer argument as the result of the execution. If the top of the stack is an operation EVAL y, we evaluate the expression y, placing the operation ADD n on top of the remaining stack to indicate that the current integer argument, n, should be added together with the result of evaluating y once this is completed. And, finally, if the top of the stack is an operation ADD n, evaluation of the two arguments of an addition expression is now complete, and we execute the remaining control stack in the context of the sum of the two resulting integer values.

Finally, we define a function that evaluates an expression to an integer, by invoking eval with the given expression and the empty control stack:

```
value :: Expr -> Int
value e = eval e []
```

The fact that our abstract machine uses two mutually recursive functions, eval and exec, reflects the fact that it has two modes of operation, depending

upon whether it is being driven by the structure of the expression or the control
stack. To illustrate the machine, here is how it evaluates $(2 + 3) + 4$:

```
    value (Add (Add (Val 2) (Val 3)) (Val 4))
=      { applying value }
    eval (Add (Add (Val 2) (Val 3)) (Val 4)) []
=      { applying eval }
    eval (Add (Val 2) (Val 3)) [EVAL (Val 4)]
=      { applying eval }
    eval (Val 2) [EVAL (Val 3), EVAL (Val 4)]
=      { applying eval }
    exec [EVAL (Val 3), EVAL (Val 4)] 2
=      { applying exec }
    eval (Val 3) [ADD 2, EVAL (Val 4)]
=      { applying eval }
    exec [ADD 2, EVAL (Val 4)] 3
=      { applying exec }
    exec [EVAL (Val 4)] 5
=      { applying exec }
    eval (Val 4) [ADD 5]
=      { applying eval }
    exec [ADD 5] 4
=      { applying exec }
    exec [] 9
=      { applying exec }
    9
```

Note how **eval** proceeds downwards to the leftmost integer in the expression,
maintaining a trail of the pending right-hand expressions on the control stack.
In turn, **exec** then proceeds upwards through the trail, transferring control back
to **eval** and performing additions as appropriate.

8.8   Chapter remarks

The abstract machine example is derived from [11], and the type of control
stacks used in this example is a special case of the zipper data structure for
traversing values of recursive types [12]. As well as the basic mechanisms for
declaring new types and classes introduced in this chapter, the GHC system
also supports a number of more advanced and experimental typing features; see
http://www.haskell.org/ghc for further details.

8.9   Exercises

1. In a similar manner to the function `add`, define a recursive multiplication function `mult :: Nat -> Nat -> Nat` for the recursive type of natural numbers: Hint: make use of `add` in your definition.

2. Although not included in appendix B, the standard prelude defines

   ```
   data Ordering = LT | EQ | GT
   ```

   together with a function

   ```
   compare :: Ord a => a -> a -> Ordering
   ```

   that decides if one value in an ordered type is less than (`LT`), equal to (`EQ`), or greater than (`GT`) another value. Using this function, redefine the function `occurs :: Ord a => a -> Tree a -> Bool` for search trees. Why is this new definition more efficient than the original version?

3. Consider the following type of binary trees:

   ```
   data Tree a = Leaf a | Node (Tree a) (Tree a)
   ```

   Let us say that such a tree is *balanced* if the number of leaves in the left and right subtree of every node differs by at most one, with leaves themselves being trivially balanced. Define a function `balanced :: Tree a -> Bool` that decides if a binary tree is balanced or not.

   Hint: first define a function that returns the number of leaves in a tree.

4. Define a function `balance :: [a]  -> Tree a` that converts a non-empty list into a balanced tree. Hint: first define a function that splits a list into two halves whose length differs by at most one.

5. Given the type declaration

   ```
   data Expr = Val Int | Add Expr Expr
   ```

   define a higher-order function

   ```
   folde :: (Int -> a) -> (a -> a -> a) -> Expr -> a
   ```

   such that `folde f g` replaces each `Val` constructor in an expression by the function `f`, and each `Add` constructor by the function `g`.

6. Using `folde`, define a function `eval :: Expr -> Int` that evaluates an expression to an integer value, and a function `size :: Expr -> Int` that calculates the number of values in an expression.

7. Complete the following instance declarations:

```
instance Eq a => Eq (Maybe a) where
   ...

instance Eq a => Eq [a] where
   ...
```

8. Extend the tautology checker to support the use of logical disjunction ($\vee$) and equivalence ($\Leftrightarrow$) in propositions.

9. Extend the abstract machine to support the use of multiplication.

Solutions to exercises 1–4 are given in appendix A.

9 The countdown problem

In this chapter we conclude part I of the book, by showing how the concepts introduced so far can be used to develop an efficient program to solve a simple numbers game. We start by defining some types and utility functions, then formalise the rules of the game in Haskell, and finally present a simple brute force solution, whose performance is then improved in two steps.

9.1 Introduction

Countdown is a popular quiz programme that has been running on British television since 1982, and includes a numbers game that we shall refer to as the *countdown problem*. The essence of the problem is as follows:

> Given a sequence of numbers and a target number, attempt to construct an expression whose value is the target, by combining one or more numbers from the sequence using addition, subtraction, multiplication, division and parentheses.

Each number in the sequence can only be used at most once in the expression, and all of the numbers involved, including intermediate values, must be positive natural numbers $(1, 2, 3, \ldots)$. In particular, the use of negative numbers, zero, and proper fractions such as $2 \div 3$, is not permitted.

For example, suppose that we are given the sequence $1, 3, 7, 10, 25, 50$, and the target 765. Then one possible solution is given by the expression $(1+50)*(25-10)$, as verified by the following simple calculation:

$$
\begin{aligned}
& (1 + 50) * (25 - 10) \\
= \quad & \{ \text{ applying } + \} \\
& 51 * (25 - 10) \\
= \quad & \{ \text{ applying } - \} \\
& 51 * 15 \\
= \quad & \{ \text{ applying } * \} \\
& 765
\end{aligned}
$$

In fact, for this example it can be shown that there are 780 different solutions. On the other hand, keeping the same sequence but changing the target to 831 gives an example that can be shown to have no solutions.

In the television version of the problem, a number of additional rules are adopted to make it suitable for human players on a quiz programme. In particular, there are always six numbers selected from the sequence 1–10, 1–10, 25, 50, 75, 100, the target is always in the range 100–999, and there is a time limit of 30 seconds. It is natural to abstract from such constraints when developing a computer player, so none of the programs that we develop enforces or depends upon these extra rules. Note, however, that we do not abstract from the positive naturals to a richer numeric domain, such as the integers or the rationals, as this would change the computational complexity of the problem.

9.2   Arithmetic operators

We start by declaring a type for the four arithmetic operators, and making values of this type showable using a simple instance declaration:

```
data Op = Add | Sub | Mul | Div

instance Show Op where
    show Add = "+"
    show Sub = "-"
    show Mul = "*"
    show Div = "/"
```

In turn, we define a function `valid` that decides if the application of an operator to two positive naturals gives another positive natural, and a function `apply` that actually performs such a valid application:

```
valid :: Op -> Int -> Int -> Bool
valid Add _ _ = True
valid Sub x y = x > y
valid Mul _ _ = True
valid Div x y = x 'mod' y == 0

apply :: Op -> Int -> Int -> Int
apply Add x y = x + y
apply Sub x y = x - y
apply Mul x y = x * y
apply Div x y = x 'div' y
```

For example, the application `Sub 2 3` is invalid because $2 - 3$ is negative, while `Div 2 3` is invalid because $2 \div 3$ is a rational number.

9.3   Numeric expressions

We now declare a type for numeric expressions, which can either be an integer value or the application of an operator to two argument expressions, together with a simple pretty-printer for expressions:

```
data Expr = Val Int | App Op Expr Expr

instance Show Expr where
   show (Val n)     = show n
   show (App o l r) = brak l ++ show o ++ brak r
                      where
                         brak (Val n) = show n
                         brak e       = "(" ++ show e ++ ")"
```

For example, $1 + (2 * 3)$ can be represented as a value of type Expr and then shown in more readable form as a string as follows:

```
> show (App Add (Val 1) (App Mul (Val 2) (Val 3)))
"1+(2*3)"
```

Using this type, we define a function that returns the list of values in an expression, and a function eval that returns the overall value of an expression, provided that this value is a positive natural number:

```
values :: Expr -> [Int]
values (Val n)     = [n]
values (App _ l r) = values l ++ values r

eval :: Expr -> [Int]
eval (Val n)     = [n | n > 0]
eval (App o l r) = [apply o x y | x <- eval l,
                                  y <- eval r,
                                  valid o x y]
```

Note that the possibility of failure within eval is handled by returning a list of results, with the convention that a singleton list denotes success, and the empty list denotes failure. For example, for $2 + 3$ and $2 - 3$, we have:

```
> eval (App Add (Val 2) (Val 3))
[5]

> eval (App Sub (Val 2) (Val 3))
[]
```

Failure within eval could also be handled by using the Maybe type, but we prefer to use the list type because the comprehension notation then provides a convenient way to define the eval function.

9.4   Combinatorial functions

We now define a number of useful combinatorial functions that return all possible lists that satisfy certain properties. The function subs returns all subsequences of a list, which are given by all possible combinations of excluding or including each element of the list, interleave returns all possible ways of inserting a new element into a list, and finally, perms returns all permutations of a list, which are given by all possible reorderings of the elements:

```
subs :: [a] -> [[a]]
subs []     = [[]]
subs (x:xs) = yss ++ map (x:) yss
              where yss = subs xs

interleave :: a -> [a] -> [[a]]
interleave x []     = [[x]]
interleave x (y:ys) = (x:y:ys) : map (y:) (interleave x ys)

perms :: [a] -> [[a]]
perms []     = [[]]
perms (x:xs) = concat (map (interleave x) (perms xs))
```

For example:

```
> subs [1,2,3]
[[],[3],[2],[2,3],[1],[1,3],[1,2],[1,2,3]]

> interleave 1 [2,3,4]
[[1,2,3,4],[2,1,3,4],[2,3,1,4],[2,3,4,1]]

> perms [1,2,3]
[[1,2,3],[2,1,3],[2,3,1],[1,3,2],[3,1,2],[3,2,1]]
```

In turn, a function that returns all choices from a list, which are given by all possible ways of selecting zero or more elements in any order, can then be defined simply by considering all permutations of all subsequences:

```
choices :: [a] -> [[a]]
choices = concat . map perms . subs
```

For example:

```
> choices [1,2,3]
[[],[3],[2],[2,3],[3,2],[1],[1,3],[3,1],[1,2],[2,1],
 [1,2,3],[2,1,3],[2,3,1],[1,3,2],[3,1,2],[3,2,1]]
```

9.5   Formalising the problem

Finally, we can now define a function `solution` that formalises what it means to solve an instance of the countdown problem:

```
solution :: Expr -> [Int] -> Int -> Bool
solution e ns n =
    elem (values e) (choices ns) && eval e == [n]
```

That is, an expression is a solution for a given list of numbers and a target if the list of values in the expression is chosen from the list of numbers, and the expression successfully evaluates to give the target. For example, if `e :: Expr` represents the expression $(1 + 50) * (25 - 10)$, then we have:

```
> solution e [1,3,7,10,25,50] 765
True
```

The efficiency of `solution` could be improved by using a function `isChoice` that decides directly if one list is chosen from another, rather than doing so indirectly using the function `choices` that returns all possible choices from a list. However, efficiency is not important at this stage, and `choices` itself is used to define a number of other functions in this chapter.

9.6   Brute force solution

Our first approach to solving the countdown problem is by brute force, using the idea of generating all possible expressions over the given list of numbers. We start by defining a function `split` that returns all possible ways of splitting a list into two non-empty lists that append to give the original list:

```
split :: [a] -> [([a],[a])]
split []     = []
split [_]    = []
split (x:xs) = ([x],xs) : [(x:ls,rs) | (ls,rs) <- split xs]
```

For example:

```
> split [1,2,3,4]
[([1],[2,3,4]),([1,2],[3,4]),([1,2,3],[4])]
```

Using `split` we can then define the key function, `exprs`, which returns all possible expressions whose list of values is precisely a given list:

```
exprs :: [Int] -> [Expr]
exprs []  = []
exprs [n] = [Val n]
exprs ns  = [e | (ls,rs) <- split ns,
```

```
l          <- exprs ls,
r          <- exprs rs,
e          <- combine l r]
```

That is, for the empty list of numbers there are no possible expressions, while for a single number there is a single expression comprising that number. Otherwise, for a list of two or more numbers we first produce all splittings of the list, then recursively calculate all possible expressions for each of these lists, and, finally, combine each pair of expressions using each of the four numeric operators, using an auxiliary function that is defined as follows:

```
combine :: Expr -> Expr -> [Expr]
combine l r = [App o l r | o <- ops]

ops :: [Op]
ops = [Add,Sub,Mul,Div]
```

In conclusion, we can now define a function `solutions` that returns all possible expressions that solve an instance of the countdown problem, by first generating all expressions over each choice from the given list of numbers, and then selecting those expressions that successfully evaluate to give the target:

```
solutions :: [Int] -> Int -> [Expr]
solutions ns n =
    [e | ns' <- choices ns, e <- exprs ns', eval e == [n]]
```

9.7   Performance testing

For the purposes of testing our countdown programs in this chapter, the performance of the GHCi interpreter is somewhat limited, so instead we use the GHC compiler. The first step is to put all the necessary definitions into a script called `countdown.hs`, together with a top-level definition `main` that applies the function `solutions` to an example and displays the result:

```
main :: IO ()
main = print (solutions [1,3,7,10,25,50] 765)
```

(The library function `print` writes a value of a showable type to the screen, and the type for `main` will be explained in further detail in chapter 10.) The compiler itself can then be executed from the command prompt simply by typing ghc, and using the -O2 flag to turn on compiler optimisations:

```
$ ghc -O2 countdown.hs
[1 of 1] Compiling Main
Linking countdown ...
```

Finally, the resulting executable file can then be run:

```
$ ./countdown
[3*((7*(50-10))-25), ((7*(50-10))-25)*3, ...]
```

For example, running some simple performance tests using GHC version 7.10.2 on a 2.8GHz Intel Core 2 Duo with 4GB of RAM, this example returns the first solution to the problem in 0.108 seconds, and all 780 solutions in 12.224 seconds, while if the target is changed to 831, the empty list of solutions is returned in 12.802 seconds. More generally, our brute force program already performs well enough to solve countdown problems from the television show within the 30 second time limit. But surely we can do better than this?

9.8 Combining generation and evaluation

The function `solutions` generates all possible expressions over the given numbers, but in practice many of these expressions will fail to evaluate, due to the fact that subtraction and division are not always valid operations for positive naturals. For example, it can be shown that there are 33,665,406 possible expressions over the numbers $1, 3, 7, 10, 25, 50$, but only 4,672,540 of these expressions evaluate successfully, which is just under 14%.

Based upon this observation, our second approach to solving the countdown problem is to improve our brute force program by combining the generation of expressions with their evaluation, such that both tasks are performed simultaneously. In this way, expressions that fail to evaluate are rejected at an earlier stage, and, more importantly, are not used to generate further expressions that will fail to evaluate. We start by declaring a type `Result` of expressions that evaluate successfully paired with their overall values:

```
type Result = (Expr,Int)
```

Using this type, we then define a function `results` that returns all possible results comprising expressions whose list of values is precisely a given list:

```
results :: [Int] -> [Result]
results []  = []
results [n] = [(Val n,n) | n > 0]
results ns  = [res | (ls,rs) <- split ns,
                     lx       <- results ls,
                     ry       <- results rs,
                     res      <- combine' lx ry]
```

That is, for the empty list there are no possible results, while for a single number there is a single result formed from that number, provided that the number itself is a positive natural number. Otherwise, for two or more numbers we first produce all splittings of the list, then recursively calculate all possible results for each of these lists, and, finally, combine each pair of results using each of the four numeric operators that are valid, by means of the following auxiliary function:

```
combine' :: Result -> Result -> [Result]
combine' (l,x) (r,y) =
   [(App o l r, apply o x y) | o <- ops, valid o x y]
```

Using **results** we can now define a new function **solutions'** that returns all possible expressions that solve an instance of the countdown problem, by first generating all results over each choice from the given numbers, and then selecting those expressions whose value is the target:

```
solutions' :: [Int] -> Int -> [Expr]
solutions' ns n =
   [e | ns' <- choices ns, (e,m) <- results ns', m == n]
```

In terms of performance, **solutions'** [1,3,7,10,25,50] 765 returns the first solution in 0.014 seconds (7 times faster than **solutions**) and all solutions in 1.312 seconds (9 times faster), while if the target is changed to 831, the empty list is returned in 1.134 seconds (11 times faster). That is, our new program is approximately 10 times faster than the original version. But we can still do better, by using some simple high-school algebra.

9.9   Exploiting algebraic properties

The function **solutions'** generates all possible expressions over the given numbers whose evaluation is successful, but in practice many of these expressions will be essentially the same, due to the fact that the numeric operators have algebraic properties. For example, the expressions $2 + 3$ and $3 + 2$ are essentially the same because the result of an addition does not depend upon the order of the two arguments, while $2 \div 1$ and 2 are essentially the same because dividing any number by one has no effect on that number.

Based upon this observation, our final approach to solving the countdown problem is to improve our second program by exploiting such algebraic properties to reduce the number of generated expressions. In particular, we exploit the following five commutativity and identity properties:

$$x + y = y + x$$
$$x * y = y * x$$
$$x * 1 = x$$
$$1 * y = y$$
$$x \div 1 = x$$

We start by recalling the function **valid** that decides if the application of an operator to two positive naturals gives another such:

```
valid :: Op -> Int -> Int -> Bool
valid Add _ _ = True
```

```
valid Sub x y = x > y
valid Mul _ _ = True
valid Div x y = x 'mod' y == 0
```

This definition can be modified to exploit the commutativity of addition and multiplication simply by requiring that their arguments are in numeric order ($x \leqslant y$), and the identity properties of multiplication and division simply by requiring that the appropriate arguments are non-unitary ($\neq 1$):

```
valid Add x y = x <= y
valid Sub x y = x > y
valid Mul x y = x /= 1 && y /= 1 && x <= y
valid Div x y = y /= 1 && x 'mod' y == 0
```

For example, using this new definition, Add 3 2 is now invalid because it is essentially the same as Add 2 3 using the commutativity property for addition, while Div 2 1 is now invalid because it is essentially the same as the number 2 on its own using the identity property for division.

Using the new version of valid gives a new version of solutions' that solves the countdown problem, which we write as solutions''. Using this new function can considerably reduce the number of generated expressions and the number of solutions. For example, solutions'' [1,3,7,10,25,50] 765 only generates 245,644 expressions, of which just 49 are solutions, which is just over 5% and 6% respectively of the numbers using solutions'.

As regards performance, solutions'' [1,3,7,10,25,50] 765 now returns the first solution in 0.007 seconds (twice as fast as solutions') and all solutions in 0.119 seconds (11 times faster), while for the target number 831 the empty list is returned in 0.115 seconds (9 times faster). More generally, given any numbers from the television version of the countdown problem, our final program usually returns all solutions in a fraction of a second, and is around 100 times faster than the original brute force version — quite an improvement!

9.10   Chapter remarks

Countdown is based upon an original version on French television called *Des Chiffres et des Lettres*, while the countdown problem itself is related to the children's arithmetic games called *krypto* and *four fours*. This chapter is based upon [13], which also includes proofs of correctness of the three programs that were produced. A number of more advanced approaches to solving the countdown problem are explored by Bird and Mu [14].

9.11   Exercises

1. Redefine the combinatorial function `choices` using a list comprehension rather than using composition, `concat` and `map`.

2. Define a recursive function `isChoice :: Eq a => [a] -> [a] -> Bool` that decides if one list is chosen from another, without using the combinatorial functions `perms` and `subs`. Hint: start by defining a function that removes the first occurrence of a value from a list.

3. What effect would generalising the function `split` to also return pairs containing the empty list have on the behaviour of `solutions`?

4. Using the functions `choices`, `exprs`, and `eval`, verify that there are 33,665,406 possible expressions over the numbers $1, 3, 7, 10, 25, 50$, and that only 4,672,540 of these expressions evaluate successfully.

5. Similarly, verify that the number of expressions that evaluate successfully increases to 10,839,369 if the numeric domain is generalised to arbitrary integers. Hint: modify the definition of `valid`.

6. Modify the final program to:

    a. allow the use of exponentiation in expressions;

    b. produce the nearest solutions if no exact solution is possible;

    c. order the solutions using a suitable measure of simplicity.

Solutions to exercises 1–3 are given in appendix A.

Part II

Going Further

10 Interactive programming

In this chapter we show how Haskell can be used to write interactive programs. We start by explaining the problem of handling interaction in a pure language, present the solution that is adopted in Haskell, introduce a range of primitives and derived functions for interactive programming, and conclude by developing three interactive games: hangman, nim and life.

10.1 The problem

In the early days of computing, most programs were *batch programs* that were run in isolation from their users, to maximise the amount of time the computer was performing useful work. For example, a compiler is a batch program that takes a high-level program as its input, silently performs a large number of operations, and then produces a low-level program as its output.

In part I of the book, we showed how Haskell can be used to write batch programs. In Haskell such programs, and more generally all programs, are modelled as *pure functions* that take all their inputs as explicit arguments, and produce all their outputs as explicit results, as depicted below:

For example, a compiler such as GHC may be modelled as a function of type `Prog -> Code` that transforms a high-level program into low-level code.

In the modern era of computing, most programs are now *interactive programs* that are run as an ongoing dialogue with their users, to provide increased flexibility and functionality. For example, an interpreter is an interactive program that allows expressions to be entered using the keyboard, and immediately displays the result of evaluating such expressions on the screen:

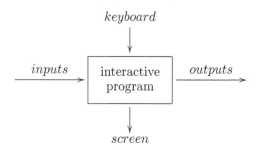

How can such programs be modelled as pure functions? At first sight, this may seem impossible, because interactive programs by their very nature require the *side effects* of taking additional inputs and producing additional outputs while the program is running. For example, how can an interpreter such as GHCi be viewed as a pure function from arguments to results?

Over the years many approaches to the problem of combining the use of pure functions with the need for side effects have been developed. In the remainder of this chapter we present the solution that is used in Haskell, which is based upon a new type together with a small number of primitive operations. As we shall see in later chapters, the underlying approach is not specific to interaction, but can also be used to program with other forms of effects.

10.2   The solution

In Haskell, an interactive program is viewed as a pure function that takes the current *state of the world* as its argument, and produces a modified world as its result, in which the modified world reflects any side effects that were performed by the program during its execution. Hence, given a suitable type World whose values represent states of the world, the notion of an interactive program can be represented by a function of type World -> World, which we abbreviate as IO (short for input/output) using the following type declaration:

```
type IO = World -> World
```

In general, however, an interactive program may return a result value in addition to performing side effects. For example, a program for reading a character from the keyboard may return the character that was read. For this reason, we generalise our type for interactive programs to also return a result value, with the type of such values being a parameter of the IO type:

```
type IO a = World -> (a,World)
```

Expressions of type IO a are called *actions*. For example, IO Char is the type of actions that return a character, while IO () is the type of actions that return the empty tuple () as a dummy result value. Actions of the latter type can be thought of as purely side-effecting actions that return no result value, and are often useful in interactive programming. For example, the countdown program in chapter 9 used a top-level definition `main` of type `IO ()`.

In addition to returning a result value, interactive programs may also require argument values. However, there is no need to generalise the `IO` type further to take account of this, because this behaviour can already be achieved by exploiting currying. For example, an interactive program that takes a character and returns an integer would have type `Char -> IO Int`, which abbreviates the curried function type `Char -> World -> (Int,World)`.

At this point the reader may, quite reasonably, be concerned about the feasibility of passing around the entire state of the world when programming with actions! Of course, this isn't possible, and in reality the type `IO a` is provided as a primitive in Haskell, rather than being represented as a function type. However, the above explanation is useful for understanding how actions can be viewed as pure functions, and the implementation of actions in Haskell is consistent with this view. For the remainder of this chapter, we will consider `IO a` as a built-in type whose implementation details are hidden:

```
data IO a = ...
```

10.3   Basic actions

We now introduce three basic `IO` actions that are provided in Haskell. First of all, the action `getChar` reads a character from the keyboard, echoes it to the screen, and returns the character as its result value.

```
getChar :: IO Char
getChar = ...
```

(The actual definition for `getChar` is built into the GHC system.) If there are no characters waiting to be read from the keyboard, `getChar` waits until one is typed. The dual action, `putChar c`, writes the character `c` to the screen, and returns no result value, represented by the empty tuple:

```
putChar :: Char -> IO ()
putChar c = ...
```

Our final basic action is `return v`, which simply returns the result value `v` without performing any interaction with the user:

```
return :: a -> IO a
return v = ...
```

The function `return` provides a bridge from pure expressions without side effects to impure actions with side effects. Crucially, there is no bridge back — once we are impure we are impure for ever, with no possibility for redemption! As a result, we may suspect that impurity quickly permeates entire programs, but in practice this is usually not the case. For most Haskell programs, the vast majority of functions do not involve interaction, with this being handled by a relatively small number of interactive functions at the outermost level.

10.4   Sequencing

In Haskell, a sequence of IO actions can be combined into a single composite action using the do notation, whose typical form is as follows:

```
do v1 <- a1
   v2 <- a2
   .
   .
   .
   vn <- an
   return (f v1 v2 ... vn)
```

Such expressions have a simple operational reading: first perform the action a1 and call its result value v1; then perform the action a2 and call its result value v2; ...; then perform the action an and call its result value vn; and finally, apply the function f to combine all the results into a single value, which is then returned as the result value from the expression as a whole.

There are three further points to note about the do notation. First of all, the layout rule applies, in the sense that each action in the sequence must begin in precisely the same column, as illustrated above. Secondly, as with list comprehensions, the expressions vi <- ai are called *generators*, because they generate values for the variables vi. And finally, if the result value produced by a generator vi <- ai is not required, the generator can be abbreviated simply by ai, which has the same meaning as writing _ <- ai.

For example, an action that reads three characters, discards the second, and returns the first and third as a pair can now be defined as follows:

```
act :: IO (Char,Char)
act = do x <- getChar
         getChar
         y <- getChar
         return (x,y)
```

Note that omitting the use of **return** in this example would give rise to a type error, because (x,y) is an expression of type (Char,Char), whereas in the above context we require an action of type IO (Char,Char).

10.5   Derived primitives

Using the three basic actions together with sequencing, we can now define a number of other useful action primitives that are provided in the standard prelude. First of all, we define an action `getLine` that reads a string of characters from the keyboard, terminated by the newline character '\n':

```
getLine :: IO String
getLine = do x <- getChar
             if x == '\n' then
                return []
             else
                do xs <- getLine
                   return (x:xs)
```

Note the use of recursion to read the rest of the string once the first character has been read. Dually, we define primitives `putStr` and `putStrLn` that write a string to the screen, and in the latter case also move to a new line:

```
putStr :: String -> IO ()
putStr []     = return ()
putStr (x:xs) = do putChar x
                   putStr xs

putStrLn :: String -> IO ()
putStrLn xs = do putStr xs
                 putChar '\n'
```

For example, using these primitives we can now define an action that prompts for a string to be entered from the keyboard, and displays its length:

```
strlen :: IO ()
strlen = do putStr "Enter a string: "
            xs <- getLine
            putStr "The string has "
            putStr (show (length xs))
            putStrLn " characters"
```

For example:

```
> strlen
Enter a string: Haskell
The string has 7 characters
```

10.6   Hangman

In the remainder of this chapter we present three extended programming examples, of increasing complexity. Our first example illustrates the basics of IO programming using a variant of the game *hangman*. At the start of the game, one player secretly enters a word. Another player then tries to deduce the word via a series of guesses. For each guess, we indicate which letters in the secret word occur in the guess, and the game ends when the guess is correct.

We implement the hangman game in a top-down manner, starting with a top-level action that prompts the first player to enter a secret word, and then asks the second player to try and guess it:

```
hangman :: IO ()
hangman = do putStrLn "Think of a word:"
             word <- sgetLine
             putStrLn "Try to guess it:"
             play word
```

It now remains to complete the definitions for sgetLine and play. First of all, the action sgetLine reads a string of characters from the keyboard in a similar manner to the basic action getLine, except that it echoes each character as a dash symbol '-' in order to keep the string secret:

```
sgetLine :: IO String
sgetLine = do x <- getCh
              if x == '\n' then
                 do putChar x
                    return []
              else
                 do putChar '-'
                    xs <- sgetLine
                    return (x:xs)
```

In turn, the action getCh used in this definition reads a single character from the keyboard without echoing it to the screen, and is defined by using the primitive hSetEcho from the library System.IO to turn input echoing off prior to reading the character, and back on again afterwards:

```
getCh :: IO Char
getCh = do hSetEcho stdin False
           x <- getChar
           hSetEcho stdin True
           return x
```

(The primitive hSetEcho can be made available by including the declaration import System.IO at the start of a script.) We now return to the function play, which implements the main game loop by repeatedly prompting the second player to enter a guess until it equals the secret word:

```
play :: String -> IO ()
play word = do putStr "? "
               guess <- getLine
               if guess == word then
                   putStrLn "You got it!!"
               else
                   do putStrLn (match word guess)
                      play word
```

In the case when the guess is not correct, we use a list comprehension to indicate which letters in the secret word occur anywhere in the guess:

```
match :: String -> String -> String
match xs ys = [if elem x ys then x else '-' | x <- xs]
```

The game is now complete, and can be tried out. For example, here is how the game might proceed if the secret word was nottingham:

```
> hangman
Think of a word:
----------
Try to guess it:
? glasgow
-o----g-a-
? utrecht
--tt---h--
? gothenburg
nott-ngh--
? nottingham
You got it!!
```

10.7   Nim

For our second example we consider a variant of the *game of nim*, played on a board comprising five numbered rows of stars, initially set up as follows:

$$1 : \star \; \star \; \star \; \star \; \star$$
$$2 : \star \; \star \; \star \; \star$$
$$3 : \star \; \star \; \star$$
$$4 : \star \; \star$$
$$5 : \star$$

Two players then take it in turn to remove one or more stars from the end of a single row. The winner is the player who makes the board empty, that is, who removes the final star or stars from the board. To contrast with the top-down development of the hangman game in the previous section, we implement nim in a bottom-up manner, starting by defining a series of utility functions, which are then used to implement the game itself.

Game utilities

For simplicity, we represent the player number (1 or 2) as an integer, and use the following function to give the next player:

```
next :: Int -> Int
next 1 = 2
next 2 = 1
```

In turn, we represent the board as a list comprising the number of stars that remain on each row, with the initial board given by the list [5,4,3,2,1], and the game being finished when all rows have no stars left:

```
type Board = [Int]

initial :: Board
initial = [5,4,3,2,1]

finished :: Board -> Bool
finished = all (== 0)
```

A move in the game is specified by a row number and the number of stars to be removed, and is valid if the row contains at least this many stars:

```
valid :: Board -> Int -> Int -> Bool
valid board row num = board !! (row-1) >= num
```

(Recall that list indexing starts from zero, hence the use of subtraction above.) For example, `valid initial 1 3` returns `True`, because the first row on the initial board contains at least three stars, whereas `valid initial 4 3` returns `False`, because the fourth row contains fewer than three stars. A valid move can then be applied to a board to give an new board by using a list comprehension to update the number of stars that remain in each row:

```
move :: Board -> Int -> Int -> Board
move board row num = [update r n | (r,n) <- zip [1..] board]
    where update r n = if r == row then n-num else n
```

For example, `move initial 1 3` returns the new board [2,4,3,2,1] in which three stars have been removed from the first row.

IO utilities

We begin by defining a function that displays a row of the board on the screen, given the row number and the number of stars remaining:

```
putRow :: Int -> Int -> IO ()
putRow row num = do putStr (show row)
                    putStr ": "
                    putStrLn (concat (replicate num "* "))
```

Recall that the library function `replicate` produces a list with a given number of identical elements. For example, we have:

```
> putRow 1 5
1: * * * * *
```

In turn, `putRow` can then be used to display the board. For simplicity, we assume that the board always contains precisely five rows:

```
putBoard :: Board -> IO ()
putBoard [a,b,c,d,e] = do putRow 1 a
                          putRow 2 b
                          putRow 3 c
                          putRow 4 d
                          putRow 5 e
```

For example:

```
> putBoard initial
1: * * * * *
2: * * * *
3: * * *
4: * *
5: *
```

We also define a utility function `getDigit` that displays a prompt and reads a single character from the keyboard. If the character is a digit, the corresponding integer is returned as the result value, otherwise an error message is displayed and the user is reprompted to enter a digit:

```
getDigit :: String -> IO Int
getDigit prompt = do putStr prompt
                     x <- getChar
                     newline
                     if isDigit x then
                        return (digitToInt x)
                     else
                        do putStrLn "ERROR: Invalid digit"
                           getDigit prompt
```

(The function `digitToInt :: Char -> Int` converts a digit to an integer, and can be made available by writing `import Data.Char` at the start of a script.) Finally, we define an action that moves onto a new line:

```
newline :: IO ()
newline = putChar '\n'
```

Game of nim

Using the above utility functions, we can now implement the main game loop, which takes the current board and player number as arguments:

```
play :: Board -> Int -> IO ()
play board player =
   do newline
      putBoard board
      if finished board then
         do newline
            putStr "Player "
            putStr (show (next player))
            putStrLn " wins!!"
      else
         do newline
            putStr "Player "
            putStrLn (show player)
            row <- getDigit "Enter a row number: "
            num <- getDigit "Stars to remove : "
            if valid board row num then
               play (move board row num) (next player)
            else
               do newline
                  putStrLn "ERROR: Invalid move"
                  play board player
```

That is, we first display the board, and then check if the game is finished. If so, we display the other player as the winner, as they were the one who made the board empty. Otherwise we prompt the current player for the move they wish to make. If the move is valid, we update the board accordingly and then continue the game with the next player, otherwise we display an error message and reprompt the current player to enter a valid move.

Finally, the game of nim itself can then be implemented simply by invoking the game loop with the initial board and player number:

```
nim :: IO ()
nim = play initial 1
```

We conclude with two further remarks about our implementation of nim. First of all, note that because Haskell is a pure language, we needed to supply the game state, which in this case comprises the current board and player number, as explicit arguments to the `play` function. And secondly, note the separation between the pure parts of our implementation, in the form of the utility functions on players and boards, from the impure parts that involve input/output. It is good practice to try and maintain this kind of separation in Haskell programs, to minimise and localise the use of side effects.

10.8   Life

Our third and final interactive programming example concerns the *game of life*. The game models a simple evolutionary system based on cells, and is played on a two-dimensional board. Each square on the board is either empty, or contains a single living cell, as illustrated in the following example:

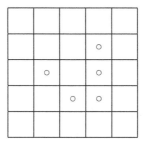

Each internal square on the board has eight immediate neighbours:

For uniformity, each external square on the board is also viewed as having eight neighbours, by assuming that the board wraps around from top-to-bottom and from left-to-right. That is, we can think of the board as really being a torus, the surface of a three-dimensional doughnut shaped object.

Given an initial configuration of the board, the next *generation* of the board is given by simultaneously applying the following rules to all squares:

- a living cell survives if it has precisely two or three neighbouring squares that contain living cells, and

- an empty square gives birth to a living cell if it has precisely three neighbours that contain living cells, and remains empty otherwise.

For example, applying these rules to the above board gives:

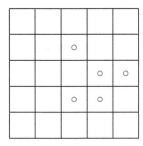

By repeating this procedure with the new board, an infinite sequence of generations can be produced. By careful design of the initial configuration, many interesting patterns of behaviour can be observed in such sequences. For example, the above arrangement of cells is called a *glider*, and over successive generations will move diagonally down the board. Despite its simplicity, the game of life is in fact computationally complete, in the sense that any computational process can be simulated within it by means of a suitable encoding. In the remainder of this section we show how the game of life can be implemented in Haskell.

Screen utilities

We begin with some useful output utilities concerning the screen on which the game will be played. First of all, we define an action that clears the screen, which can be achieved by displaying the appropriate control characters:

```
cls :: IO ()
cls = putStr "\ESC[2J"
```

By convention, the position of each character on the screen is given by a pair (x,y) of positive integers, with (1,1) being the top-left corner. We represent such coordinate positions using the following type:

```
type Pos = (Int,Int)
```

We can then define a function that displays a string at a given position by using control characters to move the cursor to this position:

```
writeat :: Pos -> String -> IO ()
writeat p xs = do goto p
                  putStr xs

goto :: Pos -> IO ()
goto (x,y) = putStr ("\ESC[" ++ show y ++ ";" ++ show x ++ "H")
```

Game of life

For simplicity, we assumed that the board size for nim was fixed. For increased flexibility, we allow the board size for life to be modified, by means of two integer values that specify the size of the board in squares:

```
width :: Int
width = 10

height :: Int
height = 10
```

We represent a board as a list of the (x,y) positions at which there is a living cell, using the same coordinate convention as the screen:

```
type Board = [Pos]
```

For example, the initial example board above would be represented by:

```
glider :: Board
glider = [(4,2),(2,3),(4,3),(3,4),(4,4)]
```

Using this representation of the board, it is easy to display the living cells on the screen, and to decide if a given position is alive or empty:

```
showcells :: Board -> IO ()
showcells b = sequence_ [writeat p "O" | p <- b]

isAlive :: Board -> Pos -> Bool
isAlive b p = elem p b

isEmpty :: Board -> Pos -> Bool
isEmpty b p = not (isAlive b p)
```

(The library function sequence_ :: [IO a] -> IO () performs a list of actions in sequence, discarding their result values and returning no result.) Next, we define a function that returns the neighbours of a position:

```
neighbs :: Pos -> [Pos]
neighbs (x,y) = map wrap [(x-1,y-1), (x,y-1),
                          (x+1,y-1), (x-1,y),
                          (x+1,y), (x-1,y+1),
                          (x,y+1), (x+1,y+1)]
```

The auxiliary function wrap takes account of the wrapping around at the edges of the board, by subtracting one from each component of the given position, taking the remainder when divided by the width and height of the board, and then adding one to each component again:

```
wrap :: Pos -> Pos
wrap (x,y) = (((x-1) 'mod' width) + 1,
              ((y-1) 'mod' height) + 1)
```

Using function composition, we can now define a function that calculates the number of live neighbours for a given position by producing the list of its neighbours, retaining those that are alive, and counting their number:

```
liveneighbs :: Board -> Pos -> Int
liveneighbs b = length . filter (isAlive b) . neighbs
```

Using this function, it is then straightforward to produce the list of living positions in a board that have precisely two or three living neighbours, and hence survive to the next generation of the game:

```
survivors :: Board -> [Pos]
survivors b = [p | p <- b, elem (liveneighbs b p) [2,3]]
```

In turn, the list of empty positions in a board that have precisely three living neighbours, and hence give birth to a new cell, can be produced as follows:

```
births :: Board -> [Pos]
births b = [(x,y) | x <- [1..width],
                    y <- [1..height],
                    isEmpty b (x,y),
                    liveneighbs b (x,y) == 3]
```

However, this definition considers every position on the board. A more refined approach, which may be more efficient for larger boards, is to only consider the neighbours of living cells, because only such cells can give rise to new births. Using this approach, the function **births** can be rewritten as follows:

```
births :: Board -> [Pos]
births b = [p | p <- rmdups (concat (map neighbs b)),
             isEmpty b p,
             liveneighbs b p == 3]
```

The auxiliary function **rmdups** removes duplicates from a list, and is used above to ensure that each potential new cell is only considered once:

```
rmdups :: Eq a => [a] -> [a]
rmdups []     = []
rmdups (x:xs) = x : rmdups (filter (/= x) xs)
```

The next generation of a board can now be produced simply by appending the list of survivors and the list of new births:

```
nextgen :: Board -> Board
nextgen b = survivors b ++ births b
```

Finally, we define a function `life` that implements the game of life itself, by clearing the screen, showing the living cells in the current board, waiting for a moment, and then continuing with the next generation:

```
life :: Board -> IO ()
life b = do cls
            showcells b
            wait 500000
            life (nextgen b)
```

The function `wait` is used to slow down the game to a reasonable speed, and can be implemented by performing a given number of dummy actions:

```
wait :: Int -> IO ()
wait n = sequence_ [return () | _ <- [1..n]]
```

For fun, you might like to try out the `life` function with the `glider` example, and experiment with some patterns of your own. Note also that most of the definitions used to implement the game of life are pure functions, with only a small number of top-level definitions involving input/output. Moreover, the definitions that do have such side effects are clearly distinguishable from those that do not, through the presence of `IO` in their types.

10.9   Chapter remarks

The use of the `IO` type to perform other forms of side effects, including reading and writing from files, is discussed in the Haskell Report [4], and a formal meaning for this type is given in [15]. For specialised applications, a bridge back from impure actions to pure expressions is in fact available via the function `unsafePerformIO :: IO a -> a` in the library `System.IO.Unsafe`. However, as suggested by the naming, this function is unsafe and should not be used in normal Haskell programs as it compromises the purity of the language.

10.10   Exercises

1. Redefine `putStr :: String -> IO ()` using a list comprehension and the library function `sequence_ :: [IO a] -> IO ()`.

2. Using recursion, define a version of `putBoard :: Board -> IO ()` that displays nim boards of any size, rather than being specific to boards with just five rows of stars. Hint: first define an auxiliary function that takes the current row number as an additional argument.

3. In a similar manner to the first exercise, redefine the generalised version of
`putBoard` using a list comprehension and `sequence_`.

4. Define an action `adder :: IO ()` that reads a given number of integers from
the keyboard, one per line, and displays their sum. For example:

```
> adder
How many numbers? 5
1
3
5
7
9
The total is 25
```

Hint: start by defining an auxiliary function that takes the current total and
how many numbers remain to be read as arguments. You will also likely need
to use the library functions `read` and `show`.

5. Redefine `adder` using the function `sequence :: [IO a] -> IO [a]` that performs a list of actions and returns a list of the resulting values.

6. Using `getCh`, define an action `readLine :: IO String` that behaves in the
same way as `getLine`, except that it also permits the delete key to be used
to remove characters. Hint: the delete character is `'\DEL'`, and the control
character for moving the cursor back one space is `'\b'`.

Solutions to exercises 1–3 are given in appendix A.

11 Unbeatable tic-tac-toe

In this chapter we illustrate the concepts introduced so far by developing an interactive program that plays the game of tic-tac-toe. We start by implementing a version that allows two human players to compete against each other, and then develop a computer player that uses game trees and the minimax algorithm to ensure that it is unbeatable, that is, always wins or draws.

11.1   Introduction

Tic-tac-toe, also known as noughts and crosses, is a game that is traditionally played on a 3×3 grid, which is initially empty:

Two players, $\bigcirc$ and $\times$, then take it in turn to place their mark in a blank space in the grid. The winner is the first player to place three of their marks in a horizontal, vertical, or diagonal line. For example, the grid below has three $\times$'s in the bottom row, and hence $\times$ is the winner:

$$
\begin{array}{c|c|c}
  & \bigcirc & \bigcirc \\
\hline
\bigcirc & \times & \bigcirc \\
\hline
\times & \times & \times
\end{array}
$$

If the grid becomes fully occupied without either player having won, then the game ends in a draw, as in the following example:

$$
\begin{array}{c|c|c}
\bigcirc & \bigcirc & \times \\
\hline
\times & \times & \bigcirc \\
\hline
\bigcirc & \times & \bigcirc
\end{array}
$$

By playing in a perfect manner, that is, always making the best possible move at each turn, a player can always force a draw, independent of whether they go first or second in the game. In the remainder of this chapter we show how to implement a perfect tic-tac-toe player in Haskell.

11.2   Basic declarations

We begin by importing standard libraries that provide functions on characters, lists and input/output actions that will be used in our implementation:

```
import Data.Char
import Data.List
import System.IO
```

Rather than assuming that the tic-tac-toe grid has a fixed size of 3×3, we allow the size to be changed to any integer value greater than zero:

```
size :: Int
size = 3
```

We represent a grid as a list of lists of player values, with the assumption that the each of the inner lists, and the outer list, all have length `size`:

```
type Grid = [[Player]]
```

In turn, a player value is either O, B or X, where the extra value B represents a blank space that has not yet been occupied:

```
data Player = O | B | X
              deriving (Eq, Ord, Show)
```

For example, the winning grid from the previous section can be represented by `[[B,O,O],[O,X,O],[X,X,X]] :: Grid`. The `deriving` clause above ensures that player values support the standard equality and ordering operators, and can be displayed on the screen. Recall that the ordering on constructors is determined by their position in the `data` declaration, hence we have O < B < X, which will be important when we consider the minimax algorithm.

The next player to move is given simply by swapping between O and X, with the case for the blank value B being included for completeness even though the function should never be applied to this value:

```
next :: Player -> Player
next O = X
next B = B
next X = O
```

11.3   Grid utilities

We make use of a number of utilities on tic-tac-toe grids. First of all, we define the empty grid by replicating the blank player value to create an empty row, and then replicating this row to create an empty grid:

```
empty :: Grid
empty = replicate size (replicate size B)
```

Conversely, a grid is full if all of its player values are non-blank:

```
full :: Grid -> Bool
full = all (/= B) . concat
```

The idea of applying `concat` to flatten a grid into a single list prior to processing its player values, as in the above definition, will be used in a number of other functions that we define. For example, we can decide whose turn it is by comparing the number of O's and X's in a flattened grid:

```
turn :: Grid -> Player
turn g = if os <= xs then O else X
          where
              os = length (filter (== O) ps)
              xs = length (filter (== X) ps)
              ps = concat g
```

Note that `turn empty = O` means that we are assuming player O goes first, which in our final implementation will be the human player.

We now turn our attention to deciding if the game has been won, that is, if a player has a complete line in any row, column, or either diagonal in the grid. Using local definitions to improve readability, this idea can be translated directly into a function that decides if a player wins in a grid:

```
wins :: Player -> Grid -> Bool
wins p g = any line (rows ++ cols ++ dias)
          where
              line = all (== p)
              rows = g
              cols = transpose g
              dias = [diag g, diag (map reverse g)]
```

The function `transpose :: [[a]] -> [[a]]` used above is provided in the library `Data.List`, and takes a grid that is represented as a list of rows and reflects it about the main diagonal that runs from top-left to bottom-right, so that the columns become rows and vice-versa. For example:

```
> transpose [[1,2,3],[4,5,6],[7,8,9]]
[[1,4,7],[2,5,8],[3,6,9]]
```

In turn, the function `diag` returns the main diagonal of a grid:

```
diag :: Grid -> [Player]
diag g = [g !! n !! n | n <- [0..size-1]]
```

The other diagonal, from top-right to bottom-left, can then be obtained by first reversing each row in the grid, as in the definition of `wins` above. Finally, we can now define a function that decides if either player has won:

```
won :: Grid -> Bool
won g = wins O g || wins X g
```

11.4   Displaying a grid

For the purposes of displaying a tic-tac-toe grid on the screen, we seek to define a function with the following example behaviour:

```
> putGrid [[B,O,O],[O,X,O],[X,X,X]]

   |   |
   | O | O
   |   |
-----------
   |   |
 O | X | O
   |   |
-----------
   |   |
 X | X | X
   |   |
```

This behaviour can readily be achieved using function composition:

```
putGrid :: Grid -> IO ()
putGrid =
  putStrLn . unlines . concat . interleave bar . map showRow
  where bar = [replicate ((size*4)-1) '-']
```

That is, we convert each row to a list of strings using `showRow`, insert a horizontal bar between each row using `interleave`, flatten the resulting nested list structure using `concat`, join all the strings together with a newline character at the each of each line using the library function `unlines :: [String] -> String`, and finally, display the resulting string on the screen using `putStrLn`.

In turn, the function `showRow` converts a row to a list of strings, with a vertical bar of length three between each entry in the row:

```
showRow :: [Player] -> [String]
showRow = beside . interleave bar . map showPlayer
          where
             beside = foldr1 (zipWith (++))
             bar    = replicate 3 "|"
```

The library function `foldr1` used above behaves in a similar manner to `foldr` but can only be applied to non-empty lists, while `zipWith` behaves in the same way as `zip` but applies a given function to each pair of values in the resulting list. For example, `showRow [O,B,X]` returns the following list:

```
["   |   |   ",
 " O |   | X ",
 "   |   |   "]
```

The two remaining functions simply convert a player value to a list of strings, and interleave a value between each element in a list:

```
showPlayer :: Player -> [String]
showPlayer O = ["   ", " O ", "   "]
showPlayer B = ["   ", "   ", "   "]
showPlayer X = ["   ", " X ", "   "]

interleave :: a -> [a] -> [a]
interleave x []     = []
interleave x [y]    = [y]
interleave x (y:ys) = y : x : interleave x ys
```

11.5   Making a move

To identify where a player wishes to make a move during the game, we index each position in the grid by a natural number, starting from zero in the top-left corner and proceeding along each row in turn:

0	1	2
3	4	5
6	7	8

Attempting to make a move at a particular index is valid if the index is within the appropriate range, and the position is currently blank:

```
valid :: Grid -> Int -> Bool
valid g i = 0 <= i && i < size^2 && concat g !! i == B
```

We now define a function that applies a move to a grid. In order to take account of the possibility that a move may be invalid, we return a list of grids as the result, with the convention that a singleton list denotes success in applying the move, and the empty list denotes failure:

```
move:: Grid -> Int -> Player -> [Grid]
move g i p =
   if valid g i then [chop size (xs ++ [p] ++ ys)] else []
   where (xs,B:ys) = splitAt i (concat g)
```

That is, if the move is valid we split the list of player values in the grid at the index where the move is being made, replace the blank player value with the given player, and then reform the grid once again. The library function `splitAt` breaks a list into two parts at a given index, and the auxiliary function `chop` breaks a list into maximal segments of a given length:

```
chop :: Int -> [a] -> [[a]]
chop n [] = []
chop n xs = take n xs : chop n (drop n xs)
```

11.6   Reading a number

To read a grid index from a human player, we define a function `getNat` that displays a prompt and reads a natural number from the keyboard. It is defined in a similar manner to the function `getDigit` for the nim game in chapter 10, except that it reads a natural number rather than a single digit:

```
getNat :: String -> IO Int
getNat prompt = do putStr prompt
                   xs <- getLine
                   if xs /= [] && all isDigit xs then
                      return (read xs)
                   else
                      do putStrLn "ERROR: Invalid number"
                         getNat prompt
```

The function `isDigit :: Char -> Bool` used above is provided in the library `Data.Char`, and decides if a character is a numeric digit.

11.7   Human vs human

We now have the necessary machinery to implement tic-tac-toe for two human players. We define an action that implements the game using two mutually recursive functions that take the current grid and player as arguments:

```
tictactoe :: IO ()
tictactoe = run empty O
```

The first function simply displays the grid and invokes the second:

```
run :: Grid -> Player -> IO ()
run g p = do cls
             goto (1,1)
             putGrid g
             run' g p
```

(The screen utilities `cls` and `goto` were defined for the game of life in chapter 10.) In turn, the second function uses a series of guards to decide if the game is finished, and if not prompts the player for a move. If the move is invalid we display an error message and reprompt the player, otherwise we invoke the first function with the updated board and the next player:

```
run' :: Grid -> Player -> IO ()
run' g p | wins O g  = putStrLn "Player O wins!\n"
         | wins X g  = putStrLn "Player X wins!\n"
         | full g    = putStrLn "It's a draw!\n"
         | otherwise =
             do i <- getNat (prompt p)
                case move g i p of
                    [] -> do putStrLn "ERROR: Invalid move"
                             run' g p
                    [g'] -> run g' (next p)
```

The auxiliary function `prompt` is defined as follows:

```
prompt :: Player -> String
prompt p = "Player " ++ show p ++ ", enter your move: "
```

You may like to try the game out with a friend now! As with all the extended examples, the code is available from the website for the book.

11.8   Game trees

We now show how to develop a computer player for tic-tac-toe, based on the use of *game trees*. The basic idea is to build a tree structure that captures all possible ways in which the game can proceed from the current grid, and then use this tree to decide on the best next move to make.

By way of example, suppose that we are given the following tic-tac-toe grid, and it is player O's turn to make a move:

The player can place their mark in any of the three remaining blank spaces at positions 1, 2 and 8, giving three possible next grids:

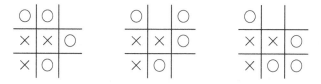

Now it is X's turn to move, and we repeat the same process for each of these three grids, stopping when there is a winner or the grid is full. In this manner, we can produce the following game tree from the starting grid:

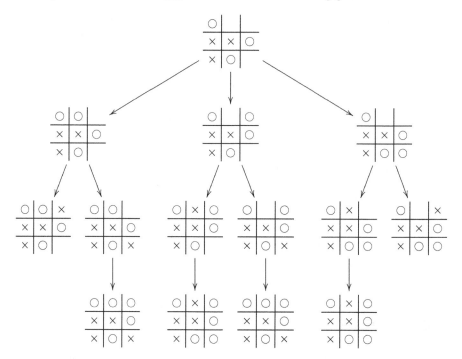

For this example, we can see that player X wins if the game proceeds down the left or right spine of the tree, and player O wins otherwise. Hence, the game tree shows that the best next move for player O is the middle of the three possible moves at the top of the tree, as this guarantees a win for O, whereas either of the other two possible next moves can result in a win for X.

A suitable type for representing such trees can be declared as follows:

```
data Tree a = Node a [Tree a]
            deriving Show
```

That is, a tree of a given type is a node that comprises a value of this type and a list of subtrees. There are three further points to note about this declaration. First of all, it is not specific to tic-tac-toe grids, but permits any type of values to be stored in the nodes; this will be important when we consider the minimax algorithm, which labels each grid in the game tree with additional information. Secondly, there is no constructor for leaves, because a node with an empty list of subtrees can play this role; this avoids having two possible representations for leaves, which could complicate the definition of functions on trees. And finally, the **deriving** clause ensures that trees can be displayed on the screen.

Using the above tree type, it is straightforward to define a function that builds a game tree from a given starting grid and player. We simply use the starting grid as the value for the root node, and then recursively build a game tree for each grid that results from the current player making a valid move, with the next player then being used to continue the process:

```
gametree :: Grid -> Player -> Tree Grid
gametree g p = Node g [gametree g' (next p) | g' <- moves g p]
```

In turn, the function **moves** that returns the list of valid moves is defined by first checking if the game is finished, in which case we return the empty list of grids, which serves to stop the recursion in **gametree**. Otherwise, we return all grids that result from making a move in a blank space:

```
moves :: Grid -> Player -> [Grid]
moves g p
   | won g     = []
   | full g    = []
   | otherwise = concat [move g i p | i <- [0..((size^2)-1)]]
```

11.9   Pruning the tree

As one may imagine, game trees can potentially become very large. For this reason, it is sometimes necessary to prune game trees to a particular depth, in order to limit the amount of time and memory that it takes to build the tree. To this end, we define a function that prunes a tree to a given depth:

```
prune :: Int -> Tree a -> Tree a
prune 0 (Node x _)  = Node x []
prune n (Node x ts) = Node x [prune (n-1) t | t <- ts]
```

For example, `prune 5 (gametree empty O)` produces a game tree of maximum depth five starting from the empty grid with player O making the first move. Note that under lazy evaluation, only as much of the tree as required by the `prune` function will actually be produced. That is, grids beyond depth five in this example will never be generated by `gametree`.

We also define a constant that specifies the maximum depth of the game tree. On a modern machine it is feasible to generate the entire tree for a 3×3 grid, so we set the default depth to the maximum value required for grids of this size. For larger grids, it may be necessary to reduce this value.

```
depth :: Int
depth = 9
```

11.10   Minimax algorithm

Once we have produced a game tree, the *minimax algorithm* can then be used to determine the best next move. The algorithm starts by labelling every node in the tree with a player value in the following manner:

- Leaves (nodes with no subtrees) are labelled with the winning player at this point if there is one, and the blank player otherwise;
- Other nodes (with subtrees) are labelled with the *minimum* or *maximum* of the player labels from the child nodes one level down, depending on whose turn it is to move at this point: on player O's turn we take the minimum of the child labels, and on X's turn we take the maximum.

For example, applying the algorithm to the game tree from the previous section results in the following tree of player labels:

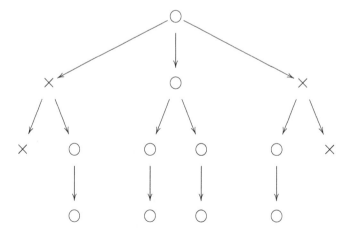

For example, the leftmost leaf in the tree is labelled X because player X has won at this point, while the root node is labelled O because it is player O's turn at this point and hence we take the minimum of the child labels X, O and X, which under the ordering O < B < X is given by the value O.

Using a series of guards to determine the label, the minimax algorithm can be translated directly into a function that labels a game tree, where the local definition ts' applies the algorithm recursively to each subtree of a node, and ps selects the top labels from the resulting trees:

```
minimax :: Tree Grid -> Tree (Grid,Player)
minimax (Node g [])
   | wins O g  = Node (g,O) []
   | wins X g  = Node (g,X) []
   | otherwise = Node (g,B) []
minimax (Node g ts)
   | turn g == O = Node (g, minimum ps) ts'
   | turn g == X = Node (g, maximum ps) ts'
               where
                  ts' = map minimax ts
                  ps  = [p | Node (_,p) _ <- ts']
```

Once the game tree has been labelled in this manner, the best next move under the minimax algorithm is given by moving to any grid with the same label as the root node. Hence for our example tree, the best move is given by the second of the three possible moves from the initial grid, because this leads to a grid with the same label as the root node, namely player O. This is the best move at this point because it guarantees a win for player O, whereas either of the two other possible moves could lead to a win for player X.

Putting all the components together, we can now define a function that returns the best next move for a given tic-tac-toe grid and player:

```
bestmove :: Grid -> Player -> Grid
bestmove g p = head [g' | Node (g',p') _ <- ts, p' == best]
            where
               tree = prune depth (gametree g p)
               Node (_,best) ts = minimax tree
```

That is, we first build the game tree up to the specified depth, then apply the minimax algorithm to label the tree, and finally select a grid whose player label is the same as that of the root node. There is always at least one 'best move', because selecting the minimum or maximum value from a non-empty (finite) list always results in a value that occurs in the list. If there is more than one best move, the above definition simply selects the first of these.

11.11   Human vs computer

It is now straightforward to modify our earlier tic-tac-toe program so that the computer takes on the role of one of the players. As with the countdown program in chapter 9, we use the GHC compiler to increase performance, and define the program using a top-level action called `main`:

```
main :: IO ()
main = do hSetBuffering stdout NoBuffering
          play empty 0
```

The function `hSetBuffering` is provided in the library `System.IO`, and is used above to turn output buffering off, which is by default turned on in GHC. As previously, the game itself is implemented using two mutually recursive functions, except that player X is now the computer player:

```
play :: Grid -> Player -> IO ()
play g p = do cls
              goto (1,1)
              putGrid g
              play' g p

play' :: Grid -> Player -> IO ()
play' g p
   | wins O g = putStrLn "Player O wins!\n"
   | wins X g = putStrLn "Player X wins!\n"
   | full g   = putStrLn "It's a draw!\n"
   | p == O   = do i <- getNat (prompt p)
                   case move g i p of
                      [] -> do putStrLn "ERROR: Invalid move"
                               play' g p
                      [g'] -> play g' (next p)
   | p == X   = do putStr "Player X is thinking... "
                   (play $! (bestmove g p)) (next p)
```

The operator `$!` used in the definition of the function `play'` forces evaluation of the best move for the computer player prior to the function `play` being invoked again, without which there may be a delay between clearing the screen and displaying the grid in `play` while the best move was then calculated under lazy evaluation. Controlling evaluation order in this manner is discussed further in chapter 15 when we consider lazy evaluation in more detail.

Finally, if all the definitions are placed into a file called `tictactoe.hs`, we can then compile the program and run the game:

```
$ ghc -O2 tictactoe.hs
[1 of 1] Compiling Main
Linking tictactoe ...
```

```
$ ./tictactoe
```

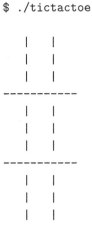

```
    Player O, enter your move:
```

On a reasonable modern machine, the computer should take around one second to make its first move, with subsequent moves becoming progressively faster as the size of the game tree reduces. Note that because the computer always chooses the first move from the list of best moves, it may not always take the quickest route to a win, but it is guaranteed to be unbeatable!

11.12   Chapter remarks

For tic-tac-toe grids of size 3 × 3, it is feasible to generate the entire game tree. For larger grids, in addition to limiting the maximum depth of the tree, it may also be useful to reduce the size of the tree using *alpha-beta pruning* [16], which avoids generating parts of the game tree that have no possibility of leading to the best next move under the minimax algorithm.

11.13   Exercises

1. Using the function **gametree**, verify that there are 549,946 nodes in the complete game tree for a 3 × 3 tic-tac-toe game starting from the empty grid, and that the maximum depth of this tree is 9.

2. Our tic-tac-toe program always chooses the first move from the list of best moves. Modify the final program to choose a random move from the list of best moves, using the function **randomRIO :: (Int,Int) -> IO Int** from **System.Random** to generate a random integer in the given range.

3. Alternatively, modify the final program to choose a move that attempts to

take the quickest route to a win, by calculating the depths of resulting game trees and selecting a move that results in a tree with the smallest depth.

4. Modify the final program to:

   a. let the user decide if they wish to play first or second;

   b. allow the length of a winning line to also be changed;

   c. generate the game tree once, rather than for each move;

   d. reduce the size of game tree using alpha-beta pruning.

Solutions to exercises 1 and 2 are given in appendix A.

12 Monads and more

In this chapter we increase the level of generality that can be achieved in Haskell, by considering functions that are generic over a range of parameterised types such as lists, trees and input/output actions. In particular, we introduce functors, applicatives and monads, which variously capture generic notions of mapping, function application and effectful programming.

12.1 Functors

All three new concepts introduced in this chapter are examples of the idea of abstracting out a common programming pattern as a definition. We begin by reviewing this idea using the following two simple functions:

```
inc :: [Int] -> [Int]
inc []     = []
inc (n:ns) = n+1 : inc ns

sqr :: [Int] -> [Int]
sqr []     = []
sqr (n:ns) = n^2 : sqr ns
```

Both functions are defined in the same manner, with the empty list being mapped to itself, and a non-empty list to some function applied to the head of the list and the result of recursively processing the tail. The only important difference is the function that is applied to each integer in the list: in the first case it is the increment function (+1), and in the second the squaring function (^2). Abstracting out this pattern gives the familiar library function map,

```
map :: (a -> b) -> [a] -> [b]
map f []     = []
map f (x:xs) = f x : map f xs
```

using which our two examples can then be defined more compactly by simply providing the function to be applied to each integer:

```
inc = map (+1)
```

```
sqr = map (^2)
```

More generally, the idea of mapping a function over each element of a data structure isn't specific to the type of lists, but can be abstracted further to a wide range of parameterised types. The class of types that support such a mapping function are called *functors*. In Haskell, this concept is captured by the following class declaration in the standard prelude:

```
class Functor f where
    fmap :: (a -> b) -> f a -> f b
```

That is, for a parameterised type `f` to be an instance of the class `Functor`, it must support a function `fmap` of the specified type. The intuition is that `fmap` takes a function of type `a -> b` and a structure of type `f a` whose elements have type `a`, and applies the function to each such element to give a structure of type `f b` whose elements now have type `b`. The fact that `f` must be a parameterised type, that is, a type that takes another type as a parameter, is determined automatically during type inference by virtue of the application of `f` to the types `a` and `b` in the specified type for `fmap` in the class declaration.

Examples

As we would expect, the type of lists can be made into a functor by simply defining `fmap` to be the function `map`:

```
instance Functor [] where
    -- fmap :: (a -> b) -> [a] -> [b]
    fmap = map
```

The symbol `[]` in this declaration denotes the list type without a type parameter, and is based upon the fact that the type `[a]` can also be written in more primitive form as the application `[] a` of the list type `[]` to the parameter type `a`. Note also that the type of `fmap` above is stated in a comment rather than explicitly, because Haskell does not permit such type information in instance declarations. However, it is useful for guiding the definition of `fmap` and for documentation purposes, so we include such types in comments.

For our second example, recall the built-in type `Maybe a` that represents values of type `a` that may either fail or succeed:

```
data Maybe a = Nothing | Just a
```

It is straightforward to make the `Maybe` type into a functor by defining a function `fmap` of the appropriate type, as follows:

```
instance Functor Maybe where
    -- fmap :: (a -> b) -> Maybe a -> Maybe b
    fmap _ Nothing  = Nothing
    fmap g (Just x) = Just (g x)
```

(We call the argument function g to avoid confusion with the use of f for a functor in this section.) That is, mapping a function over a failed value results in the failure being propagated, while for success we apply the function to the underlying value and retag the result. For example:

```
> fmap (+1) Nothing
Nothing

> fmap (*2) (Just 3)
Just 6

> fmap not (Just False)
Just True
```

User-defined types can also be made into functors. For example, suppose that we declare a type of binary trees that have data in their leaves:

```
data Tree a = Leaf a | Node (Tree a) (Tree a)
              deriving Show
```

The `deriving` clause ensures that trees can be displayed on the screen. The parameterised type `Tree` can then be made into a functor by defining a function `fmap` that applies a given function to each leaf value in a tree:

```
instance Functor Tree where
   -- fmap :: (a -> b) -> Tree a -> Tree b
   fmap g (Leaf x)   = Leaf (g x)
   fmap g (Node l r) = Node (fmap g l) (fmap g r)
```

For example:

```
> fmap length (Leaf "abc")
Leaf 3

> fmap even (Node (Leaf 1) (Leaf 2))
Node (Leaf False) (Leaf True)
```

Many functors f that are used in Haskell are similar to the three examples above, in the sense that f a is a data structure that contains elements of type a, which is sometimes called a *container type*, and `fmap` applies a given function to each such element. However, not all instances fit this pattern. For example, the IO type is not a container type in the normal sense of the term because its values represent input/output actions whose internal structure we do not have access to, but it can readily be made into a functor:

```
instance Functor IO where
   -- fmap :: (a -> b) -> IO a -> IO b
   fmap g mx = do {x <- mx; return (g x)}
```

In this case, `fmap` applies a function to the result value of the argument action, and hence provides a means of processing such values. For example:

```
> fmap show (return True)
"True"
```

We conclude by noting two key benefits of using functors. First of all, the function `fmap` can be used to process the elements of any structure that is functorial. That is, we can use the same name for functions that are essentially the same, rather than having to invent a separate name for each instance. And secondly, we can define generic functions that can be used with any functor. For example, our earlier function that increments each integer in a list can be generalised to any functorial type by simply using `fmap` rather than `map`:

```
inc :: Functor f => f Int -> f Int
inc = fmap (+1)
```

For example:

```
> inc (Just 1)
Just 2

> inc [1,2,3,4,5]
[2,3,4,5,6]

> inc (Node (Leaf 1) (Leaf 2))
Node (Leaf 2) (Leaf 3)
```

Functor laws

In addition to providing a function `fmap` of the specified type, functors are also required to satisfy two equational laws:

```
fmap id       =    id
fmap (g . h)  =    fmap g . fmap h
```

The first equation states that `fmap` preserves the identity function, in the sense that applying `fmap` to this function returns the same function as the result. Note, however, that the two occurrences of `id` in this equation have different types: on the left-hand side `id` has type `a -> a` and hence `fmap id` has type `f a -> f a`, which means that the `id` on the right-hand side must also have type `f a -> f a` in order for the equation to be well-typed.

In turn, the second equation above states that `fmap` also preserves function composition, in the sense that applying `fmap` to the composition of two functions gives the same result as applying `fmap` to the two functions separately and then composing. In order for the compositions to be well-typed, the component functions `g` and `h` must have types `b -> c` and `a -> b`.

In combination with the polymorphic type for `fmap`, the functor laws ensure that `fmap` does indeed perform a mapping operation. In the case of lists, for instance, they ensure that the structure of the argument list is preserved by `fmap`, in the sense that elements are not added, removed or rearranged. For example, suppose that we replaced the built-in list functor by an alternative version in which `fmap` reverses the order of the list elements:

```
instance Functor [] where
   -- fmap :: (a -> b) -> f a -> f b
   fmap g []     = []
   fmap g (x:xs) = fmap g xs ++ [g x]
```

(If you wish to try out this example in GHCi, you must first declare your own list type and modify the above declaration accordingly, to avoiding clashing with the built-in list functor.) This declaration is type correct, but fails to satisfy the functor laws, as shown by the following examples:

```
> fmap id [1,2]
[2,1]

> id [1,2]
[1,2]

> fmap (not . even) [1,2]
[False,True]

> (fmap not . fmap even) [1,2]
[True,False]
```

All the functors that we defined in the examples section satisfy the functor laws. We will see how to formally prove such properties when we consider techniques for reasoning about programs in chapter 16. In fact, for any parameterised type in Haskell, there is at most one function `fmap` that satisfies the required laws. That is, if it is possible to make a given parameterised type into a functor, there is only one way to achieve this. Hence, the instances that we defined for lists, `Maybe`, `Tree` and `IO` were all uniquely determined.

12.2   Applicatives

Functors abstract the idea of mapping a function over each element of a structure. Suppose now that we wish to generalise this idea to allow functions with any number of arguments to be mapped, rather than being restricted to functions with a single argument. More precisely, suppose that we wish to define a hierarchy of `fmap` functions with the following types:

```
fmap0 :: a -> f a

fmap1 :: (a -> b) -> f a -> f b

fmap2 :: (a -> b -> c) -> f a -> f b -> f c

fmap3 :: (a -> b -> c -> d) -> f a -> f b -> f c -> f d
```

        .

        .

        .

Note that `fmap1` is just another name for `fmap`, and `fmap0` is the degenerate case when the function being mapped has no arguments. One approach would be to declare a special version of the functor class for each case: `Functor0`, `Functor1`, `Functor2`, and so on. Then, for example, we could write:

```
> fmap2 (+) (Just 1) (Just 2)
Just 3
```

However, this would be unsatisfactory in a number of different ways. First of all, we would have to manually declare each version of the `Functor` class even they all follow a similar pattern. Secondly, it is not clear how many such classes we should declare, as there are infinitely many but we can only declare a finite number. And finally, if we view `fmap` of type `(a -> b) -> f a -> f b` as being a generalisation of the built-in function application operator of type `(a -> b) -> a -> b`, we might expect that some form of currying can be used to achieve the desired behaviour. In particular, we don't require special versions of application for functions with different numbers of arguments, instead relying on currying in definitions such as `add x y = x + y`.

In fact, using the idea of currying, it turns out that a version of `fmap` for functions with any desired number of arguments can be constructed in terms of two basic functions with the following types:

```
pure :: a -> f a

(<*>) :: f (a -> b) -> f a -> f b
```

That is, `pure` converts a value of type `a` into a structure of type `f a`, while `<*>` is a generalised form of function application for which the argument function, the argument value, and the result value are all contained in `f` structures. As with normal function application, the `<*>` operator is written between its two arguments and is assumed to associate to the left. For example,

```
g <*> x <*> y <*> z
```

means

```
((g <*> x) <*> y) <*> z
```

A typical use of `pure` and `<*>` has the following form:

```
pure g <*> x1 <*> x2 <*> ... <*> xn
```

Such expressions are said to be in *applicative style*, because of the similarity to normal function application notation `g x1 x2 ... xn`. In both cases, `g` is a curried function that takes `n` arguments of type `a1 ... an` and produces a result of type `b`. However, in applicative style, each argument `xi` has type `f ai` rather than just `ai`, and the overall result has type `f b` rather than `b`. Using this idea, we can now define the hierarchy of mapping functions:

```
fmap0 :: a -> f a
fmap0 = pure

fmap1 :: (a -> b) -> f a -> f b
fmap1 g x = pure g <*> x

fmap2 :: (a -> b -> c) -> f a -> f b -> f c
fmap2 g x y = pure g <*> x <*> y

fmap3 :: (a -> b -> c -> d) -> f a -> f b -> f c -> f d
fmap3 g x y z = pure g <*> x <*> y <*> z
```

.

.

.

It is a useful exercise to check the types of these definitions for yourself. In practice, however, there is usually no need to define such mapping functions explicitly as they can be constructed as required, as we shall see in the next section. The class of functors that support `pure` and `<*>` functions are called *applicative functors*, or *applicatives* for short. In Haskell, this concept is captured by the following built-in class declaration:

```
class Functor f => Applicative f where
    pure  :: a -> f a
    (<*>) :: f (a -> b) -> f a -> f b
```

Examples

Using the fact that `Maybe` is a functor and hence supports `fmap`, it is straightforward to make this type into an applicative functor:

```
instance Applicative Maybe where
    -- pure :: a -> Maybe a
```

```
pure = Just

-- (<*>) :: Maybe (a -> b) -> Maybe a -> Maybe b
Nothing  <*> _  = Nothing
(Just g) <*> mx = fmap g mx
```

That is, the function `pure` transforms a value into a successful result, while the operator `<*>` applies a function that may fail to an argument that may fail to produce a result that may fail. For example:

```
> pure (+1) <*> Just 1
Just 2

> pure (+) <*> Just 1 <*> Just 2
Just 3

> pure (+) <*> Nothing <*> Just 2
Nothing
```

In this manner, the applicative style for `Maybe` supports a form of *exceptional* programming in which we can apply pure functions to arguments that may fail without the need to manage the propagation of failure ourselves, as this is taken care of automatically by the applicative machinery.

We now turn our attention to the list type, for which the standard prelude contains the following instance declaration:

```
instance Applicative [] where
   -- pure :: a -> [a]
   pure x = [x]

   -- (<*>) :: [a -> b] -> [a] -> [b]
   gs <*> xs = [g x | g <- gs, x <- xs]
```

That is, `pure` transforms a value into a singleton list, while `<*>` takes a list of functions and a list of arguments, and applies each function to each argument in turn, returning all the results in a list. For example:

```
> pure (+1) <*> [1,2,3]
[2,3,4]

> pure (+) <*> [1] <*> [2]
[3]

> pure (*) <*> [1,2] <*> [3,4]
[3,4,6,8]
```

How should we understand these examples? The key is to view the type [a] as a generalisation of Maybe a that permits multiple results in the case of success. More precisely, we can think of the empty list as representing failure, and a non-empty list as representing all the possible ways in which a result may succeed. Hence, in the last example above there are two possible values for the first argument (1 or 2), two possible values for the second (3 or 4), which gives four possible results for the multiplication (3, 4, 6 or 8).

More generally, consider a function that returns all possible ways of multiplying two lists of integers, defined using a list comprehension:

```
prods :: [Int] -> [Int] -> [Int]
prods xs ys = [x*y | x <- xs, y <- ys]
```

Using the fact that lists are applicative, we can now also give an applicative definition, which avoids having to name the intermediate results:

```
prods :: [Int] -> [Int] -> [Int]
prods xs ys = pure (*) <*> xs <*> ys
```

In summary, the applicative style for lists supports a form of *non-deterministic* programming in which we can apply pure functions to multi-valued arguments without the need to manage the selection of values or the propagation of failure, as this is taken care of by the applicative machinery.

The final type that we consider in this section is the IO type, which can be made into an applicative functor using the following declaration:

```
instance Applicative IO where
   -- pure :: a -> IO a
   pure = return

   -- (<*>) :: IO (a -> b) -> IO a -> IO b
   mg <*> mx = do {g <- mg; x <- mx; return (g x)}
```

In this case, pure is given by the return function for the IO type, and <*> applies an impure function to an impure argument to give an impure result. For example, a function that reads a given number of characters from the keyboard can be defined in applicative style as follows:

```
getChars :: Int -> IO String
getChars 0 = return []
getChars n = pure (:) <*> getChar <*> getChars (n-1)
```

That is, in the base case we simply return the empty list, and in the recursive case we apply the cons operator to the result of reading the first character and the remaining list of characters. Note that in the latter case there is no need to name the arguments that are supplied to the cons function, which there would be if the function was defined using the do notation.

More generally, the applicative style for IO supports a form of *interactive* programming in which we can apply pure functions to impure arguments without the need to manage the sequencing of actions or the extraction of result values, as this is taken care of automatically by the applicative machinery.

Effectful programming

Our original motivation for applicatives was the desire the generalise the idea of mapping to functions with multiple arguments. This is a valid interpretation of the concept of applicatives, but from the three instances we have seen it becomes clear that there is also another, more abstract view.

The common theme between the instances is that they all concern programming with *effects*. In each case, the applicative machinery provides an operator <*> that allows us to write programs in a familiar applicative style in which functions are applied to arguments, with one key difference: the arguments are no longer just plain values but may also have effects, such as the possibility of failure, having many ways to succeed, or performing input/output actions. In this manner, applicative functors can also be viewed as abstracting the idea of applying pure functions to effectful arguments, with the precise form of effects that are permitted depending on the nature of the underlying functor.

In addition to providing a uniform approach to a form of effectful programming, using applicatives also has the important benefit that we can define generic functions that can be used with any applicative functor. By way of example, the standard library provides the following function:

```
sequenceA :: Applicative f => [f a] -> f [a]
sequenceA []     = pure []
sequenceA (x:xs) = pure (:) <*> x <*> sequenceA xs
```

This function transforms a list of applicative actions into a single such action that returns a list of result values, and captures a common pattern of applicative programming. For example, the function getChars can now be defined in a simpler manner by replicating the basic action getChar the required number of times, and executing the resulting sequence:

```
getChars :: Int -> IO String
getChars n = sequenceA (replicate n getChar)
```

Applicative laws

In addition to providing the functions **pure** and <*>, applicative functors are also required to satisfy four equational laws:

```
pure id <*> x      =   x

pure (g x)         =   pure g <*> pure x

x <*> pure y       =   pure (\g -> g y) <*> x

x <*> (y <*> z)    =   (pure (.) <*> x <*> y) <*> z
```

The first equation states that **pure** preserves the identity function, in the sense that applying **pure** to this function gives an applicative version of the identity function. The second equation states that **pure** also preserves function application, in the sense that it distributes over normal function application to give applicative application. The third equation states that when an effectful function is applied to a pure argument, the order in which we evaluate the two components doesn't matter. And finally, the fourth equation states that, modulo the types that are involved, the operator **<*>** is associative. It is a useful exercise to work out the types for the variables in each of these laws.

The applicative laws together formalise our intuition regarding the function **pure :: a -> f a**, namely that it embeds values of type **a** into the pure fragment of an effectful world of type **f a**. The laws also ensure that every well-typed expression that is built using the function **pure** and the operator **<*>** can be rewritten in applicative style, that is in the form:

```
pure g <*> x1 <*> x2 <*> ... <*> xn
```

In particular, the fourth law reassociates applications to the left, the third law moves occurrences of **pure** to the left, and the remaining two laws allow zero or more consecutive occurrences of **pure** to be combined into one.

All the applicative functors that we defined in the examples section satisfy the above laws. Moreover, each of these instances also satisfies the equation **fmap g x = pure g <*> x**, which shows how **fmap** can be defined in terms of the two applicative primitives. In fact, this latter law comes for free, by virtue of the fact that (as noted at the end of section 12.1) there is only one way to make any given parameterised type into a functor, and hence any function with the same polymorphic type as **fmap** must be equal to **fmap**.

We conclude by noting that Haskell also provides an infix version of **fmap**, defined by **g <$> x = fmap g x**, which in combination with the above law for **fmap** gives an alternative formulation of applicative style:

```
g <$> x1 <*> x2 <*> ... <*> xn
```

While this is slightly more concise, for expository purposes we prefer the version in which **pure** is used explicitly, to emphasise the fact that applicative programming is about applying pure functions to effectful arguments. However, the version using **<$>** is often used in practical applications.

12.3   Monads

The final new concept in this chapter captures another pattern of effectful programming. By way of example, consider the following type of expressions that are built up from integer values using a division operator:

```
data Expr = Val Int | Div Expr Expr
```

Such expressions can be evaluated as follows:

```
eval :: Expr -> Int
eval (Val n)   = n
eval (Div x y) = eval x `div` eval y
```

However, this function does not take account of the possibility of division by zero, and will produce an error in this case:

```
> eval (Div (Val 1) (Val 0))
*** Exception: divide by zero
```

In order to address this, we can use the `Maybe` type to define a safe version of division that returns `Nothing` when the second argument is zero,

```
safediv :: Int -> Int -> Maybe Int
safediv _ 0 = Nothing
safediv n m = Just (n `div` m)
```

and modify our evaluator to explicitly handle the possibility of failure when the function is called recursively on the two argument expressions:

```
eval :: Expr -> Maybe Int
eval (Val n)   = Just n
eval (Div x y) = case eval x of
                   Nothing -> Nothing
                   Just n  -> case eval y of
                                Nothing -> Nothing
                                Just m  -> safediv n m
```

Now, for example, we have:

```
> eval (Div (Val 1) (Val 0))
Nothing
```

The new definition for `eval` resolves the division by zero issue, but is rather verbose. Aiming to simplify the definition, we might use the fact that `Maybe` is applicative and attempt to redefine `eval` in applicative style:

```
eval :: Expr -> Maybe Int
eval (Val n)   = pure n
eval (Div x y) = pure safediv <*> eval x <*> eval y
```

However, this definition is not type correct. In particular, the function `safediv` has type `Int -> Int -> Maybe Int`, whereas in the above context a function of type `Int -> Int -> Int` is required. Replacing `pure safediv` by a custom-defined function would not help either, because this function would need to have type `Maybe (Int -> Int -> Int)`, which does not provide any means to indicate failure when the second integer argument is zero.

The conclusion is that the function `eval` does not fit the pattern of effectful programming that is captured by applicative functors. The applicative style restricts us to applying pure functions to effectful arguments: `eval` does not fit this pattern because the function `safediv` that is used to process the resulting values is not a pure function, but may itself fail.

How then can we rewrite `eval :: Expr -> Maybe Int` in a simpler manner? The key is to observe the common pattern that occurs twice in its definition, namely performing a case analysis on a `Maybe` value, mapping `Nothing` to itself and `Just x` to some result depending on x. Abstracting out this pattern gives a new operator `>>=` that is defined as follows:

```
(>>=) :: Maybe a -> (a -> Maybe b) -> Maybe b
mx >>= f = case mx of
                Nothing -> Nothing
                Just x  -> f x
```

That is, `>>=` takes an argument of type `a` that may fail and a function of type `a -> b` whose result may fail, and returns a result of type `b` that may fail. If the argument fails we propagate the failure, otherwise we apply the function to the resulting value. In this manner, `>>=` integrates the sequencing of values of type `Maybe` with the processing of their results. The `>>=` operator is often called *bind*, because the second argument binds the result of the first.

Using the bind operator and the lambda notation, we can now redefine the function `eval` in a more compact manner as follows:

```
eval :: Expr -> Maybe Int
eval (Val n)   = Just n
eval (Div x y) = eval x >>= \n ->
                 eval y >>= \m ->
                 safediv n m
```

The case for division states that we first evaluate x and call its result value n, then evaluate y and call its result value m, and finally combine the two results by applying `safediv`. This case can also be written on a single line, but has been broken into separate lines to emphasise its operational reading.

Generalising from the above example, a typical expression that is built using the `>>=` operator has the following structure:

```
m1 >>= \x1 ->
m2 >>= \x2 ->
```

```
        .
        .
        .
mn >>= \xn ->
f x1 x2 ... xn
```

That is, we evaluate each of the expressions m1 ... mn in turn, and then combine their result values x1 ... xn by applying the function f. The definition of the >>= operator ensures that such an expression only succeeds if every component mi in the sequence succeeds. Moreover, the user does not have to worry about dealing with the possibility of failure at any point in the sequence, as this is handled automatically by the definition of the >>= operator.

Haskell provides a special notation for expressions of the above form, allowing them to be written in a simpler manner as follows:

```
do x1 <- m1
   x2 <- m2
     .
     .
     .
   xn <- mn
   f x1 x2 ... xn
```

This is the same notation that is also used for interactive programming. As in this setting, each item in the sequence must begin in the same column, and xi <- mi can be abbreviated by mi if its result value xi is not required. Using this notation, eval can now be redefined simply as:

```
eval :: Expr -> Maybe Int
eval (Val n)   = Just n
eval (Div x y) = do n <- eval x
                    m <- eval y
                    safediv n m
```

More generally, the do notation is not specific to the types IO and Maybe, but can be used with any applicative type that forms a *monad*. In Haskell, the concept of a monad is captured by the following built-in declaration:

```
class Applicative m => Monad m where
   return :: a -> m a
   (>>=)  :: m a -> (a -> m b) -> m b

   return = pure
```

That is, a monad is an applicative type m that supports return and >>= functions of the specified types. The default definition return = pure means that return is normally just another name for the applicative function `pure`, but can be overridden in instances declarations if desired.

The function `return` is included in the `Monad` class for historical reasons, and to ensure backwards compatibility with existing code, articles and textbooks that assume the class declaration includes both `return` and `>>=` functions. However, at some point in the future `return` may be removed from the `Monad` class and become a library function instead, with the following definition:

```
return :: Applicative f => a -> f a
return = pure
```

If this change is implemented, it will no longer be possible to define `return` in instance declarations, but most of our examples would be unaffected as we generally just use the default definition `return = pure`. Any adjustments that are required will be explained on the book's website.

Examples

In the standard prelude, the bind operator for the `Maybe` type is defined using pattern matching rather than case analysis for simplicity:

```
instance Monad Maybe where
    -- (>>=) :: Maybe a -> (a -> Maybe b) -> Maybe b
    Nothing  >>= _ = Nothing
    (Just x) >>= f = f x
```

It is because of this declaration that the `do` notation can be used to program with `Maybe` values, as in the function `eval` from the previous section. In turn, lists can be made into a monadic type as follows:

```
instance Monad [] where
    -- (>>=) :: [a] -> (a -> [b]) -> [b]
    xs >>= f = [y | x <- xs, y <- f x]
```

That is, `xs >>= f` applies the function `f` to each of the results in the list `xs`, collecting all the resulting values in a list. In this manner, the bind operator for lists provides a means of sequencing expressions that may produce multiple results. For example, a function that returns all possible ways of pairing elements from two lists can now be defined using the `do` notation:

```
pairs :: [a] -> [b] -> [(a,b)]
pairs xs ys = do x <- xs
                 y <- ys
                 return (x,y)
```

For example:

```
> pairs [1,2] [3,4]
[(1,3),(1,4),(2,3),(2,4)]
```

Note that we could have written `pure (x,y)` in the final line for `pairs` because of the default definition `return = pure`, but in monadic programming the convention is to use the function `return` instead. It is also interesting to note the similarity to a definition using the comprehension notation:

```
pairs :: [a] -> [b] -> [(a,b)]
pairs xs ys = [(x,y) | x <- xs, y <- ys]
```

However, whereas the comprehension notation is specific to the type of lists, the do notation can be used with an arbitrary monad.

The prelude also includes an instance for the IO type, which supports the use of the do notation for interactive programming. Unlike the other examples above, in this case the definitions for `return` and `>>=` are built-in to the language, rather than being defined within Haskell itself:

```
instance Monad IO where
   -- return :: a -> IO a
   return x = ...

   -- (>>=) :: IO a -> (a -> IO b) -> IO b
   mx >>= f = ...
```

The state monad

Now let us consider the problem of writing functions that manipulate some form of state that can be changed over time. For simplicity, we assume that the state is just an integer value, but this can be modified as required:

```
type State = Int
```

The most basic form of function on this type is a *state transformer*, abbreviated by ST, which takes an input state as its argument and produces an output state as its result, in which the output state reflects any updates that were made to the state by the function during its execution:

```
type ST = State -> State
```

In general, however, we may wish to return a result value in addition to updating the state. For example, if the state represents a counter, a function for incrementing the counter may also wish to return its current value. For this reason, we generalise the type of state transformers to also return a result value, with the type of such values being a parameter of the ST type:

```
type ST a = State -> (a,State)
```

Such functions can be displayed in pictorial form as follows, where **s** is the input state, **s'** is the output state, and **v** is the result value:

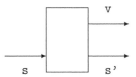

Conversely, a state transformer may also wish to take argument values. However, there is no need to further generalise the ST type to take account of this, because this behaviour can already be achieved by exploiting currying. For example, a state transformer that takes a character and returns an integer would have type `Char -> ST Int`, which abbreviates the curried function type `Char -> State -> (Int,State)`, as illustrated below:

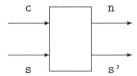

Given that `ST` is a parameterised type, it is natural to try and make it into a monad so that the `do` notation can then be used to write stateful programs. However, types declared using the `type` mechanism cannot be made into instances of classes. Hence, we first redefine `ST` using the `newtype` mechanism, which requires introducing a dummy constructor, which we call `S`:

```
newtype ST a = S (State -> (a,State))
```

It is also convenient to define a special-purpose application function for this type, which simply removes the dummy constructor:

```
app :: ST a -> State -> (a,State)
app (S st) x = st x
```

As a first step towards making the parameterised type `ST` into a monad, it is straightforward to make this type into a functor:

```
instance Functor ST where
    -- fmap :: (a -> b) -> ST a -> ST b
    fmap g st = S (\s -> let (x,s') = app st s in (g x, s'))
```

That is, `fmap` allows us to apply a function to the result value of a state transformer, as in the following picture:

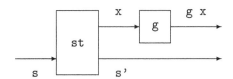

The `let` mechanism of Haskell used in the above definition is similar to the `where` mechanism, except that it allows local definitions to be made at the level of expressions rather than at the level of function definitions. In turn, the type `ST` can then be made into an applicative functor:

```
instance Applicative ST where
   -- pure :: a -> ST a
   pure x = S (\s -> (x,s))

   -- (<*>) :: ST (a -> b) -> ST a -> ST b
   stf <*> stx = S (\s ->
      let (f,s')  = app stf s
          (x,s'') = app stx s' in (f x, s''))
```

In this case, the function `pure` transforms a value into a state transformer that simply returns this value without modifying the state:

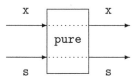

In turn, the operator `<*>` applies a state transformer that returns a function to a state transformer that returns an argument to give a state transformer that returns the result of applying the function to the argument:

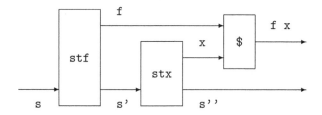

The symbol `$` denotes normal function application, defined by `f $ x = f x`. Finally, the monadic instance for `ST` is declared as follows:

```
instance Monad ST where
   -- (>>=) :: ST a -> (a -> ST b) -> ST b
   st >>= f = S (\s -> let (x,s') = app st s in app (f x) s')
```

That is, `st >>= f` applies the state transformer `st` to an initial state `s`, then applies the function `f` to the resulting value `x` to give a new state transformer `f x`, which is then applied to the new state `s'` to give the final result:

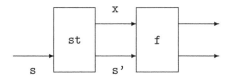

In this manner, the bind operator for the state monad integrates the sequencing of state transformers with the processing of their result values. Note that within the definition for `>>=` we produce a new state transformer `f x` whose behaviour may depend on the result value of the first argument `x`, whereas with `<*>` we are restricted to using state transformers that are explicitly supplied as arguments. As such, using the `>>=` operator provides extra flexibility.

Relabelling trees

As an example of stateful programming, we develop a relabelling function for trees, for which purposes we use the following type:

```
data Tree a = Leaf a | Node (Tree a) (Tree a)
              deriving Show
```

For example, we can define:

```
tree :: Tree Char
tree = Node (Node (Leaf 'a') (Leaf 'b')) (Leaf 'c')
```

Now consider the problem of defining a function that relabels each leaf in such a tree with a unique or *fresh* integer. This can be implemented in a pure language such as Haskell by taking the next fresh integer as an additional argument, and returning the next fresh integer as an additional result:

```
rlabel :: Tree a -> Int -> (Tree Int, Int)
rlabel (Leaf _)   n = (Leaf n, n+1)
rlabel (Node l r) n = (Node l' r', n'')
                      where
                        (l',n')  = rlabel l n
                        (r',n'') = rlabel r n'
```

Then, for example, we have:

```
> fst (rlabel tree 0)
Node (Node (Leaf 0) (Leaf 1)) (Leaf 2)
```

However, the definition for `rlabel` is complicated by the need to explicitly thread an integer state through the computation. To obtain a simpler definition, we first note that the type `Tree a -> Int -> (Tree Int, Int)` can be rewritten using the type of state transformers by `Tree a -> ST (Tree Int)`, where the state is the next fresh integer. The next such integer can be generated by defining a state transformer that simply returns the current state as its result, and the next integer as the new state:

```
fresh :: ST Int
fresh = S (\n -> (n, n+1))
```

Using the fact that `ST` is an applicative functor, we can now define a new version of the relabelling function that is written in applicative style:

```
alabel :: Tree a -> ST (Tree Int)
alabel (Leaf _)  = Leaf <$> fresh
alabel (Node l r) = Node <$> alabel l <*> alabel r
```

(Recall that `g <$> x` behaves in the same way as `pure g <*> x`.) The new version gives the same result as previously:

```
> fst (app (alabel tree) 0)
Node (Node (Leaf 0) (Leaf 1)) (Leaf 2)
```

However, its definition is much simpler. In the base case we now simply apply the `Leaf` constructor to the next `fresh` integer, while in the recursive case we apply the `Node` constructor to the result of labelling the two subtrees. In particular, the programmer no longer has to worry about the tedious and error-prone task of threading an integer state through the computation, as this is handled automatically by the applicative machinery.

Using the fact that `ST` is also a monad, we can define an equivalent monadic version of the relabelling function using the `do` notation:

```
mlabel :: Tree a -> ST (Tree Int)
mlabel (Leaf _)  = do n <- fresh
                      return (Leaf n)
mlabel (Node l r) = do l' <- mlabel l
                       r' <- mlabel r
                       return (Node l' r')
```

This definition is similar to the applicative version, except that we are now required to give names to the intermediate results. When a non-generic function such as `rlabel` can be defined in both applicative and monadic style, it is largely a matter of taste which definition is preferred.

Generic functions

An important benefit of abstracting out the concept of monads is the ability to define generic functions that can be used with any monad. A number of such functions are provided in the library `Control.Monad`. For example, a monadic version of the `map` function on list can be defined as follows:

```
mapM :: Monad m => (a -> m b) -> [a] -> m [b]
```

```
mapM f []     = return []
mapM f (x:xs) = do y  <- f x
                   ys <- mapM f xs
                   return (y:ys)
```

Note that `mapM` has the same type as `map`, except that the argument function and the function itself now have monadic return types. To illustrate how it might be used, consider a function that converts a digit character to its numeric value, provided that the character is indeed a digit:

```
conv :: Char -> Maybe Int
conv c | isDigit c = Just (digitToInt c)
       | otherwise = Nothing
```

(The functions `isDigit` and `digitToInt` are provided in `Data.Char`.) Then applying `mapM` to the `conv` function gives a means of converting a string of digits into the corresponding list of numeric values, which succeeds if every character in the string is a digit, and fails otherwise:

```
> mapM conv "1234"
Just [1,2,3,4]

> mapM conv "123a"
Nothing
```

In turn, a monadic version of the `filter` function on lists is defined by generalising its type and definition in a similar manner to `mapM`:

```
filterM :: Monad m => (a -> m Bool) -> [a] -> m [a]
filterM p []     = return []
filterM p (x:xs) = do b  <- p x
                      ys <- filterM p xs
                      return (if b then x:ys else ys)
```

For example, in the case of the list monad, using `filterM` provides a particularly concise means of computing the *powerset* of a list, which is given by all possible ways of including or excluding each element of the list:

```
> filterM (\x -> [True,False]) [1,2,3]
[[1,2,3],[1,2],[1,3],[1],[2,3],[2],[3],[]]
```

As a final example, the prelude function `concat :: [[a]] -> [a]` on lists is generalised to an arbitrary monad as follows:

```
join :: Monad m => m (m a) -> m a
join mmx = do mx <- mmx
              x  <- mx
              return x
```

This function flattens a nested monadic value to a normal monadic value. For the list monad it behaves in the same way as `concat`, while for the `Maybe` monad it only succeeds if both the outer and inner values succeed:

```
> join [[1,2],[3,4],[5,6]]
[1,2,3,4,5,6]

> join (Just (Just 1))
Just 1

> join (Just Nothing)
Nothing

> join Nothing
Nothing
```

Monad laws

In a similar manner to functors and applicatives, the two monadic primitives are required to satisfy some equational laws:

$$
\begin{aligned}
\text{return x >>= f} \quad &= \quad \text{f x} \\
\text{mx >>= return} \quad &= \quad \text{mx} \\
\text{(mx >>= f) >>= g} \quad &= \quad \text{mx >>= (\textbackslash x -> (f x >>= g))}
\end{aligned}
$$

The first two equations concern the link between `return` and `>>=`. The first equation states that if we `return` a value and then feed this into a monadic function, this should give the same result as simply applying the function to the value. Dually, the second equation states that if we feed the result of a monadic computation into the function `return`, this should give the same result as simply performing the computation. Together, these two equations state, modulo the fact that the second argument to `>>=` involves a binding operation, that `return` is the identity for the `>>=` operator.

The third equation concerns the link between `>>=` and itself, and expresses (again modulo binding) that `>>=` is associative. Note that we cannot simply write `mx >>= (f >>= g)` on the right-hand side of this equation, as this would not be type correct. All the monads we have seen satisfy the above laws.

12.4   Chapter remarks

Functors and monads come from *category theory* [17], a mathematical approach to the study of algebraic structure. Having at most one way to make a parameterised type into a functor in Haskell assumes that we don't use special language features that force evaluation, such as `seq` and `$!`. The use of monads in functional programming was developed by Wadler [18], and applicatives were introduced in [19]. An more in-depth exploration of the `IO` monad is given in [15], and the tree relabelling example comes from [20].

12.5   Exercises

1. Define an instance of the `Functor` class for the following type of binary trees that have data in their nodes:

   ```
   data Tree a = Leaf | Node (Tree a) a (Tree a)
                 deriving Show
   ```

2. Complete the following instance declaration to make the partially-applied function type (a ->) into a functor:

   ```
   instance Functor ((->) a) where
      ...
   ```

   Hint: first write down the type of `fmap`, and then think if you already know a library function that has this type.

3. Define an instance of the `Applicative` class for the type (a ->). If you are familiar with combinatory logic, you might recognise `pure` and `<*>` for this type as being the well-known K and S combinators.

4. There may be more than one way to make a parameterised type into an applicative functor. For example, the library `Control.Applicative` provides an alternative 'zippy' instance for lists, in which the function `pure` makes an infinite list of copies of its argument, and the operator `<*>` applies each argument function to the corresponding argument value at the same position. Complete the following declarations that implement this idea:

   ```
   newtype ZipList a = Z [a] deriving Show

   instance Functor ZipList where
      -- fmap :: (a -> b) -> ZipList a -> ZipList b
      fmap g (Z xs) = ...

   instance Applicative ZipList where
      -- pure :: a -> ZipList a
      pure x = ...

      -- <*> :: ZipList (a -> b) -> ZipList a -> ZipList b
      (Z gs) <$> (Z xs) = ...
   ```

The `ZipList` wrapper around the list type is required because each type can only have at most one instance declaration for a given class.

5. Work out the types for the variables in the four applicative laws.

6. Define an instance of the `Monad` class for the type `(a ->)`.

7. Given the following type of expressions

   ```
   data Expr a = Var a | Val Int | Add (Expr a) (Expr a)
                 deriving Show
   ```

   that contain variables of some type a, show how to make this type into instances of the `Functor`, `Applicative` and `Monad` classes. With the aid of an example, explain what the `>>=` operator for this type does.

8. Rather than making a parameterised type into instances of the `Functor`, `Applicative` and `Monad` classes in this order, in practice it is sometimes simpler to define the functor and applicative instances in terms of the monad instance, relying on the fact that the order in which declarations are made is not important in Haskell. Complete the missing parts in the following declarations for the `ST` type using the do notation.

   ```
   instance Functor ST where
      -- fmap :: (a -> b) -> ST a -> ST b
      fmap g st = do ...

   instance Applicative ST where
      -- pure :: a -> ST a
      pure x = S (\s -> (x,s))

      -- (<*>) :: ST (a -> b) -> ST a -> ST b
      stf <*> stx = do ...

   instance Monad ST where
      -- (>>=) :: ST a -> (a -> ST b) -> ST b
      st >>= f = S (\s ->
         let (x,s') = app st s in app (f x) s')
   ```

Solutions to exercises 1–4 are given in appendix A.

13 Monadic parsing

In this chapter we illustrate how monads can be used to implement parsers. We start by explaining what parsers are and why they are useful, show how parsers can naturally be viewed as functions, introduce a range of primitives and derived functions for writing parsers, and conclude by developing an arithmetic expression parser and an interactive calculator.

13.1   What is a parser?

A *parser* is a program that takes a string of characters as input, and produces some form of tree that makes the syntactic structure of the string explicit. For example, given the string 2*3+4, a parser for arithmetic expressions might produce a tree of the following form, in which the numbers appear at the leaves of the tree, and the operators appear at the nodes:

The structure of this tree makes explicit that + and * are operators with two arguments, and that * has higher priority than +.

Parsers are an important topic in computing, because most real-life programs use a parser to preprocess their input. For example, a calculator program parses numeric expressions prior to evaluating them, while the GHC system parses Haskell programs prior to executing them. In each case, making the structure of the input explicit considerably simplifies its further processing. For example, once a numeric expression has been parsed into a tree structure as in the example above, evaluating the expression is then straightforward.

13.2   Parsers as functions

In Haskell, a parser can naturally be viewed directly as a function that takes a string and produces a tree. Hence, given a suitable type Tree of trees, the notion of a parser can be represented as a function of type `String -> Tree`, which we abbreviate as `Parser` using the following declaration:

```
type Parser = String -> Tree
```

In general, however, a parser might not always consume its entire argument string. For example, a parser for numbers might be applied to a string comprising a number followed by a word. For this reason, we generalise our type for parsers to also return any unconsumed part of the argument string:

```
type Parser = String -> (Tree,String)
```

Similarly, a parser might not always succeed. For example, a parser for numbers might be applied to a string comprising a word. To handle this, we further generalise our type for parsers to return a list of results, with the convention that the empty list denotes failure, and a singleton list denotes success:

```
type Parser = String -> [(Tree,String)]
```

Returning a list also opens up the possibility of returning more than one result if the argument string can be parsed in more than one way. For simplicity, however, we only consider parsers that return at most one result.

Finally, different parsers will likely return different kinds of trees, or more generally, any kind of value. For example, a parser for numbers might return an integer value. Hence, it is useful to abstract from the specific type `Tree` of result values, and make this into a parameter of the `Parser` type:

```
type Parser a = String -> [(a,String)]
```

In summary, this declaration states that a parser of type `a` is a function that takes an input string and produces a list of results, each of which is a pair comprising a result value of type `a` and an output string. Alternatively, the parser type can also be read as a rhyme in the style of Dr Seuss!

> *A parser for things*
> *Is a function from strings*
> *To lists of pairs*
> *Of things and strings*

We conclude by noting that the type `String -> [(a,String)]` for parsers is similar to the type `State -> (a,State)` for state transformers from the previous chapter, where the state being manipulated is a string. The key difference is that a parser also has the possibility to fail by returning a list of results, whereas a state transformer always returns a single result. In this manner, a parser can be viewed as a generalised form of state transformer.

13.3   Basic definitions

We begin by importing two standard libraries for applicative functors and characters that will be used in our implementation:

```
import Control.Applicative
import Data.Char
```

To allow the `Parser` type to be made into instances of classes, it is first redefined using `newtype`, with a dummy constructor called P:

```
newtype Parser a = P (String -> [(a,String)])
```

Parser of this type can then be applied to an input string using a function that simply removes the dummy constructor:

```
parse :: Parser a -> String -> [(a,String)]
parse (P p) inp = p inp
```

Our first parsing primitive is called `item`, which fails if the input string is empty, and succeeds with the first character as the result value otherwise:

```
item :: Parser Char
item = P (\inp -> case inp of
                     []     -> []
                     (x:xs) -> [(x,xs)])
```

The `item` parser is the basic building block from which all other parsers that consume characters from the input will ultimately be constructed. Its behaviour is illustrated by the following two examples:

```
> parse item ""
[]

> parse item "abc"
[('a',"bc")]
```

13.4   Sequencing parsers

We now make the parser type into an instance of the functor, applicative and monad classes, in order that the do notation can then be used to combine parsers in sequence. The declarations are similar to those for state transformers, except that we also need to take account of the possibility that a parser may fail. The first step is to make the `Parser` type into a functor:

```
instance Functor Parser where
    -- fmap :: (a -> b) -> Parser a -> Parser b
```

```
fmap g p = P (\inp -> case parse p inp of
                        []        -> []
                        [(v,out)] -> [(g v, out)])
```

That is, `fmap` applies a function to the result value of a parser if the parser succeeds, and propagates the failure otherwise. For example:

```
> parse (fmap toUpper item) "abc"
[('A',"bc")]
```

```
> parse (fmap toUpper item) ""
[]
```

(The function `toUpper` is provided in the library `Data.Char`.) The `Parser` type can then be made into an applicative functor as follows:

```
instance Applicative Parser where
   -- pure :: a -> Parser a
   pure v = P (\inp -> [(v,inp)])

   -- <*> :: Parser (a -> b) -> Parser a -> Parser b
   pg <*> px = P (\inp -> case parse pg inp of
                           []        -> []
                           [(g,out)] -> parse (fmap g px) out)
```

In this case, `pure` transforms a value into a parser that always succeeds with this value as its result, without consuming any of the input string:

```
> parse (pure 1) "abc"
[(1,"abc")]
```

In turn, `<*>` applies a parser that returns a function to a parser that returns an argument to give a parser that returns the result of applying the function to the argument, and only succeeds if all the components succeed. For example, a parser that consumes three characters, discards the second, and returns the first and third as a pair can now be defined in applicative style :

```
three :: Parser (Char,Char)
three = pure g <*> item <*> item <*> item
        where g x y z = (x,z)
```

Then, for example, we have:

```
> parse three "abcdef"
[(('a','c'),"def")]
```

```
> parse three "ab"
[]
```

Note that the applicative machinery automatically ensures that the above parser fails if the input string is too short, without the need to detect or manage this ourselves. Finally, we make the `Parser` type into a monad:

```
instance Monad Parser where
   -- (>>=) :: Parser a -> (a -> Parser b) -> Parser b
   p >>= f = P (\inp -> case parse p inp of
                           []        -> []
                           [(v,out)] -> parse (f v) out)
```

That is, the parser `p >>= f` fails if the application of the parser `p` to the input string `inp` fails, and otherwise applies the function `f` to the result value `v` to give another parser `f v`, which is then applied to the output string `out` that was produced by the first parser to give the final result.

Because `Parser` is a monadic type, the `do` notation can now be used to sequence parsers and process their result values. For example, the parser `three` can be defined in an alternative manner as follows:

```
three :: Parser (Char,Char)
three = do x <- item
           item
           z <- item
           return (x,z)
```

Recall that the monadic function `return` is just another name for the applicative function `pure`, which in this case builds parsers that always succeed.

For the remainder of this chapter we adopt a monadic approach to writing parsers using the `do` notation, and generally avoid using the the functorial `fmap` and applicative `<*>` primitives on parsers. However, some users prefer writing parsers in applicative style, and using an applicative approach can sometimes be beneficial for optimising the performance of parsers.

13.5   Making choices

The `do` notation combines parsers in sequence, with the output string from each parser in the sequence becoming the input string for the next. Another natural way of combining parsers is to apply one parser to the input string, and if this fails to then apply another to the same input instead. We now consider how such a choice operator can be defined for parsers.

Making a choice between two alternatives isn't specific to parsers, but can be generalised to a range of applicative types. This concept is captured by the following class declaration in the library `Control.Applicative`:

```
class Applicative f => Alternative f where
   empty :: f a
   (<|>) :: f a -> f a -> f a
```

That is, for an applicative functor to be an instance of the **Alternative** class, it must support `empty` and `<|>` primitives of the specified types. (The class also provides two further primitives, which will be discussed in the next section.) The intuition is that `empty` represents an alternative that has failed, and `<|>` is an appropriate choice operator for the type. The two primitives are also required to satisfy the following identity and associativity laws:

$$
\begin{aligned}
\text{empty <|> x} &= \text{x} \\
\text{x <|> empty} &= \text{x} \\
\text{x <|> (y <|> z)} &= \text{(x <|> y) <|> z}
\end{aligned}
$$

The motivating example of an **Alternative** type is the **Maybe** type, for which `empty` is given by the failure value `Nothing`, and `<|>` returns its first argument if this succeeds, and its second argument otherwise:

```
instance Alternative Maybe where
   -- empty :: Maybe a
   empty = Nothing

   -- (<|>) :: Maybe a -> Maybe a -> Maybe a
   Nothing  <|> my = my
   (Just x) <|> _  = Just x
```

The instance for the **Parser** type is a natural extension of this idea, where `empty` is the parser that always fails regardless of the input string, and `<|>` is a choice operator that returns the result of the first parser if it succeeds on the input, and applies the second parser to the same input otherwise:

```
instance Alternative Parser where
   -- empty :: Parser a
   empty = P (\inp -> [])

   -- (<|>) :: Parser a -> Parser a -> Parser a
   p <|> q = P (\inp -> case parse p inp of
                          []        -> parse q inp
                          [(v,out)] -> [(v,out)])
```

For example:

```
> parse empty "abc"
[]

> parse (item <|> return 'd') "abc"
[('a',"bc")]

> parse (empty <|> return 'd') "abc"
[('d',"abc")]
```

We conclude by noting that the library file `Control.Monad` provides a class `MonadPlus` that plays the same role as `Alternative` but for monadic types, with primitives called `mzero` and `mplus`. However, we prefer to use the applicative choice primitives `empty` and `<|>` for parsers because of their similarity to the corresponding symbols for grammars, which we discuss later on.

13.6   Derived primitives

We now have three basic parsers: `item` consumes a single character if the input string is non-empty, `return v` always succeeds with the result value v, and `empty` always fails. In combination with sequencing and choice, these primitives can be used to define a number of other useful parsers. First of all, we define a parser `sat p` for single characters that satisfy the predicate p:

```
sat :: (Char -> Bool) -> Parser Char
sat p = do x <- item
           if p x then return x else empty
```

Using `sat` and appropriate predicates from the library `Data.Char`, we can now define parsers for single digits, lower-case letters, upper-case letters, arbitrary letters, alphanumeric characters, and specific characters:

```
digit :: Parser Char
digit = sat isDigit

lower :: Parser Char
lower = sat isLower

upper :: Parser Char
upper = sat isUpper

letter :: Parser Char
letter = sat isAlpha

alphanum :: Parser Char
alphanum = sat isAlphaNum

char :: Char -> Parser Char
char x = sat (== x)
```

For example:

```
> parse (char 'a') "abc"
[('a',"bc")]
```

In turn, using `char` we can define a parser `string xs` for the string of characters `xs`, with the string itself returned as the result value:

```
string :: String -> Parser String
string []     = return []
string (x:xs) = do char x
                   string xs
                   return (x:xs)
```

That is, the empty string can always be parsed, while for a non-empty string we parse the first character, recursively parse the remaining characters, and return the string as the result value. Note that `string` only succeeds if the entire target string is consumed from the input. For example:

```
> parse (string "abc") "abcdef"
[("abc","def")]

> parse (string "abc") "ab1234"
[]
```

Our next two parsers, `many p` and `some p`, apply a parser p as many times as possible until it fails, with the result values from each successful application of p being returned in a list. The difference between these two repetition primitives is that `many` permits zero or more applications of p, whereas `some` requires at least one successful application. For example:

```
> parse (many digit) "123abc"
[("123","abc")]

> parse (many digit) "abc"
[("","abc")]

> parse (some digit) "abc"
[]
```

In fact, there is no need to define `many` and `some` ourselves, as suitable default definitions are already provided in the `Alternative` class:

```
class Applicative f => Alternative f where
   empty :: f a
   (<|>) :: f a -> f a -> f a
   many  :: f a -> f [a]
   some  :: f a -> f [a]

   many x = some x <|> pure []
   some x = pure (:) <*> x <*> many x
```

Note that the two new functions are defined using mutual recursion. In particular, the above definition for **many** x states that x can either be applied at least once or not at all, while the definition for **some** x states that x can be applied once and then zero or more times, with the results being returned in a list. These functions are provided for any applicative type that is an instance of the class, but are primarily intended for use with parsers.

Using **many** and **some**, we can now define parsers for identifiers (variable names) comprising a lower-case letter followed by zero or more alphanumeric characters, natural numbers comprising one or more digits, and spacing comprising zero or more space, tab, and newline characters:

```
ident :: Parser String
ident = do x  <- lower
           xs <- many alphanum
           return (x:xs)


nat :: Parser Int
nat = do xs <- some digit
         return (read xs)


space :: Parser ()
space = do many (sat isSpace)
           return ()
```

For example:

```
> parse ident "abc def"
[("abc"," def")]

> parse nat "123 abc"
[(123," abc")]

> parse space "   abc"
[((),"abc")]
```

Note that **nat** converts the number that was read into an integer, and **space** returns the empty tuple () as a dummy result value, reflecting the fact that the details of spacing are not usually important. Finally, using **nat** it is now straightforward to define a parser for integer values:

```
int :: Parser Int
int = do char '-'
         n <- nat
         return (-n)
       <|> nat
```

For example:

```
> parse int "-123 abc"
[(-123," abc")]
```

13.7   Handling spacing

Most real-life parsers allow spacing to be freely used around the basic tokens in their input string. For example, the strings 1+2 and 1 + 2 are both parsed in the same way by GHC. To handle such spacing, we define a new primitive that ignores any space before and after applying a parser for a token:

```
token :: Parser a -> Parser a
token p = do space
             v <- p
             space
             return v
```

Using `token`, we can now define parsers that ignore spacing around identifiers, natural numbers, integers and special symbols:

```
identifier :: Parser String
identifier = token ident

natural :: Parser Int
natural = token nat

integer :: Parser Int
integer = token int

symbol :: String -> Parser String
symbol xs = token (string xs)
```

For example, using these primitives a parser for a non-empty list of natural numbers that ignores spacing around tokens can be defined as follows:

```
nats :: Parser [Int]
nats = do symbol "["
          n  <- natural
          ns <- many (do symbol ","
                         natural)
          symbol "]"
          return (n:ns)
```

This definition states that such a list begins with an opening square bracket and a natural number, followed by zero or more commas and natural numbers, and concludes with a closing square bracket. Note that **nats** only succeeds if a complete list in precisely this format is consumed:

```
> parse nats " [1, 2, 3] "
[([1,2,3],"")]

> parse nats "[1,2,]"
[]
```

13.8   Arithmetic expressions

We conclude this chapter with two extended programming examples concerning arithmetic expressions. For our first example, consider a simple form of expressions that are built up from natural numbers using addition, multiplication and parentheses. We assume that addition and multiplication associate to the right, and that multiplication has higher priority than addition. For example, 2+3+4 means 2+(3+4), while 2*3+4 means (2*3)+4.

The syntactic structure of a language can be formalised using the mathematical notion of a *grammar*, which is a set of rules that describes how strings of the language can be constructed. For example, a grammar for our language of arithmetic expressions can be defined by the following two rules:

$$expr \quad ::= \quad expr + expr \mid expr * expr \mid (\ expr\ ) \mid nat$$

$$nat \quad ::= \quad 0 \mid 1 \mid 2 \mid \cdots$$

The first rule states that an expression is either the addition or multiplication of two expressions, a parenthesised expression, or a natural number. In turn, the second rule states that a natural number is either zero, one, two, etc.

For example, using the above grammar the construction of the expression 2*3+4 can be represented by the following *parse tree*, in which the tokens in the expression appear at the leaves, and the grammatical rules applied to construct the expression give rise to the branching structure:

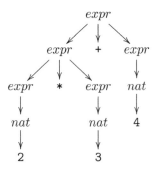

The structure of this tree makes explicit that 2*3+4 can be constructed from the addition of two expressions, the first given by the multiplication of two further expressions which are in turn given by the numbers two and three, and the second expression given by the number four. However, the grammar also permits another possible parse tree for this example, which corresponds to the erroneous interpretation of the expression as 2*(3+4):

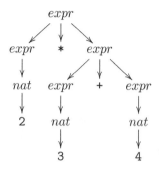

The problem is that our grammar for expressions does not take account of the fact that multiplication has higher priority than addition. However, this can easily be addressed by modifying the grammar to have a separate rule for each level of priority, with addition at the lowest level of priority, multiplication at the middle level, and parentheses and numbers at the highest level:

$$
\begin{aligned}
expr &\quad ::= \quad expr + expr \mid term \\
term &\quad ::= \quad term * term \mid factor \\
factor &\quad ::= \quad (\ expr\ ) \mid nat \\
nat &\quad ::= \quad 0 \mid 1 \mid 2 \mid \cdots
\end{aligned}
$$

Using this new grammar, 2*3+4 indeed has a single parse tree, which corresponds to the correct interpretation of the expression as (2*3)+4:

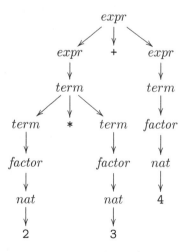

We have now dealt with the issue of priority, but our grammar does not yet take account of the fact that addition and multiplication associate to the right.

For example, the expression 2+3+4 currently has two possible parse trees, corresponding to (2+3)+4 and 2+(3+4). However, this can easily be rectified by modifying the rules for addition and multiplication to be recursive in their right argument only, rather than in both arguments:

$$expr \quad ::= \quad term + expr \mid term$$

$$term \quad ::= \quad factor * term \mid factor$$

Using these new rules, 2+3+4 now has a single parse tree, which corresponds to the correct interpretation of the expression as 2+(3+4):

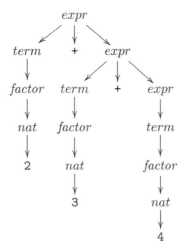

In fact, our grammar for expressions is now *unambiguous*, in the sense that every well-formed expression has precisely one parse tree.

Our final modification to the grammar is a simplification. Consider the rule *expr ::= term + expr | term*, which states that an expression is either the addition of a term and an expression, or is a term. In other words, an expression always begins with a term, which can then be followed by the addition of an expression or by nothing. Hence, the rule for expressions can be simplified to *expr ::= term (+ expr | ϵ)*, in which the symbol ϵ denotes the empty string. Simplifying the rule for terms in a similar manner gives our final grammar:

$$expr \quad ::= \quad term \ (+ \ expr \mid \epsilon \,)$$

$$term \quad ::= \quad factor \ (* \ term \mid \epsilon \,)$$

$$factor \quad ::= \quad (\ expr \,) \mid nat$$

$$nat \quad ::= \quad 0 \mid 1 \mid 2 \mid \cdots$$

It is now straightforward to translate this grammar directly into a parser for expressions, by simply rewriting the rules using the parsing primitives we have introduced. Sequencing in the grammar is translated into the do notation, choice | is translated into the <|> operator, the empty string ϵ becomes the empty parser, special symbols such as + and * are handled using the `symbol` function, and natural numbers are parsed using the `natural` primitive:

```
expr :: Parser Int
expr = do t <- term
          do symbol "+"
             e <- expr
             return (t + e)
          <|> return t


term :: Parser Int
term = do f <- factor
          do symbol "*"
             t <- term
             return (f * t)
          <|> return f


factor :: Parser Int
factor = do symbol "("
            e <- expr
            symbol ")"
            return e
         <|> natural
```

Note that each of the above parsers returns the integer value of the expression that was parsed, rather than some form of expression tree. Combining parsing and evaluation in this manner is easy to achieve using our approach. For example, `expr` first parses a term with integer value `t`, then parses an addition symbol followed by an expression with value `e` and returns the value `t + e`, or else parses nothing further and simply returns the value `t`.

Finally, using `expr` we define a function that returns the integer value that results from parsing and evaluating an expression. To handle the cases of unconsumed and invalid input, we use the library function `error :: String -> a` that displays an error message and then terminates the program:

```
eval :: String -> Int
eval xs = case (parse expr xs) of
             [(n,[])]  -> n
             [(_,out)] -> error ("Unused input " ++ out)
             []        -> error "Invalid input"
```

For example:

```
> eval "2*3+4"
10

> eval "2*(3+4)"
14

> eval "2*3^4"
*** Exception: Unused input ^4

> eval "one plus two"
*** Exception: Invalid input
```

13.9   Calculator

In the previous section we developed a parser for arithmetic expressions. We now extend this example to a simple calculator program, which allows the user to enter expressions interactively using the keyboard, and displays the value of such expressions on the screen. Our calculator will handle expressions built up from integer values using addition, subtraction, multiplication, division and parentheses. A suitable parser `expr :: Parser Int` for such expressions can be obtained by solving one of the exercises for this chapter.

We begin by considering the user interface of the calculator, for which purpose we use the input/output utilities `cls`, `writeat`, `goto` and `getCh` from chapter 10. First of all, we define the calculator box as a list of strings:

```
box :: [String]
box = ["+---------------+",
       "|               |",
       "+---+---+---+---+",
       "| q | c | d | = |",
       "+---+---+---+---+",
       "| 1 | 2 | 3 | + |",
       "+---+---+---+---+",
       "| 4 | 5 | 6 | - |",
       "+---+---+---+---+",
       "| 7 | 8 | 9 | * |",
       "+---+---+---+---+",
       "| 0 | ( | ) | / |",
       "+---+---+---+---+"]
```

The first four buttons on the calculator, q, c, d, and =, allow the user to quit, clear the display, delete a character, and evaluate an expression, while the remaining sixteen buttons allow the user to enter expressions.

We also define the buttons on the calculator as a list of characters, comprising both the twenty standard buttons that appear on the box itself, together with a number of extra characters that will be allowed for flexibility, namely Q, C, D, space, escape, backspace, delete and newline:

```
buttons :: String
buttons = standard ++ extra
             where
                 standard = "qcd=123+456-789*0()/"
                 extra    = "QCD \ESC\BS\DEL\n"
```

Using a list comprehension together with the library function that performs a list of input/output actions in sequence, we can define an action that displays the calculator box in the top-left corner of the screen:

```
showbox :: IO ()
showbox = sequence_ [writeat (1,y) b | (y,b) <- zip [1..] box]
```

The last part of the user interface is to define a function that shows a string in the display of the calculator, by first clearing the display and then showing the last thirteen characters of the string:

```
display xs = do writeat (3,2) (replicate 13 ' ')
                writeat (3,2) (reverse (take 13 (reverse xs)))
```

In this manner, if the user deletes characters from the string they will automatically be removed from the display, and if the user types more than thirteen characters the display will appear to scroll to the left.

The calculator itself is controlled by a function `calc` that displays the current string, and then reads a character from the keyboard without echoing it. If this character is a valid button, then it is processed, otherwise we sound a beep to indicate an error and continue with the same string:

```
calc :: String -> IO ()
calc xs = do display xs
             c <- getCh
             if elem c buttons then
                 process c xs
             else
                 do beep
                    calc xs
```

The action `beep :: IO ()` used above is defined by `beep = putStr "\BEL"`. In turn, the function `process` takes a valid character and the current string, and performs the appropriate action depending upon the character:

```
process :: Char -> String -> IO ()
process c xs | elem c "qQ\ESC"   = quit
```

```
                    | elem c "dD\BS\DEL" = delete xs
                    | elem c "=\n"       = eval xs
                    | elem c "cC"        = clear
                    | otherwise          = press c xs
```

We now consider each of the five possible actions:

- Quitting moves the cursor below the calculator box and terminates:

```
        quit :: IO ()
        quit = goto (1,14)
```

- Deleting a character has no effect if the current string is empty, and otherwise removes the last character from this string:

```
        delete :: String -> IO ()
        delete [] = calc []
        delete xs = calc (init xs)
```

- Evaluation displays the result of parsing and evaluating the current string, sounding a beep if this process is unsuccessful:

```
        eval :: String -> IO ()
        eval xs = case parse expr xs of
                     [(n,[])] -> calc (show n)
                     _        -> do beep
                                    calc xs
```

- Clearing the display resets the current string to empty:

```
        clear :: IO ()
        clear = calc []
```

- Any other character is appended to the end of the current string:

```
        press :: Char -> String -> IO ()
        press c xs = calc (xs ++ [c])
```

Finally, we define a top-level function that runs the calculator, by clearing the screen, displaying the box, and starting with an empty display:

```
    run :: IO ()
    run = do cls
             showbox
             clear
```

13.10   Chapter remarks

A library file comprising the parsing primitives from this chapter is available online from the book's website. Further details about the monadic approach to parsing can be found in [21, 22], upon which this chapter is based. A more detailed introduction to grammars is given in [23], and more sophisticated approaches to building parsers in Haskell are provided in [24, 25]. The reading of the parser type as a rhyme is due to Fritz Ruehr.

13.11   Exercises

1. Define a parser `comment :: Parser ()` for ordinary Haskell comments that begin with the symbol `--` and extend to the end of the current line, which is represented by the control character `'\n'`.

2. Using our second grammar for arithmetic expressions, draw the two possible parse trees for the expression 2+3+4.

3. Using our third grammar for arithmetic expressions, draw the parse trees for the expressions 2+3, 2*3*4 and (2+3)+4.

4. Explain why the final simplification of the grammar for arithmetic expressions has a dramatic effect on the efficiency of the resulting parser. Hint: begin by considering how an expression comprising a single number would be parsed if this simplification step had not been made.

5. Define a suitable type `Expr` for arithmetic expressions and modify the parser for expressions to have type `expr :: Parser Expr`.

6. Extend the parser `expr :: Parser Int` to support subtraction and division, and to use integer values rather than natural numbers, based upon the following revisions to the grammar:

$$
\begin{aligned}
expr   &\;::=\; term\;(\,+\,expr \mid -\,expr \mid \epsilon\,) \\
term   &\;::=\; factor\;(\,*\,term \mid \,/\;term \mid \epsilon\,) \\
factor &\;::=\; (\,expr\,) \mid int \\
int   &\;::=\; \cdots \mid -1 \mid 0 \mid 1 \mid \cdots
\end{aligned}
$$

7. Further extend the grammar and parser for arithmetic expressions to support exponentiation ^, which is assumed to associate to the right and have higher priority than multiplication and division, but lower priority than parentheses

and numbers. For example, 2^3*4 means (2^3)*4. Hint: the new level of priority requires a new rule in the grammar.

8. Consider expressions built up from natural numbers using a subtraction operator that is assumed to associate to the left.

   a. Translate this description directly into a grammar.

   b. Implement this grammar as a parser expr :: Parser Int.

   c. What is the problem with this parser?

   d. Show how it can be fixed. Hint: rewrite the parser using the repetition primitive **many** and the library function foldl.

9. Modify the calculator program to indicate the approximate position of an error rather than just sounding a beep, by using the fact that the parser returns the unconsumed part of the input string.

Solutions to exercises 1–4 are given in appendix A.

14 Foldables and friends

In this chapter we introduce three common patterns for processing the values in a data structure. We start with monoids, which capture the idea of combining values using an associative operator, then consider foldables, which generalise the concept of folding from lists to a range of parameterised types, and conclude with traversables, which further generalise the notion of mapping.

14.1 Monoids

In mathematics, a *monoid* is a set together with an associative operator that combines two elements from the set, and an identity element for the operator. For example, the set of integers forms a monoid with the operator given by addition and the identity element by the value zero. In Haskell, the notion of a monoid is captured by the following built-in class declaration:

```
class Monoid a where
   mempty  :: a
   mappend :: a -> a -> a

   mconcat :: [a] -> a
   mconcat = foldr mappend mempty
```

That is, for a type `a` to be an instance of the class `Monoid`, it must support a value `mempty` and a function `mappend` of the specified types, which respectively play the role of the identity element and the operator for the monoid. In practice, the function `mappend` is often written as an infix operator by enclosing its name in single back quotes, as in `x 'mappend' y`.

As well as the two primitives, the above class also provides a function `mconcat` that combines a list of values within a monoid, with a default definition that replaces each cons in the list by `mappend` and the empty list by `mempty`. For example, applying `mconcat` to a list of the form `[x,y,z]` gives:

```
x 'mappend' (y 'mappend' (z 'mappend' mempty))
```

As in mathematics, the two primitives in the `Monoid` class are required to satisfy the following identity and associativity laws:

```
mempty 'mappend' x                = x

x 'mappend' mempty                = x

x 'mappend' (y 'mappend' z)   =   (x 'mappend' y) 'mappend' z
```

For example, using these laws the result of mconcat [x,y,z] can be written in a simpler manner as follows, without the need for parentheses or mempty, because the monoid laws ensure that these do not affect the result:

```
x 'mappend' y 'mappend' z
```

At some point in the future the Monoid class in Haskell may be divided up into two separate classes, one that provides an associative operator, and one that provides an identity element. If this change is implemented, any adjustments that are required will be explained on the book's website.

Examples

A number of standard monoids are provided in the library Data.Monoid. The simplest example is the list monoid, for which mempty and mappend are respectively given by the empty list and the append operator for lists:

```
instance Monoid [a] where
   -- mempty :: [a]
   mempty = []

   -- mappend :: [a] -> [a] -> [a]
   mappend = (++)
```

The method names mempty and mappend are inspired by this instance, but the choice of names is unfortunate as in general the monoid primitives do not need to correspond to an empty value or provide a means of appending values. All that is required is two primitives that satisfy the monoid laws.

For our second example, the type Maybe a can also be made into a monoid, provided that the parameter type a is a monoid:

```
instance Monoid a => Monoid (Maybe a) where
   -- mempty :: Maybe a
   mempty = Nothing

   -- mappend :: Maybe a -> Maybe a -> Maybe a
   Nothing 'mappend' my        = my
   mx      'mappend' Nothing    = mx
   Just x  'mappend' Just y   = Just (x 'mappend' y)
```

That is, mempty is given by the failure value Nothing, while mappend combines the results of two arguments that may fail. In the latter case, if either argument

fails the other argument is returned, and if both arguments succeed the two
result values are combined using `mappend` for the parameter type `a`.

A particular type may give rise to a monoid in a number of different ways. For
example, we have already seen that the integers form a monoid under addition,
so we could declare the following simple instance:

```
instance Monoid Int where
   -- mempty :: Int
   mempty = 0

   -- mappend :: Int -> Int -> Int
   mappend = (+)
```

The integers also form a monoid under multiplication, with the identity element
given by the value one, so we could also declare:

```
instance Monoid Int where
   -- mempty :: Int
   mempty = 1

   -- mappend :: Int -> Int -> Int
   mappend = (*)
```

However, multiple instance declarations of the same type for the same class are
not permitted in Haskell, so attempting to declare two separate instances for
`Monoid Int` in this manner will result in an error. The solution is to introduce
special-purpose wrapper types for each of the two instances.

In the case of addition, the monoid library declares a new type `Sum a` with
a dummy constructor also called `Sum` that takes a single argument of type `a`,
together with a function that removes the constructor:

```
newtype Sum a = Sum a
   deriving (Eq, Ord, Show, Read)

getSum :: Sum a -> a
getSum (Sum x) = x
```

The `deriving` clause above ensures that values of type `Sum a` support the standard equality and ordering operators, and can be converted to and from strings.
Now for any parameter type `a` that is a numeric (such as `Int`), the type `Sum a`
can be made into a monoid by taking `mempty` as the value `Sum 0`, and `mappend`
as the addition operator for values of type `Sum a`:

```
instance Num a => Monoid (Sum a) where
   -- mempty :: Sum a
   mempty = Sum 0
```

```
-- mappend :: Sum a -> Sum a -> Sum a
Sum x `mappend` Sum y = Sum (x+y)
```

For example, using this instance we have:

```
> mconcat [Sum 2, Sum 3, Sum 4]
Sum 9
```

(If you wish to try out such examples in GHCi, you must first load the monoid library by entering import Data.Monoid.) In particular, applying Sum to each number in the list ensures that mconcat uses the monoid for summation. We will see in the next section how the use of such wrappers can be simplified.

In turn, in the case of multiplication of numbers, the monoid library declares a new type Product a using the same approach as for addition:

```
newtype Product a = Product a
    deriving (Eq, Ord, Show, Read)

getProduct :: Product a -> a
getProduct (Product x) = x
```

The type Product a can then be made into an instance of the Monoid class by defining the two primitives in the appropriate way for multiplication:

```
instance Num a => Monoid (Product a) where
    -- mempty :: Product a
    mempty = Product 1

    -- mappend :: Product a -> Product a -> Product a
    Product x `mappend` Product y = Product (x*y)
```

For example:

```
> mconcat [Product 2, Product 3, Product 4]
Product 24
```

In a similar manner, the type of logical values forms a monoid under both logical conjunction and disjunction, for which purpose the monoid library provides wrapper types for Bool called All and Any (see appendix B for the details.) For example, the function mconcat for All decides if all logical values in a list are True, while for Any decides if any such value is True:

```
> mconcat [All True, All True, All True]
All True

> mconcat [Any False, Any False, Any False]
Any False
```

We conclude this section by noting that the library also provides an infix version of `mappend`, defined by `x <> y = x 'mappend' y`, which allows monoid expressions to be written more concisely, as in `x <> y <> z`. This operator is often used in practical applications, however for expository purposes in this chapter we prefer to use the `mappend` primitive directly.

14.2   Foldables

One of the primary applications of monoids in Haskell is to combine all the values in a data structure to give a single value. For example, in the case of lists we could define a function `fold` that implements this idea as follows:

```
fold :: Monoid a => [a] -> a
fold []     = mempty
fold (x:xs) = x 'mappend' fold xs
```

That is, applying `fold` to an empty list gives the identity element `mempty` of the monoid, while for a non-empty list we use the monoid operator `mappend` to combine the head of the list with the result of recursively processing the tail. For example, applying `fold` to a list of the form `[x,y,z]` gives:

```
x 'mappend' (y 'mappend' (z 'mappend' mempty))
```

In other words, `fold` provides a simple means of 'folding up' a list using a monoid, hence the choice of name for the function. Note that `fold` behaves in the same way as `mconcat` from the `Monoid` class, but is defined using explicit recursion rather than using `foldr`. In a similar manner, we can also define a version of `fold` for the type of binary trees that have data in their leaves:

```
data Tree a = Leaf a | Node (Tree a) (Tree a)
              deriving Show

fold :: Monoid a => Tree a -> a
fold (Leaf x)   = x
fold (Node l r) = fold l 'mappend' fold r
```

That is, for a leaf we simply return the value that it contains, while for a node we recursively fold the two subtrees and combine the resulting values using `mappend`. For this example there is no need to use the identity element `mempty` in the definition, because trees of this type are always non-empty.

More generally, the idea of folding up the values in data structure using a monoid isn't specific to types such as lists and binary trees, but can be abstracted to a range of parameterised types. In Haskell, this concept is captured by the following class declaration in the library `Data.Foldable`:

```
class Foldable t where
   fold    :: Monoid a => t a -> a
   foldMap :: Monoid b => (a -> b) -> t a -> b
   foldr   :: (a -> b -> b) -> b -> t a -> b
   foldl   :: (a -> b -> a) -> a -> t b -> a
```

That is, for a parameterised type to be an instance of the class `Foldable`, it must support a range of fold functions of the specified types. As in the above declaration, by convention foldable types are usually denoted by `t`.

Intuitively, the generalised version of `fold` in the `Foldable` class takes a data structure of type `t a` whose elements have type `a`, and combines the elements using the monoid primitives for this type to give a single value of type `a`. In turn, `foldMap` generalises `fold` by taking a function of type `a -> b` as an additional argument, which is applied to each element in the structure prior to combining the resulting values using the monoid primitives for the type `b`.

The final two functions in the class declaration above, `foldr` and `foldl`, generalise the higher-order functions for lists that we introduced in chapter 7 to other data structures. Note that for these latter two functions there is no need to have an underlying monoid, because a starting value and function to combine two values are explicitly supplied as arguments.

The full version of the `Foldable` class also includes a number of other useful functions, together with a number of default definitions, but we begin by considering the cut-down version presented above.

Examples

As we would expect, the type of lists can be made into a foldable type by defining the folding primitives in the appropriate manner:

```
instance Foldable [] where
   -- fold :: Monoid a => [a] -> a
   fold []     = mempty
   fold (x:xs) = x 'mappend' fold xs

   -- foldMap :: Monoid b => (a -> b) -> [a] -> b
   foldMap _ []     = mempty
   foldMap f (x:xs) = f x 'mappend' foldMap f xs

   -- foldr :: (a -> b -> b) -> b -> [a] -> b
   foldr _ v []     = v
   foldr f v (x:xs) = f x (foldr f v xs)

   -- foldl :: (a -> b -> a) -> a -> [b] -> a
   foldl _ v []     = v
   foldl f v (x:xs) = foldl f (f v x) xs
```

For example, using the numeric monoids from the previous section, `foldMap` can now be used to calculate the sum and product of a list of numbers:

```
> getSum (foldMap Sum [1..10])
55

> getProduct (foldMap Product [1..10])
3628800
```

(If trying such examples, make sure to import `Data.Monoid` and `Data.Foldable`.) An instance for binary trees can be defined in a similar manner, except that we need to take care to ensure that `foldr` and `foldl` combine the values in the tree in right-to-left and left-to-right order, respectively:

```
instance Foldable Tree where
   -- fold :: Monoid a => Tree a -> a
   fold (Leaf x)   = x
   fold (Node l r) = fold l `mappend` fold r

   -- foldMap :: Monoid b => (a -> b) -> Tree a -> b
   foldMap f (Leaf x)   = f x
   foldMap f (Node l r) = foldMap f l `mappend` foldMap f r

   -- foldr :: (a -> b -> b) -> b -> Tree a -> b
   foldr f v (Leaf x)   = f x v
   foldr f v (Node l r) = foldr f (foldr f v r) l

   -- foldl :: (a -> b -> a) -> a -> Tree b -> a
   foldl f v (Leaf x)   = f v x
   foldl f v (Node l r) = foldl f (foldl f v l) r
```

For example, consider the following tree of integers:

```
tree :: Tree Int
tree = Node (Node (Leaf 1) (Leaf 2)) (Leaf 3)
```

Then evaluating `foldr (+) 0 tree` gives the result `1+(2+(3+0))`, in which the additions are performed from right-to-left, whereas `foldl (+) 0 tree` gives `((0+1)+2)+3`, in which they are performed from left-to-right. Of course, in this case the result is the same, because addition is associative. However, as we will see in chapter 15, using `foldl` may be more efficient.

Other primitives and defaults

In addition to the four basic folding primitives, the `Foldable` class also includes a range of other useful functions for combining the values in a data structure. The first group generalise familiar functions on lists:

```
null     :: t a -> Bool
length   :: t a -> Int
elem     :: Eq a => a -> t a -> Bool
maximum  :: Ord a => t a -> a
minimum  :: Ord a => t a -> a
sum      :: Num a => t a -> a
product  :: Num a => t a -> a
```

For example, `null` decides if a structure is empty (has no elements), and `length` counts the number of elements of type `a` in a structure of type `t a`. Hence, these functions can be applied to both lists and trees:

```
> null []
True

> null (Leaf 1)
False

> length [1..10]
10

> length (Node (Leaf 'a') (Leaf 'b'))
2
```

In turn, the class also includes versions of `foldr` and `foldl` for structures that contain at least one element, and hence do not require a starting value:

```
foldr1 :: (a -> a -> a) -> t a -> a
foldl1 :: (a -> a -> a) -> t a -> a
```

For example:

```
> foldr1 (+) [1..10]
55

> foldl1 (+) (Node (Leaf 1) (Leaf 2))
3
```

The final primitive in the class flattens a data structure to a list, such as transforming the tree `Node (Leaf 1) (Leaf 2)` into the list `[1,2]`:

```
toList :: t a -> [a]
```

In fact, the function `toList` plays a special role in the declaration of the `Foldable` class, as it can be used to provide default definitions for most of the other primitives in the class in terms of the corresponding primitives for lists. In particular, we have the following collection of default definitions:

```
foldr f v = foldr f v . toList
```

```
foldl f v = foldl f v . toList
foldr1 f  = foldr1 f . toList
foldl1 f  = foldl1 f . toList

null    = null . toList
length  = length . toList
elem x  = elem x . toList
maximum = maximum . toList
minimum = minimum . toList
sum     = sum . toList
product = product . toList
```

For example, the definition `null = null . toList` states that we can decide if a data structure is empty by first flattening the structure to a list, and then checking if this list is empty using the instance of `null` for lists. The other definitions have a similarly straightforward interpretation.

The final three default definitions in the foldable class establish important relationships between the primitives `fold`, `foldMap` and `toList`:

```
fold      = foldMap id
foldMap f = foldr (mappend . f) mempty
toList    = foldMap (\x -> [x])
```

That is, `fold` can be viewed as a special case of `foldMap` where the identity function is applied to each element prior to combining them. In turn, `foldMap` can be defined in terms of `foldr` by applying the function `f` to each element before they are combined using the monoid primitives. And finally, `toList` can be defined in terms of `foldMap` by first transforming each element into a singleton list, and then concatenating the resulting lists using the list monoid.

In summary, the `Foldable` class provides a range of useful functions for processing the values in a data structure, most of which have default definitions in terms of the specific instance for lists, or other generic functions in the class. There are three natural questions to ask at this point.

1. Why are there so many functions in the class? In particular, one might ask why additional primitives such as `null`, `length`, and so on are provided as methods in the `Foldable` class, rather than as definitions in the foldable library. The reason is to allow the default definitions to be overridden if required, which would not be possible if they were defined as top-level functions.

2. What do we need to define manually? The minimal complete definition for an instance of the `Foldable` class is to define either `foldMap` or `foldr`, as all other functions in the class can be derived from either of these two using the default definitions and the instance for lists. As we have already seen with lists and trees, it is often simplest to define the function `foldMap`.

3. What about efficiency? For many applications using the default definitions that are provided in the class will suffice, but if greater efficiency is required these can be overridden, as noted above. In practice, the GHC system uses more efficient default definitions than the simple versions we have presented, but these are functionally equivalent to our simpler versions.

We conclude this section by noting that GHC automatically imports the library `Data.Foldable`, but currently hides the `fold` and `toList` methods of the class. For this reason, we generally prefer to explicitly import `Data.Foldable` when programming with foldable types, rather than relying on the cut-down version that is automatically provided. For reference, the complete definition for the `Foldable` class can be found in appendix B.

Generic functions

An important benefit of abstracting out the concept of foldable types is the ability to use the primitives in the `Foldable` class to define generic functions that can be used with any such type. For example, recall that in chapter 2 we defined a function that calculates the average of a list of integers:

```
average :: [Int] -> Int
average ns = sum ns 'div' length ns
```

As we have now seen, the functions `sum` and `length` are not specific to lists, but can be used with any foldable type, so the type of `average` can be generalised, without any change being required to the definition itself:

```
average :: Foldable t => t Int -> Int
average ns = sum ns 'div' length ns
```

As such, it can now be applied to both lists and trees:

```
> average [1..10]
5

> average (Node (Leaf 1) (Leaf 3))
2
```

In a similar manner, the library `Data.Foldable` provides generic versions of a number of familiar functions that operate on lists of logical values:

```
and :: Foldable t => t Bool -> Bool
and = getAll . foldMap All

or :: Foldable t => t Bool -> Bool
or = getAny . foldMap Any

all :: Foldable t => (a -> Bool) -> t a -> Bool
```

```
all p = getAll . foldMap (All . p)

any :: Foldable t => (a -> Bool) -> t a -> Bool
any p = getAny . foldMap (Any . p)
```

In each case, using `foldMap` together with the appropriate monoid primitives allows us to obtain the desired behaviour in a generic manner:

```
> and [True,False,True]
False

> or (Node (Leaf True) (Leaf False))
True

> all even [1,2,3]
False

> any even (Node (Leaf 1) (Leaf 2))
True
```

As a final example, the function `concat :: [[a]] -> [a]` that concatenates a list of lists can now be generalised to any foldable type whose elements are lists by simply folding the elements using the list monoid:

```
concat :: Foldable t => t [a] -> [a]
concat = fold
```

For example:

```
> concat ["ab","cd","ef"]
"abcdef"

> concat (Node (Leaf [1,2]) (Leaf [3]))
[1,2,3]
```

In conclusion, when declaring a new type in Haskell it is useful to consider whether it can be made into a foldable type, for which it suffices to define either of the primitives `foldMap` or `foldr`. The advantage of doing so is that we are then provided with a range of useful functions for the type essentially 'for free', by means of the default definitions that are included in the `Foldable` class, as well as any other generic functions defined in terms of these primitives.

14.3   Traversables

As we saw in chapter 12, the idea of mapping a function over each element of a data structure is captured by the notion of a functor:

```
class Functor f where
    fmap :: (a -> b) -> f a -> f b
```

For example, in the case of lists the primitive `fmap` is given by the familiar library function `map`, which can be defined recursively as follows:

```
map :: (a -> b) -> [a] -> [b]
map g []     = []
map g (x:xs) = g x : map g xs
```

However, the idea of mapping a function over a list can be generalised further. For example, suppose that the function `g` that is applied to each element may fail, in the sense that it has type `a -> Maybe b` rather than simply `a -> b`, and that the mapping as a whole only succeeds if every such application succeeds. Using the fact that `Maybe` is applicative, as we also saw in chapter 12, it easy to define a function that implements this behaviour:

```
traverse :: (a -> Maybe b) -> [a] -> Maybe [b]
traverse g []     = pure []
traverse g (x:xs) = pure (:) <*> g x <*> traverse g xs
```

The recursive structure of this definition is essentially the same as that for `map`, except that the applicative machinery is used to manage the possibility of failure. In this manner, `traverse` provides a simple means of traversing the elements of a list using a function that may fail, hence the choice of name for the function. By way of example, suppose that we use the `Maybe` type to define a function that decrements an integer, provided it is strictly positive:

```
dec :: Int -> Maybe Int
dec n = if n > 0 then Just (n-1) else Nothing
```

Then we have:

```
> traverse dec [1,2,3]
Just [0,1,2]

> traverse dec [2,1,0]
Nothing
```

(If you wish to try out these examples in GHCi, note that `traverse` is already defined in the standard library, as shown in the next section.)

Not surprisingly, the idea of traversing a data structure in the above manner isn't specific to the type of lists, and isn't specific to argument functions that may fail. The class of types that support such a generalised mapping function are called *traversable types*, or *traversables* for short. In Haskell, this concept is captured by the following built-in class declaration:

```
class (Functor t, Foldable t) => Traversable t where
    traverse :: Applicative f => (a -> f b) -> t a -> f (t b)
```

That is, for a parameterised type `t` that is both functorial and foldable to be an instance of the class `Traversable`, it must support a `traverse` function of the specified type. The requirement that `t` is a functor reflects the fact that traversables generalise the idea of mapping, and are hence expected to support the `fmap` primitive. The requirement that `t` is foldable ensures that values in a traversable type can also be folded up if desired.

Examples

Because lists are functorial and foldable, the list type can be made traversable by simply generalising `traverse` for the `Maybe` type to an arbitrary applicative. That is, the definition remains the same, but the type is generalised:

```
instance Traversable [] where
   -- traverse :: Applicative f => (a -> f b) -> [a] -> f [b]
   traverse g []     = pure []
   traverse g (x:xs) = pure (:) <*> g x <*> traverse g xs
```

An instance for trees can be defined in a similar manner, except that the application of the argument function then takes place in the base case:

```
instance Traversable Tree where
   -- traverse :: Applicative f =>
   --      (a -> f b) -> Tree a -> f (Tree b)
   traverse g (Leaf x)   = pure Leaf <*> g x
   traverse g (Node l r) =
       pure Node <*> traverse g l <*> traverse g r
```

For example, `traverse` can now be used to map a function that may fail, such as `dec` from the previous section, over both lists and trees:

```
> traverse dec [1,2,3]
Just [0,1,2]

> traverse dec [2,1,0]
Nothing

> traverse dec (Node (Leaf 1) (Leaf 2))
Just (Node (Leaf 0) (Leaf 1))

> traverse dec (Node (Leaf 0) (Leaf 1))
Nothing
```

Other primitives and defaults

In addition to the `traverse` primitive, the `Traversable` class also includes the following extra function and default definition:

```
sequenceA :: Applicative f => t (f a) -> f (t a)
sequenceA = traverse id
```

The type expresses that **sequenceA** transforms a data structure whose elements are applicative actions into a single such action that returns a data structure, while the definition states that this can be achieved by traversing the elements of the structure using the identity function, which in this case has type `f a -> f a`. For example, **sequenceA** can be used to transform a data structure whose elements may fail into a data structure that may fail:

```
> sequenceA [Just 1, Just 2, Just 3]
Just [1,2,3]

> sequenceA [Just 1, Nothing, Just 3]
Nothing

> sequenceA (Node (Leaf (Just 1)) (Leaf (Just 2)))
Just (Node (Leaf 1) (Leaf 2))

> sequenceA (Node (Leaf (Just 1)) (Leaf Nothing))
Nothing
```

Conversely, the class declaration also includes a default definition for `traverse` in terms of `sequenceA`, which expresses that to traverse a data structure using an effectful function we can first apply the function to each element using `fmap`, and then combine all the effects using `sequenceA`:

```
-- traverse :: Applicative f => (a -> f b) -> t a -> f (t b)
traverse g = sequenceA . fmap g
```

In this manner, to declare an instance of the `Traversable` class it suffices to define either `traverse` or `sequenceA`, as each can be derived from the other using the above defaults. However, as the default for `traverse` notionally makes two passes over the data structure, one using `fmap` and one using `sequenceA`, it is generally preferable to define `traverse` rather than `sequenceA`.

Finally, the class also provides special names for the two traversable primitives for the special case when the effects that are involved are monadic rather than applicative, as shown below. For reference, the complete definition for the `Traversable` class can be found in appendix B.

```
mapM     :: Monad m => (a -> m b) -> t a -> m (t b)
sequence :: Monad m => t (m a) -> m (t a)
```

```
mapM     = traverse
sequence = sequenceA
```

In conclusion, when declaring a new type it is also useful to consider whether it can be made into a traversable type, by defining either of the primitives `traverse` or `sequenceA`. The advantage of doing so is that we are then provided with a number of useful functions for effectful programming with the type, by means of the default definitions in the `Traversable` class.

14.4   Chapter remarks

Further information on the use of monoids in Haskell can be found in [26]. There are two standard ways to generalise `foldr` from lists to other data structures, known in the literature as *catamorphisms* [27] and *crush operators* [28]. The generalised form of folding that is captured by the `Foldable` class corresponds to a crush, hence it can be argued that the `Foldable` class should really be called `Crushable`, and the `fold` primitive should be called `crush`. Traversables were introduced in [19], which also discusses the issue of laws.

14.5   Exercises

1. Complete the following instance declaration from `Data.Monoid` to make a pair type into a monoid provided the two component types are monoids:

   ```
   instance (Monoid a, Monoid b) => Monoid (a,b) where
      -- mempty :: (a,b)
      mempty = ...

      -- mappend :: (a,b) -> (a,b) -> (a,b)
      (x1,y1) `mappend` (x2,y2) = ...
   ```

2. In a similar manner, show how a function type `a -> b` can be made into a monoid provided that the result type `b` is a monoid.

3. Show how the `Maybe` type can be made foldable and traversable, by giving explicit definitions for `fold`, `foldMap`, `foldr`, `foldl` and `traverse`.

4. In a similar manner, show how the following type of binary trees with data in their nodes can be made into a foldable and traversable type:

   ```
   data Tree a = Leaf | Node (Tree a) a (Tree a)
               deriving Show
   ```

5. Using `foldMap`, define a generic version of the higher-order function `filter` on lists that can be used with any foldable type:

```
filterF :: Foldable t => (a -> Bool) -> t a -> [a]
```

Solutions to exercises 1 and 2 are given in appendix A.

15 Lazy evaluation

In this chapter we introduce lazy evaluation, the mechanism used to evaluate expressions in Haskell. We start by reviewing the notion of evaluation, then consider evaluation strategies and their properties, discuss infinite structures and modular programming, and conclude with a special form of function application that can improve the space performance of programs.

15.1   Introduction

As we have seen throughout this book, the basic method of computation in Haskell is the application of functions to arguments. For example, suppose that we define a function that increments an integer:

```
inc :: Int -> Int
inc n = n + 1
```

Then the expression `inc (2*3)` can be evaluated as follows:

```
    inc (2*3)
=      { applying * }
    inc 6
=      { applying inc }
    6 + 1
=      { applying + }
    7
```

Alternatively, the same final result can also be obtained by performing the first two function applications in the opposite order:

```
    inc (2*3)
=      { applying inc }
    (2*3) + 1
=      { applying * }
    6 + 1
=      { applying + }
    7
```

The fact that changing the order in which functions are applied does not affect the final result is not specific to simple examples such as the above, but is an important general property of function application in Haskell. More formally, in Haskell any two different ways of evaluating the same expression will always produce the same final value, provided that they both terminate. We will return to the issue of termination later on in this chapter.

We also note that the above property does not hold for most imperative programming languages, in which the basic method of computation is changing stored values. For example, consider the imperative expression n + (n = 1) that adds the current value of the variable n to the result of changing its value to one. Assuming that n initially has the value zero, this expression can be evaluated by first performing the left-hand side of the addition

$$
\begin{array}{ll}
& \texttt{n + (n = 1)} \\
= & \quad \{ \text{ applying } \texttt{n} \} \\
& \texttt{0 + (n = 1)} \\
= & \quad \{ \text{ applying } \texttt{=} \} \\
& \texttt{0 + 1} \\
= & \quad \{ \text{ applying } \texttt{+} \} \\
& \texttt{1}
\end{array}
$$

or alternatively, by first performing the right-hand side:

$$
\begin{array}{ll}
& \texttt{n + (n = 1)} \\
= & \quad \{ \text{ applying } \texttt{=} \} \\
& \texttt{n + 1} \\
= & \quad \{ \text{ applying } \texttt{n} \} \\
& \texttt{1 + 1} \\
= & \quad \{ \text{ applying } \texttt{+} \} \\
& \texttt{2}
\end{array}
$$

The final value is different in each case. The general problem illustrated by this example is that the precise time at which an assignment is performed in an imperative language may affect the value that results from a computation. In contrast, the time at which a function is applied to an argument in Haskell never affects the value that results from a computation. Nonetheless, as we shall see in the remainder of this chapter, there are important practical issues concerning the order and nature of the evaluation process.

15.2   Evaluation strategies

An expression that has the form of a function applied to one or more arguments that can be 'reduced' by performing the application is called a *reducible expression*, or *redex* for short. As indicated by the use of quotations marks in the preceding sentence, such reductions do not necessarily decrease the size of an expression, although in practice this is often the case.

By way of example, suppose that we define a function `mult` that takes a pair of integers and returns their product:

```
mult :: (Int,Int) -> Int
mult (x,y) = x * y
```

Now consider the expression `mult (1+2,2+3)`. This expression contains three redexes, namely the sub-expressions `1+2` and `2+3`, which have the form of the addition operator `+` applied to two arguments, and the entire expression itself `mult (1+2,2+3)`, which has the form of the function `mult` applied to a pair of arguments. Performing the corresponding reductions gives the expressions `mult (3,2+3)`, `mult (1+2,5)`, and `(1+2) * (2+3)`.

When evaluating an expression, in what order should the reductions be performed? One common strategy, known as *innermost evaluation*, is to always choose a redex that is innermost, in the sense that it contains no other redex. If there is more than one innermost redex, by convention we choose the one that begins at the leftmost position in the expression.

For example, both of the sub-expressions `1+2` and `2+3` contain no other redexes and are hence innermost within the expression `mult (1+2,2+3)`, with the redex `1+2` beginning at the leftmost position. More generally, our example expression is evaluated using innermost evaluation as follows:

```
    mult (1+2, 2+3)
=      { applying the first + }
    mult (3, 2+3)
=      { applying + }
    mult (3, 5)
=      { applying mult }
    3 * 5
=      { applying * }
    15
```

Innermost evaluation can also be characterised in terms of how arguments are passed to functions. In particular, using this strategy ensures that arguments are always fully evaluated before functions are applied. That is, arguments are passed *by value*. For example, as shown above, evaluating `mult (1+2,2+3)` using innermost evaluation proceeds by first evaluating the arguments `1+2` and `2+3`, and then applying `mult`. The fact that we always choose the leftmost innermost redex ensures that the first argument is evaluated before the second.

Another common strategy for evaluating an expression, dual to innermost evaluation, is to always choose a redex that is outermost, in the sense that it is contained in no other redex. If there is more than one such redex then as previously we choose that which begins at the leftmost position. Not surprisingly, this evaluation strategy is known as *outermost evaluation*.

For example, the expression `mult (1+2,2+3)` is contained in no other redex and is hence outermost within itself. More generally, evaluating this expression using outermost evaluation proceeds as follows:

```
    mult (1+2, 2+3)
=      { applying mult }
    (1+2) * (2+3)
=      { applying the first + }
    3 * (2+3)
=      { applying + }
    3 * 5
=      { applying * }
    15
```

In terms of how arguments are passed to functions, using outermost evaluation allows functions to be applied before their arguments are evaluated. For this reason, we say that arguments are passed *by name*. For example, as shown above, evaluating `mult (1+2,2+3)` using outermost evaluation proceeds by first applying the function `mult` to the two unevaluated arguments 1+2 and 2+3, and then evaluating these two expressions in turn.

We conclude this section by noting that many built-in functions require their arguments to be evaluated before being applied, even when using outermost evaluation. For example, as illustrated in the calculation above, built-in arithmetic operators such as * and + cannot be applied until their two arguments have been evaluated to numbers. Functions with this property are called *strict*, and will be discussed in further detail at the end of this chapter.

Lambda expressions

Let us now define a curried version of `mult` that takes its arguments one at a time, using a lambda expression to make the use of currying explicit:

```
mult :: Int -> Int -> Int
mult x = \y -> x * y
```

Then using innermost evaluation, for example, we have:

```
    mult (1+2) (2+3)
=      { applying the first + }
    mult 3 (2+3)
=      { applying mult }
    (\y -> 3 * y) (2+3)
=      { applying + }
    (\y -> 3 * y) 5
=      { applying the lambda }
```

$$3 * 5$$
$$= \quad \{ \text{applying } * \}$$
$$15$$

That is, the two arguments are now substituted into the body of the function `mult` one at a time, as we would expect using currying, rather than at the same time as in the previous section. This behaviour arises because `mult 3` is the leftmost innermost redex in the expression `mult 3 (2+3)`, as opposed to `2+3` in the expression `mult (3,2+3)`. Performing a reduction on `mult 3` in the second step of the calculation above gives the lambda expression `\y -> 3 * y`, which awaits the result of evaluating the second argument.

Note that in Haskell, the selection of redexes within the bodies lambda expressions is prohibited. The rationale for not 'reducing under lambdas' is that functions are viewed as black boxes that we are not permitted to look inside. More formally, the only operation that can be performed on a function is that of applying it to an argument. As such, reduction within the body of a function is only permitted once the function has been applied.

For example, the function `\x -> 1 + 2` is deemed to already be fully evaluated, even though its body contains the redex `1 + 2`, but once this function has been applied to an argument, evaluation of this redex can then proceed:

$$(\backslash \text{x} \, \text{->} \, 1 \, + \, 2) \, 0$$
$$= \quad \{ \text{applying the lambda} \}$$
$$1 + 2$$
$$= \quad \{ \text{applying } + \}$$
$$3$$

Using innermost and outermost evaluation, but not within lambda expressions, is normally referred to as *call-by-value* and *call-by-name* evaluation, respectively. In the next two sections we explore how these two evaluation strategies compare in terms of two important properties, namely their termination behaviour and the number of reduction steps that they require.

15.3   Termination

Consider the following recursive definition:

```
inf :: Int
inf = 1 + inf
```

That is, the integer `inf` (abbreviating *infinity*) is defined as the successor of itself. Evaluating `inf` produces a larger and larger expression, regardless of the evaluation strategy, and hence does not terminate:

```
inf
```
$$= \quad \{ \text{applying inf} \}$$

```
      1 + inf
   =      { applying inf }
      1 + (1 + inf)
   =      { applying inf }
      1 + (1 + (1 + inf))
   =      { applying inf }
      :
```

Now consider the expression `fst (0,inf)` that contains the value `inf`, where `fst` is the library function that selects the first component of a pair, defined by `fst (x,y) = x`. Using call-by-value evaluation with this expression results in non-termination in a similar manner to `inf` itself:

```
      fst (0, inf)
   =      { applying inf }
      fst (0, 1 + inf)
   =      { applying inf }
      fst (0, 1 + (1 + inf))
   =      { applying inf }
      fst (0, 1 + (1 + (1 + inf)))
   =      { applying inf }
      :
```

In contrast, using call-by-name evaluation results in termination with the result zero in just one step, by immediately applying the definition of `fst` and hence avoiding the evaluation of the non-terminating expression `inf`:

```
      fst (0, inf)
   =      { applying fst }
      0
```

This simple example shows that call-by-name evaluation may produce a result when call-by-value evaluation fails to terminate. More generally, we have the following important property: if there exists any evaluation sequence that terminates for a given expression, then call-by-name evaluation will also terminate for this expression, and produce the same final result.

In summary, call-by-name evaluation is preferable to call-by-value for the purpose of ensuring that evaluation terminates as often as possible.

15.4   Number of reductions

Now consider the following definition:

```
   square :: Int -> Int
   square n = n * n
```

For example, using call-by-value evaluation, we have:

```
    square (1+2)
=       { applying + }
    square 3
=       { applying square }
    3 * 3
=       { applying * }
    9
```

In contrast, using call-by-name evaluation requires one extra reduction step, due to the fact that the argument expression 1+2 is duplicated when the function square is applied, and hence must be evaluated twice:

```
    square (1+2)
=       { applying square }
    (1+2) * (1+2)
=       { applying the first + }
    3 * (1+2)
=       { applying + }
    3 * 3
=       { applying * }
    9
```

This example shows that call-by-name evaluation may require more reduction steps than call-by-value evaluation, in particular when an argument is used more than once in the body of a function. More generally, we have the following property: arguments are evaluated precisely once using call-by-value evaluation, but may be evaluated many times using call-by-name.

Fortunately, the above efficiency problem with call-by-name evaluation can easily be solved, by using pointers to indicate sharing of expressions during evaluation. That is, rather than physically copying an argument if it is used many times in the body of a function, we simply keep one copy of the argument and make many pointers to it. In this manner, any reductions that are performed on the argument are automatically shared between each of the pointers to that argument. For example, using this strategy we have:

```
    square (1+2)

=       { applying square }


    • * •      1+2

=       { applying + }


    • * •      3
```

$$= \quad \{ \text{applying} * \}$$
$$9$$

That is, when applying the definition `square n = n * n` in the first step, we keep a single copy of the argument expression `1+2`, and make two pointers to it. In this manner, when the expression `1+2` is reduced in the second step, both pointers in the expression share the result.

The use of call-by-name evaluation in conjunction with sharing is known as *lazy evaluation*. This is the evaluation strategy that is used in Haskell, as a result of which Haskell is known as a lazy programming language. Being based upon call-by-name evaluation, lazy evaluation has the property that it ensures that evaluation terminates as often as possible. Moreover, using sharing ensures that lazy evaluation never requires more steps than call-by-value evaluation. The use of the term 'lazy' will be explained in the next section.

15.5 Infinite structures

An additional property of call-by-name evaluation, and hence lazy evaluation, is that it allows what at first may seem impossible: programming with infinite structures. We have already seen a simple example of this idea earlier in this chapter, in the form of the evaluation of `fst (0,inf)` avoiding the production of the infinite structure `1 + (1 + (1 + ...))` defined by `inf`.

More interesting forms of behaviour occur when we consider infinite lists. For example, consider the following recursive definition:

```
ones :: [Int]
ones = 1 : ones
```

That is, the list `ones` is defined as a single one followed by itself. As with `inf`, evaluating `ones` does not terminate, regardless of the strategy used:

```
    ones
=      { applying ones }
    1 : ones
=      { applying ones }
    1 : (1 : ones)
=      { applying ones }
    1 : (1 : (1 : ones))
=      { applying ones }
    ⋮
```

In practice, evaluating `ones` using GHCi will produce a never-ending list of ones, until the user eventually decides to terminate this process:

```
> ones
[1,1,1,1,1,1,1,1,1,1,1,...
```

Now consider the expression **head ones**, where **head** is the library function that selects the first element of a list, defined by **head (x:_) = x**. Using call-by-value evaluation in this case also results in non-termination:

```
    head ones
=       { applying ones }
    head (1 : ones)
=       { applying ones }
    head (1 : (1 : ones))
=       { applying ones }
    head (1 : (1 : (1 : ones)))
=       { applying ones }
    ⋮
```

In contrast, using lazy evaluation (or call-by-name evaluation, as sharing is not required in this example) results in termination in two steps:

```
    head ones
=       { applying ones }
    head (1 : ones)
=       { applying head }
    1
```

This behaviour arises because lazy evaluation proceeds in a lazy manner as its name suggests, only evaluating arguments as and when this is strictly necessary in order to produce results. For example, when selecting the first element of a list, the remainder of the list is not required, and hence in **head (1 : ones)** the further evaluation of the infinite list **ones** is avoided. More generally, we have the following property: using lazy evaluation, expressions are only evaluated as much as required by the context in which they are used.

Using this idea, we now see that under lazy evaluation **ones** is not an infinite list as such, but rather a *potentially infinite* list, which is only evaluated as much as required by the context. This idea is not restricted to lists, but applies equally to any form of data structure in Haskell. For example, infinite trees are considered in the exercises for this chapter.

15.6   Modular programming

Lazy evaluation also allows us to separate *control* from *data* in our computations. For example, a list of three ones can be produced by selecting the first three elements (control) of the infinite list of ones (data):

```
> take 3 ones
[1,1,1]
```

Using the definition of **take** from the standard prelude

```
take 0 _      = []
take _ []     = []
take n (x:xs) = x : take (n-1) xs
```

this behaviour arises using lazy evaluation as follows:

```
    take 3 ones
=       { applying ones }
    take 3 (1 : ones)
=       { applying take }
    1 : take 2 ones
=       { applying ones }
    1 : take 2 (1 : ones)
=       { applying take }
    1 : 1 : take 1 ones
=       { applying ones }
    1 : 1 : take 1 (1 : ones)
=       { applying take }
    1 : 1 : 1 : take 0 ones
=       { applying take }
    1 : 1 : 1 : []
=       { list notation }
    [1,1,1]
```

That is, the data is only evaluated as much as required by the control, and these two parts take it in turn to perform reductions. Without lazy evaluation, the control and data parts would need to be combined in the form of a single function that produces a list of n identical elements, such as:

```
replicate :: Int -> a -> [a]
replicate 0 _ = []
replicate n x = x : replicate (n-1) x
```

Being able to modularise programs by separating them into logically distinct parts is an important goal in programming, and being able to separate control from data is one of the most important benefits of lazy evaluation.

Note that care is still required when programming with infinite lists, to avoid non-termination. For example, the expression

```
filter (<= 5) [1..]
```

(where [n..] produces the infinite list of integers beginning with n) will produce the integers $1, 2, 3, 4, 5$ and then loop forever, because the function filter (<= 5) keeps testing elements of the infinite list in a vain attempt to find another that is less than or equal to five. In contrast, the expression

```
takeWhile (<= 5) [1..]
```

will produce the same integers and then terminate, because `takeWhile (<= 5)` stops as soon as it finds an element that is greater than five.

We conclude this section with an example concerning prime numbers. Recall that in chapter 5, we wrote a function to generate prime numbers up to a given limit. In contrast, here is a simple procedure for generating the infinite sequence of all prime numbers, as opposed to a finite prefix of this sequence:

- write down the infinite sequence $2, 3, 4, 5, 6, \cdots$;
- mark the first number, p, in the sequence as prime;
- delete all multiples of p from the sequence;
- return to the second step.

Note that the first and third steps each require an infinite amount of work, and hence in practice the steps must be interleaved. The first few iterations of this procedure can be illustrated as follows:

②	3	4̲	5	6̲	7	8̲	9	10̲	11	12̲	13	14̲	15	⋯
	③		5	_	7		9̲		11	_	13		15̲	⋯
		⑤		7			_		11		13		_	⋯
			⑦						11		13	_		⋯
				⑪							13			⋯
					⑬									⋯

Each row corresponds to one iteration of the procedure, with the first row being the initial sequence (step one), the first number in each row being circled to indicate its primality (step two), and all multiples of this number being underlined to indicate their deletion (step three) prior to the next iteration. In this manner, we can imagine the initial sequence of numbers falling downwards, with certain numbers being sieved out at each stage by the underlining, and the circled numbers forming the infinite sequence of primes:

$$2, 3, 5, 7, 11, 13, \cdots$$

The above procedure for generating prime numbers is known as the *sieve of Eratosthenes*, after the Greek mathematician who first described it. This procedure can be translated directly into Haskell:

```
primes :: [Int]
primes = sieve [2..]
```

```
sieve :: [Int] -> [Int]
sieve (p:xs) = p : sieve [x | x <- xs, x 'mod' p /= 0]
```

That is, starting with the infinite list [2..] (step one), we apply the function sieve that retains the first number p as being prime (step two), and then calls itself recursively with a new list obtained by filtering all multiples of p from this list (steps three and four). Lazy evaluation ensures that this program does indeed produce the infinite list of all prime numbers:

```
> primes
[2,3,5,7,11,13,17,19,23,29,31,37,41,43,47,53,59,61,67,...
```

By freeing the generation of prime numbers from the constraint of finiteness, we have obtained a modular program on which different control parts can be used in different situations. For example, the first ten prime numbers, and the prime numbers less than ten, can be produced as follows:

```
> take 10 primes
[2,3,5,7,11,13,17,19,23,29]

> takeWhile (< 10) primes
[2,3,5,7]
```

15.7   Strict application

Haskell uses lazy evaluation by default, but also provides a special *strict* version of function application, written as $!, which can sometimes be useful. Informally, an expression of the form f $! x behaves in the same way as the normal functional application f x, except that the top-level of evaluation of the argument expression x is forced before the function f is applied.

For example, if the argument has a basic type, such as Int or Bool, then top-level evaluation is simply complete evaluation. On the other hand, for a pair type such as (Int,Bool), evaluation is performed until a pair of expressions is obtained, but no further. Similarly, for a list type, evaluation is performed until the empty list or the cons of two expressions is obtained.

More formally, an expression of the form f $! x is only a redex once evaluation of the argument x, using lazy evaluation as normal, has reached the point where it is known that the result is not an undefined value, at which point the expression can be reduced to the normal application f x. For example, using the definition square n = n * n, evaluation of the application square $! (1+2) proceeds in a call-by-value manner, by first evaluating the argument expression 1+2 to give the value 3, and then applying the function square:

```
square $! (1+2)
```

```
=      { applying + }
   square $! 3
=      { applying $! }
   square 3
=      { applying square }
   3 * 3
=      { applying * }
   9
```

When used with a curried function with multiple arguments, strict application can be used to force top-level evaluation of any combination of arguments. For example, if f is a curried function with two arguments, an application of the form f x y can be modified to have three different behaviours:

> (f $! x) y forces top-level evaluation of x
>
> (f x) $! y forces top-level evaluation of y
>
> (f $! x) $! y forces top-level evaluation of x and y

In Haskell, strict application is mainly used to improve the space performance of programs. For example, consider a function sumwith that calculates the sum of a list of integers using an accumulator value:

```
sumwith :: Int -> [Int] -> Int
sumwith v []     = v
sumwith v (x:xs) = sumwith (v+x) xs
```

Then, using lazy evaluation, we have:

```
   sumwith 0 [1,2,3]
=      { applying sumwith }
   sumwith (0+1) [2,3]
=      { applying sumwith }
   sumwith ((0+1)+2) [3]
=      { applying sumwith }
   sumwith (((0+1)+2)+3) []
=      { applying sumwith }
   ((0+1)+2)+3
=      { applying the first + }
   (1+2)+3
=      { applying the first + }
   3+3
=      { applying + }
   6
```

Note that the entire summation ((0+1)+2)+3 is constructed before any of the component additions are actually performed. More generally, sumwith will construct a summation whose size is proportional to the number of integers in the original list, which for a long list may require a significant amount of space. In practice, it would be preferable to perform each addition as soon as it is introduced, to improve the space performance of the function.

This behaviour can be achieved by redefining `sumwith` using strict application, to force evaluation of its accumulator value:

```
sumwith v []     = v
sumwith v (x:xs) = (sumwith $! (v+x)) xs
```

For example, we now have:

```
      sumwith 0 [1,2,3]
=        { applying sumwith }
      (sumwith $! (0+1)) [2,3]
=        { applying + }
      (sumwith $! 1) [2,3]
=        { applying $! }
      sumwith 1 [2,3]
=        { applying sumwith }
      (sumwith $! (1+2)) [3]
=        { applying + }
      (sumwith $! 3) [3]
=        { applying $! }
      sumwith 3 [3]
=        { applying sumwith }
      (sumwith $! (3+3)) []
=        { applying + }
      (sumwith $! 6) []
=        { applying $! }
      sumwith 6 []
=        { applying sumwith }
      6
```

This evaluation requires more steps than previously, due to the additional overhead of using strict application, but now performs each addition as soon as it is introduced, rather than constructing a large summation.

Generalising from the above example, the library `Data.Foldable` provides a strict version of the higher-order library function `foldl` that forces evaluation of its accumulator prior to processing the tail of the list:

```
foldl' :: (a -> b -> a) -> a -> [b] -> a
foldl' f v []     = v
foldl' f v (x:xs) = ((foldl' f) $! (f v x)) xs
```

For example, using this function we can define `sumwith = foldl' (+)`. It is important to note, however, that strict application is not a silver bullet that automatically improves the space behaviour of Haskell programs. Even for relatively simple examples, the use of strict application is a specialist topic that requires careful consideration of the behaviour of lazy evaluation.

15.8   Chapter remarks

Further details about evaluation orders and their properties can be found in [29], and further examples of the use of lazy evaluation for modular programming in the classic article *Why Functional Programming Matters* [30]. A formal meaning for lazy evaluation is given in [31], and a comprehensive tutorial on the efficient implementation of lazy evaluation in [32].

15.9   Exercises

1. Identify the redexes in the following expressions, and determine whether each redex is innermost, outermost, neither, or both:

   ```
   1 + (2*3)
   ```

   ```
   (1+2) * (2+3)
   ```

   ```
   fst (1+2, 2+3)
   ```

   ```
   (\x -> 1 + x) (2*3)
   ```

2. Show why outermost evaluation is preferable to innermost for the purposes of evaluating the expression `fst (1+2,2+3)`.

3. Given the definition `mult = \x -> (\y -> x * y)`, show how the evaluation of `mult 3 4` can be broken down into four separate steps.

4. Using a list comprehension, define an expression `fibs :: [Integer]` that generates the infinite sequence of Fibonacci numbers

   $$0, 1, 1, 2, 3, 5, 8, 13, 21, 34, \cdots$$

   using the following simple procedure:

   - the first two numbers are 0 and 1;
   - the next is the sum of the previous two;
   - return to the second step.

   Hint: make use of the library functions `zip` and `tail`. Note that numbers in the Fibonacci sequence quickly become large, hence the use of the type

`Integer` of arbitrary-precision integers above.

5. Define appropriate versions of the library functions

   ```
   repeat :: a -> [a]
   repeat x = xs where xs = x:xs

   take :: Int -> [a] -> [a]
   take 0 _     = []
   take _ []    = []
   take n (x:xs) = x : take (n-1) xs

   replicate :: Int -> a -> [a]
   replicate n = take n . repeat
   ```

   for the following type of binary trees:

   ```
   data Tree a = Leaf | Node (Tree a) a (Tree a)
                 deriving Show
   ```

6. *Newton's method* for computing the square root of a (non-negative) floating-point number `n` can be expressed as follows:

   - start with an initial approximation to the result;
   - given the current approximation `a`, the next approximation is defined by the function `next a = (a + n/a) / 2`;
   - repeat the second step until the two most recent approximations are within some desired distance of one another, at which point the most recent value is returned as the result.

   Define a function `sqroot :: Double -> Double` that implements this procedure. Hint: first produce an infinite list of approximations using the library function `iterate`. For simplicity, take the number `1.0` as the initial approximation, and `0.00001` as the distance value.

Solutions to exercises 1–3 are given in appendix A.

16 Reasoning about programs

In this chapter we introduce the idea of reasoning about Haskell programs. We start by reviewing the notion of equational reasoning, then consider how it can be applied in Haskell, introduce the important technique of induction, show how induction can be used to eliminate uses of the append operator, and conclude by proving the correctness of a simple compiler.

16.1 Equational reasoning

At school we learn basic algebraic properties of numbers, such as the fact that multiplication is commutative, addition is associative, and multiplication distributes over addition on both the left- and right-hand sides:

$$
\begin{aligned}
x\,y &= y\,x \\
x + (y + z) &= (x + y) + z \\
x\,(y + z) &= x\,y + x\,z \\
(x + y)\,z &= x\,z + y\,z
\end{aligned}
$$

For example, using these properties we can show that a product of the form $(x + a)\,(x + b)$ can be expanded to a summation $x^2 + (a + b)\,x + a\,b$:

$$
\begin{aligned}
&(x + a)\,(x + b) \\
=\quad &\{ \text{left distributivity} \} \\
&(x + a)\,x + (x + a)\,b \\
=\quad &\{ \text{right distributivity} \} \\
&x\,x + a\,x + x\,b + a\,b \\
=\quad &\{ \text{squaring} \} \\
&x^2 + a\,x + x\,b + a\,b \\
=\quad &\{ \text{commutativity} \} \\
&x^2 + a\,x + b\,x + a\,b \\
=\quad &\{ \text{right distributivity} \} \\
&x^2 + (a + b)\,x + a\,b
\end{aligned}
$$

Note that in this calculation we follow the common practice of implicitly exploiting associativity properties, in this case the associativity of addition by omitting parentheses when more than one addition is used in sequence.

As well as being interesting in their own right, algebraic properties can also have a computational significance. For example, the expression $x\,(y + z)$ requires two operations (one multiplication and one addition), whereas the equivalent expression $x\,y + x\,z$ requires three operations (two multiplications and one addition). Hence even though these two expressions are algebraically equal, in terms of efficiency the former is preferable to the latter.

16.2   Reasoning about Haskell

The same style of equational reasoning can also be used in Haskell. For example, in this context the equation `x * y = y * x` means that for any expressions `x` and `y` of the same numeric types, evaluation of `x * y` and `y * x` will always produce the same numeric value. Note that we use the mathematical equality operator $=$ when stating such properties, rather than the equality operator `==` provided within Haskell itself, because we are aiming to use mathematics as a language to reason about Haskell, rather than using Haskell as a language to reason about itself, which would be somewhat circular.

When reasoning about Haskell, we do not just use properties of built-in operations of the language such as addition and multiplication, but also use the equations from which user-defined functions are constructed. For example, consider the following function that doubles an integer:

```
double :: Int -> Int
double x = x + x
```

As well as being viewed as the *definition* of a function, this equation can also be viewed as a *property* that can be used when reasoning about this function. In particular, as a logical property the above equation states that for any integer expression `x`, the expression `double x` can freely be replaced by `x + x`, and, conversely, that the expression `x + x` can freely be replaced by `double x`. In this manner, when reasoning about programs, function definitions can be both *applied* from left-to-right and *unapplied* from right-to-left.

However, some care is required when reasoning about functions that are defined using multiple equations. For example, consider a function that decides if an integer is zero, defined using two equations:

```
isZero :: Int -> Bool
isZero 0 = True
isZero n = False
```

The first equation, `isZero 0 = True`, can freely be viewed as a logical property that can be applied in both directions. However, this is not the case for the second equation, `isZero n = False`. In particular, because the order in which the equations are written is significant in Haskell, an expression of the form `isZero n` can only be replaced by `False` provided that $n \neq 0$, as in the case when n = 0 the first equation applies. Dually, it is only valid to unapply the equation isZero n = False and replace False by an expression of the form isZero n in the case when $n \neq 0$, for the same reason.

More generally, when a function is defined using multiple equations, the equations cannot be viewed as logical properties in isolation from one another, but need to be interpreted in light of the order in which patterns are matched within the equations. For this reason, it is preferable to define functions in a manner that does not rely on the order in which their equations are written. For example, if we rewrite the above definition using a guard

```
isZero 0          = True
isZero n | n /= 0 = False
```

then it is now made explicit that isZero n can only be replaced by False, and conversely that False can only be replaced by isZero n, when the guard n /= 0 is satisfied. Patterns that do not rely on the order in which they are matched are called *non-overlapping*. In order to simplify the process of reasoning about programs, it is good practice to use non-overlapping patterns whenever possible when defining functions. For example, most of the functions in the standard prelude given in appendix B are defined in this manner.

16.3   Simple examples

As a simple first example of equational reasoning in Haskell, recall the following definition of the library function that reverses a list:

```
reverse :: [a] -> [a]
reverse []     = []
reverse (x:xs) = reverse xs ++ [x]
```

Using this definition, we can show that reverse has no effect on singleton lists, in the sense that reverse [x] = [x] for any value x:

```
      reverse [x]
  =      { list notation }
      reverse (x : [])
  =      { applying reverse }
      reverse [] ++ [x]
  =      { applying reverse }
      [] ++ [x]
  =      { applying ++ }
      [x]
```

Hence any expression of the form reverse [x] in a program can freely be replaced by [x] without change in meaning, but with a change in efficiency by avoiding the need to apply the reverse function.

Equational reasoning is often combined with some form of case analysis. For example, consider the logical negation function:

```
not :: Bool -> Bool
not False = True
not True  = False
```

Because this function is defined by pattern matching, properties of not are normally proved by case analysis on its argument. For example, the fact that not is its own inverse, not (not b) = b for all logical values b, can be shown by case analysis on the two possible values for b. For example, the case when b = False is verified below, and b = True follows similarly:

```
    not (not False)
=      { applying the inner not }
    not True
=      { applying not }
    False
```

16.4 Induction on numbers

Most interesting Haskell programs involve some form of recursion. Reasoning about such programs normally proceeds using the simple but powerful technique of *induction*. Let us begin by recalling the simplest example of a recursive type, namely the type of natural numbers:

```
data Nat = Zero | Succ Nat
```

This declaration states that Zero is a value of type Nat (the base case), and that if n is a value of type Nat, then so is Succ n (the recursive case). Implicit in the declaration is the fact that Zero and Succ are the only constructors for the type Nat. Hence, the values of Nat can be enumerated as follows:

```
Zero
Succ Zero
Succ (Succ Zero)
Succ (Succ (Succ Zero))
  .
  .
  .
```

For simplicity, we only consider the *finite* natural numbers, obtained by starting with Zero and applying Succ a finite number of times. In particular, we do not consider the infinite value Succ (Succ (Succ ...)), which can be defined recursively by inf = Succ inf. A similar comment applies to all the other recursive types that we consider in this chapter.

Now suppose we want to prove that some property, p say, holds for all (finite) natural numbers. Then the principle of induction states that it is sufficient to show that p holds for Zero, called the *base case*, and that p is preserved by Succ, called the *inductive case*. More precisely, in the inductive case one is required to show that if the property p holds for any natural number n, called the *induction hypothesis*, then it also holds for Succ n.

Why is induction sufficient to show that p holds for all natural numbers? For example, how does it then follow that p holds for Succ (Succ Zero). Starting from the base case that p holds for Zero, we can apply the inductive case once to conclude that p holds for Succ Zero, by taking n = Zero, and then apply the inductive case a second time to conclude that p holds for Succ (Succ Zero), by taking n = Succ Zero. In a similar manner, it can be established that the property p holds for any natural number.

It is useful to draw an analogy with the *domino effect*. Suppose there is a line of dominoes standing on end and you know that the first domino will fall, and that whenever a domino falls then its next neighbour will also fall. Then it is clear that all the dominoes will fall, by applying the first fact to get the process started, and repeatedly applying the second to keep it going. The same pattern of reasoning occurs with induction: we first verify the required property for Zero (the first domino falls), then that the property is preserved by Succ (if any domino falls, then so will its neighbour), and conclude that the property holds for all natural numbers (all dominoes fall).

As a concrete example, consider the definition of a recursive function that takes two natural numbers and adds them together:

```
add :: Nat -> Nat -> Nat
add Zero     m = m
add (Succ n) m = Succ (add n m)
```

From the first equation, it is immediate that add Zero m = m holds for any natural number m. Now let us show that the dual property, add n Zero = n, which we abbreviate by p, also holds for all natural numbers n. We proceed by induction on n. The base case, showing that p Zero holds, amounts to showing that add Zero Zero = Zero, which is immediate:

```
    add Zero Zero
=      { applying add }
    Zero
```

For the inductive case, we must show that if p holds for any natural number n, then p (Succ n) also holds. That is, using the induction hypothesis add n Zero = n as an assumption, we must show that the equation add (Succ n) Zero = Succ n holds, which can be verified as follows:

```
    add (Succ n) Zero
=      { applying add }
```

```
      Succ (add n Zero)
=         { induction hypothesis }
      Succ n
```

$\square$

Because proofs by induction normally involve more than one calculation, it is useful to explicitly indicate the end of the proof. For this purpose, we use a square box $\square$ in the right-hand margin, as illustrated above.

As another example, let us show that addition of natural numbers is associative. That is, add x (add y z) = add (add x y) z for all x, y and z. There are three variables, so which should induction be performed over? Note that the add function is defined by pattern matching on its first argument, so it is natural to try induction on x, which appears twice as the first argument to add in the associativity equation, whereas y only appears once as such and z never. Using induction on x, the proof of the associativity of add proceeds as follows.

Base case:

```
      add Zero (add y z)
=         { applying the outer add }
      add y z
=         { unapplying add }
      add (add Zero y) z
```

Inductive case:

```
      add (Succ x) (add y z)
=         { applying the outer add }
      Succ (add x (add y z))
=         { induction hypothesis }
      Succ (add (add x y) z)
=         { unapplying the outer add }
      add (Succ (add x y)) z
=         { unapplying the inner add }
      add (add (Succ x) y) z
```

$\square$

Note that both cases in the proof start by applying definitions, and conclude by unapplying definitions. This pattern is typical in proofs by induction, but the latter part may seem somewhat mysterious at first sight. In particular, knowing which definitions to unapply seems to require a degree of foresight. In practice, however, if one becomes stuck at a certain point during such a calculation, progress can often be made by focusing on the desired end result and trying to work backwards to the point where one became stuck.

For example, after applying the induction hypothesis in the inductive case above to obtain Succ (add (add x y) z), it may not be clear how to proceed, as there are no more definitions that can be applied. However, if we then focus on the expression that we are aiming towards, add (add (Succ x) y) z, we can simply apply the inner add and then the outer add to produce the expression at which we became stuck, which process can then be reversed (turning applying into unapplying) to complete the calculation.

Although we have introduced induction using the recursive type Nat, the same principle can also be used with the type of integers that is built-in to Haskell. In particular, to prove that some property p holds for all integers $n \geqslant 0$, it is sufficient to show that p holds for 0, the base case, and that if p holds for any $n \geqslant 0$, then it also holds for n+1, the inductive case.

For example, consider the following recursive definition for the library function replicate that produces a list with n identical elements:

```
replicate :: Int -> a -> [a]
replicate 0 _ = []
replicate n x = x : replicate (n-1) x
```

It is easy to show that this function does indeed produce a list with n elements, that is length (replicate n x) = n, by induction on $n \geqslant 0$.

Base case:

```
    length (replicate 0 x)
=      { applying replicate }
    length []
=      { applying length }
    0
```

Inductive case:

```
    length (replicate (n+1) x)
=      { applying replicate }
    length (x : replicate n x)
=      { applying length }
    1 + length (replicate n x)
=      { induction hypothesis }
    1 + n
=      { commutativity of + }
    n + 1
```

$\square$

16.5 Induction on lists

Induction is not restricted to natural numbers, but can also be used to reason about other recursive types, such as the type of lists. Just as natural numbers

are built up recursively from zero by applying the successor function, so lists are
built up from the empty list by applying the cons operator.

Suppose we want to prove that some property p holds for all lists. Then the
induction principle for lists states that it is sufficient to show that p holds for
the empty list [], the base case, and that if p holds for any list xs, then it also
holds for x:xs for any element x, the inductive case. Of course, both the element
x and the list xs must be of the appropriate types.

As a first example, let us show that the function reverse defined earlier in
this chapter is its own inverse, reverse (reverse xs) = xs, by induction on
xs. The base case is verified simply by applying the definition:

```
    reverse (reverse [])
=      { applying the inner reverse }
    reverse []
=      { applying reverse }
    []
```

For the inductive case, using the assumption reverse (reverse xs) = xs, we
show that reverse (reverse (x:xs)) = x:xs, as follows:

```
    reverse (reverse (x:xs))
=      { applying the inner reverse }
    reverse (reverse xs ++ [x])
=      { distributivity – see below }
    reverse [x] ++ reverse (reverse xs)
=      { singleton lists – see below }
    [x] ++ reverse (reverse xs)
=      { induction hypothesis }
    [x] ++ xs
=      { applying ++ }
    x : xs
```

□

The above calculation uses two auxiliary properties of the function reverse,
namely our earlier result that reverse preserves singleton lists, reverse [x] =
[x], together with a new result that reverse distributes over append, except
that the order of the two argument lists is then swapped:

```
    reverse (xs ++ ys) = reverse ys ++ reverse xs
```

Technically, we say that the distribution is *contravariant*. Because the append
operator ++ is defined by pattern matching on its first argument, it is natural to
attempt to verify this property by induction on xs.

Base case:

```
    reverse ([] ++ ys)
```

```
=      { applying ++ }
   reverse ys
=      { identity for ++ }
   reverse ys ++ []
=      { unapplying reverse }
   reverse ys ++ reverse []
```

Inductive case:

```
   reverse ((x:xs) ++ ys)
=      { applying ++ }
   reverse (x : (xs ++ ys))
=      { applying reverse }
   reverse (xs ++ ys) ++ [x]
=      { induction hypothesis }
   (reverse ys ++ reverse xs) ++ [x]
=      { associativity of ++ }
   reverse ys ++ (reverse xs ++ [x])
=      { unapplying the second reverse }
   reverse ys ++ reverse (x:xs)
```

□

The above calculations in turn use the fact that ++ is associative with [] as its identity, which can be verified by induction in a similar manner to our earlier results concerning add and Zero (see the exercises section.)

When we introduced the concept of a functor in chapter 12, we noted that the function fmap is required to satisfy two equational laws:

$$\text{fmap id} \quad = \quad \text{id}$$

$$\text{fmap (g . h)} \quad = \quad \text{fmap g . fmap h}$$

As another example of the use of induction on lists, we now show how these laws can be verified for the list functor, for which purpose we use the following recursive definition for the function fmap on lists:

```
fmap :: (a -> b) -> [a] -> [b]
fmap g []     = []
fmap g (x:xs) = g x : fmap g xs
```

By definition, two functions of the same type are equal if they always return the same results for the same arguments. Hence, to verify the first functor law fmap id = id for the case of lists, which has the form of an equality between functions, we must show that fmap id xs = id xs for any list xs. Using the definition for the identity function, id x = x, this equation simplifies to fmap id xs = xs, which can then be verified by induction on xs.

Base case:

```
        fmap id []
   =       { applying fmap }
        []
```

Inductive case:

```
        fmap id (x : xs)
   =       { applying fmap }
        id x : fmap id xs
   =       { applying id }
        x : fmap id xs
   =       { induction hypothesis }
        x : xs
```

□

In turn, for the second functor law we must show that `fmap (g . h) xs =`
`(fmap g . fmap h) xs` for any `xs`. Using the definition for function composition, `(f . g) x = f (g x)`, this equation simplifies to `fmap (g . h) xs =`
`fmap g (fmap h xs)`, which can then be verified by induction.

Base case:

```
        fmap (g . h) []
   =       { applying fmap }
        []
   =       { unapplying fmap }
        fmap g []
   =       { unapplying fmap }
        fmap g (fmap h [])
```

Inductive case:

```
        fmap (g . h) (x : xs)
   =       { applying fmap }
        (g . h) x : fmap (g . h) xs
   =       { applying . }
        g (h x) : fmap (g . h) xs
   =       { induction hypothesis }
        g (h x) : fmap g (fmap h xs)
   =       { unapplying fmap }
        fmap g (h x : fmap h xs)
   =       { unapplying fmap }
        fmap g (fmap h (x : xs))
```

□

The exercises for this chapter include a number of other examples of verifying
the functor laws, together with the applicative and monad laws.

16.6   Making append vanish

Many recursive functions are naturally defined using the append operator ++ on lists, but this operator carries a considerable efficiency cost when used recursively. In this section, we show how induction can be used to eliminate such uses of append, and hence make functions more efficient. As a first example, consider again the following simple recursive definition:

```
reverse :: [a] -> [a]
reverse []     = []
reverse (x:xs) = reverse xs ++ [x]
```

How efficient is this version of reverse? First of all, it is easy to show that the number of reduction steps required to evaluate xs ++ ys is one greater than the length of xs, assuming for simplicity that both xs and ys are already fully evaluated. As a result, we say that ++ takes linear time in the length of its first argument. In turn, the number of steps required by reverse xs for a list of length n can be shown to be the sum of the integers from 1 to $n + 1$, which is $(n + 1)(n + 2)/2$. Multiplying out the brackets using the equation verified at the start of this chapter gives $(n^2 + 3n + 2)/2$, as a result of which we say that reverse takes quadratic time in the length of its argument.

Quadratic time is bad. For example, reversing a list with ten thousand elements will take approximately fifty million reduction steps. Fortunately, however, through the use of induction it is easy to eliminate the use of append in the definition of reverse, and hence improve its efficiency.

The trick is to attempt to define a *more general* function, which combines the behaviours of reverse and ++. In particular, we seek to define a recursive function reverse' that satisfies the following equation:

```
reverse' xs ys  =  reverse xs ++ ys
```

That is, applying reverse' to two lists should give the result of reversing the first list, appended together with the second list. If we can define such a function, then reverse itself can be redefined by reverse xs = reverse' xs [], using the fact that the empty list is the identity for append.

Rather than giving the definition for reverse', and then showing that it satisfies the above equation, we can in fact use this equation as the driving force for *constructing* the definition itself. In particular, we attempt to verify this equation by induction on xs. The base case results in an equation that gives the definition for reverse' [] ys, while the inductive case results in an equation that gives the definition for reverse' (x:xs) ys.

Base case:

```
reverse' [] ys
```

```
=      { specification of reverse' }
    reverse [] ++ ys
=      { applying reverse }
    [] ++ ys
=      { applying ++ }
    ys
```

Inductive case:

```
    reverse' (x:xs) ys
=      { specification of reverse' }
    reverse (x:xs) ++ ys
=      { applying reverse }
    (reverse xs ++ [x]) ++ ys
=      { associativity of ++ }
    reverse xs ++ ([x] ++ ys)
=      { induction hypothesis }
    reverse' xs ([x] ++ ys)
=      { applying ++ }
    reverse' xs (x : ys)
```

□

We conclude from this proof that the definition

```
reverse' :: [a] -> [a] -> [a]
reverse' []     ys = ys
reverse' (x:xs) ys = reverse' xs (x : ys)
```

suffices to show that reverse' xs ys = reverse xs ++ ys by induction. Note that the definition for reverse' does not refer to the original reverse function, or append. Hence, reverse itself can now be redefined as follows:

```
reverse :: [a] -> [a]
reverse xs = reverse' xs []
```

For example, we have:

```
    reverse [1,2,3]
=      { applying reverse }
    reverse' [1,2,3] []
=      { applying reverse' }
    reverse' [2,3] (1:[])
=      { applying reverse' }
    reverse' [3] (2:(1:[]))
=      { applying reverse' }
    reverse' [] (3:(2:(1:[])))
=      { applying reverse' }
    3:(2:(1:[]))
```

That is, the list is reversed by using an extra argument to accumulate the final result. The new definition for `reverse` is perhaps less clear than the original version, but it is much more efficient. In particular, the number of reduction steps required to evaluate `reverse xs` for a list of length n using the new definition is simply $n + 2$, and hence `reverse` now takes linear time in the length of its argument. For example, reversing a list with ten thousand elements will now take approximately ten thousand steps, in contrast to some fifty million with the original definition – quite an improvement!

Note that we have already seen the use of accumulation to improve the efficiency of functions, by means of the function `foldl` in chapters 7 and 15. For example, the accumulator version of `reverse` can also be obtained by defining `reverse = foldl (\xs x -> x:xs) []`. However, it is instructive to see how the same kind of behaviour can be obtained using induction.

As another example of the elimination of append, which also illustrates the use of induction on tree-like types, consider the following type of binary trees, together with a function that flattens such trees to a list:

```
data Tree = Leaf Int | Node Tree Tree

flatten :: Tree -> [Int]
flatten (Leaf n)   = [n]
flatten (Node l r) = flatten l ++ flatten r
```

Because of the use of append, the function `flatten` is inefficient. Let us now construct a more efficient version, by using the same trick as for `reverse`. That is, we seek to define a more general function, `flatten'`, that combines the behaviours of the functions `flatten` and `++`:

```
flatten' t ns = flatten t ++ ns
```

In order to prove that some property holds for all trees, the induction principle for the type `Tree` states that it is sufficient to show that it holds for all trees of the form `Leaf n`, and that if the property holds for any trees `l` and `r`, then it also holds for `Node l r`. Using this principle, we construct a definition for `flatten'` that satisfies the above equation as follows.

Base case:

```
    flatten' (Leaf n) ns
=       { specification of flatten' }
    flatten (Leaf n) ++ ns
=       { applying flatten }
    [n] ++ ns
=       { applying ++ }
    n : ns
```

Inductive case:

```
    flatten' (Node l r) ns
  =       { specification of flatten' }
    (flatten l ++ flatten r) ++ ns
  =       { associativity of ++ }
    flatten l ++ (flatten r ++ ns)
  =       { induction hypothesis for l }
    flatten' l (flatten r ++ ns)
  =       { induction hypothesis for r }
    flatten' l (flatten' r ns)
```

$\square$

We conclude that the definition

```
flatten' :: Tree -> [Int] -> [Int]
flatten' (Leaf n)   ns = n : ns
flatten' (Node l r) ns = flatten' l (flatten' r ns)
```

satisfies the specification for flatten', and hence that the original function flatten can now be redefined as follows:

```
flatten :: Tree -> [Int]
flatten t = flatten' t []
```

Once again, the new definition for flatten is perhaps less clear than the original version, but is much more efficient, by using an extra argument to accumulate the final result, rather than using append.

16.7   Compiler correctness

We conclude this chapter with an extended example. Recall that in chapter 8 we defined a type of simple arithmetic expressions built up from integers using an addition operator, together with a function (here called eval) that evaluates an expression directly to an integer value:

```
data Expr = Val Int | Add Expr Expr

eval :: Expr -> Int
eval (Val n)   = n
eval (Add x y) = eval x + eval y
```

Such expressions can also be evaluated indirectly, by means of code that executes using a stack. In this context, a stack is simply a list of integers, and code comprises a list of push and add operations on the stack:

```
type Stack = [Int]

type Code = [Op]

data Op = PUSH Int | ADD
          deriving Show
```

The meaning of such code is given by defining a function that executes a piece of code using an initial stack to give a final stack:

```
exec :: Code -> Stack -> Stack
exec []              s         = s
exec (PUSH n : c) s            = exec c (n : s)
exec (ADD : c)    (m : n : s) = exec c (n+m : s)
```

That is, the push operation places a new integer on the top of the stack, while add replaces the top two integers by their sum. Using these operations, it is now straightforward to define a function that compiles an expression into code. An integer value is compiled by simply pushing that value, while an addition is compiled by first compiling the two argument expressions x and y, and then adding the resulting two integers on the stack:

```
comp :: Expr -> Code
comp (Val n)   = [PUSH n]
comp (Add x y) = comp x ++ comp y ++ [ADD]
```

Note that when an add operation is performed, the value of expression y will be the top of the stack, and the value of x will be the second top, hence the swapping of these two values in the definition of `exec`.

To illustrate the behaviour of the three functions defined above, if we consider an expression that represents $(2 + 3) + 4$, then we have:

```
> let e = Add (Add (Val 2) (Val 3)) (Val 4)

> eval e
9

> comp e
[PUSH 2, PUSH 3, ADD, PUSH 4, ADD]

> exec (comp e) []
[9]
```

Generalising from this example, the correctness of our compiler for expressions can be expressed by the following equation:

```
exec (comp e) [] = [eval e]
```

That is, compiling an expression and then executing the resulting code using an empty initial stack gives the same final stack as evaluating the expression and then converting the resulting integer into a singleton stack. For the purposes of proving this result, however, we will see that it is necessary to generalise from the empty initial stack to an arbitrary initial stack:

```
exec (comp e) s = eval e : s
```

Using induction for the type `Expr`, which is the same as induction for the type `Tree` in the previous section except that the names of the constructors are different, the compiler correctness equation can be verified as follows.

Base case:

```
    exec (comp (Val n)) s
=       { applying comp }
    exec [PUSH n] s
=       { applying exec }
    n : s
=       { unapplying eval }
    eval (Val n) : s
```

Inductive case:

```
    exec (comp (Add x y)) s
=       { applying comp }
    exec (comp x ++ comp y ++ [ADD]) s
=       { associativity of ++ }
    exec (comp x ++ (comp y ++ [ADD])) s
=       { distributivity – see below }
    exec (comp y ++ [ADD]) (exec (comp x) s)
=       { induction hypothesis for x }
    exec (comp y ++ [ADD]) (eval x : s)
=       { distributivity again }
    exec [ADD] (exec (comp y) (eval x : s))
=       { induction hypothesis for y }
    exec [ADD] (eval y : eval x : s)
=       { applying exec }
    (eval x + eval y) : s
=       { unapplying eval }
    eval (Add x y) : s
```

□

Note that without having generalised the result to an arbitrary stack, the second induction hypothesis step would not be applicable, because the stack becomes non-empty at this point. The distributivity property used in the inductive case states that executing two pieces of code appended together gives the same result as executing the two pieces of code in sequence:

```
exec (c ++ d) s = exec d (exec c s)
```

The proof of this property proceeds by induction on the code c, with the inductive case being split into two separate cases, depending upon whether the first operation in the code is a push or an add.

Base case:

```
    exec ([] ++ d) s
=      { applying ++ }
    exec d s
=      { unapplying exec }
    exec d (exec [] s)
```

Inductive case:

```
    exec ((PUSH n : c) ++ d) s
=      { applying ++ }
    exec (PUSH n : (c ++ d)) s
=      { applying exec }
    exec (c ++ d) (n : s)
=      { induction hypothesis }
    exec d (exec c (n : s))
=      { unapplying exec }
    exec d (exec (PUSH n : c) s)
```

Inductive case:

```
    exec ((ADD : c) ++ d) s
=      { applying ++ }
    exec (ADD : (c ++ d)) s
=      { assume s of the form m : n : s' }
    exec (ADD : (c ++ d)) (m : n : s')
=      { applying exec }
    exec (c ++ d) (n+m : s')
=      { induction hypothesis }
    exec d (exec c (n+m : s'))
=      { unapplying exec }
    exec d (exec (ADD : c) (m : n : s'))
```

□

The stack not having the assumed form in the second inductive case corresponds to a stack *underflow error*. In practice, this will never arise, because the structure of the compiler ensures that the stack will always contain at least two integers at the point when an add operation is performed.

In fact, however, both the distributivity property and its consequent underflow issue can be avoided altogether by applying the technique of the previous section to eliminate the use of append. In particular, we seek to define a generalised function comp' with the following property:

```
comp' e c = comp e ++ c
```

By induction on e, we can construct the definition

```
comp' :: Expr -> Code -> Code
comp' (Val n)   c = PUSH n : c
comp' (Add x y) c = comp' x (comp' y (ADD : c))
```

from which it follows that we can redefine comp e = comp' e []. In turn, the correctness of the new version of the compiler with respect to our semantics for expressions can now be stated as follows:

```
exec (comp' e c) s = exec c (eval e : s)
```

That is, compiling an expression and then executing the resulting code together with arbitrary additional code gives the same result as executing the additional code with the value of the expression on top of the original stack. The proof of this result is by induction on the expression e.

Base case:

```
      exec (comp' (Val n) c) s
=        { applying comp' }
      exec (PUSH n : c) s
=        { applying exec }
      exec c (n:s)
=        { unapplying eval }
      exec c (eval (Val n) : s)
```

Inductive case:

```
      exec (comp' (Add x y) c) s
=        { applying comp' }
      exec (comp' x (comp' y (ADD : c))) s
=        { induction hypothesis for x }
      exec (comp' y (ADD : c)) (eval x : s)
=        { induction hypothesis for y }
      exec (ADD : c) (eval y : eval x : s)
=        { applying exec }
      exec c ((eval x + eval y) : s)
```

$=$ { unapplying `eval` }
       `exec c (eval (Add x y) : s)`

☐

Note that with `s = c = []`, this new compiler correctness result simplifies to `exec (comp e) [] = [eval e]`, our original statement of correctness. In addition to avoiding the problem of stack underflow in the correctness proof, the accumulator version of the compiler has two further benefits. First of all, it avoids the use of `++`, and is hence more efficient. And, secondly, the new proof is less than half the combined length of our previous two proofs. As is often the case in formal reasoning, generalising a result in the appropriate manner can considerably simplify its proof. Mathematics is an excellent tool for guiding the development of efficient programs with simple proofs!

16.8   Chapter remarks

Reasoning about functional programs is a subject for a book in its own right, and we have only touched the surface here. Topics for further reading include reasoning about partial and infinite structures [33, 34], automated testing of program properties [35], reasoning about computational effects [36], and techniques that avoid induction [10]. The compiler example is adapted from [37], and the phrase *making append vanish* is inspired by [38].

16.9   Exercises

1. Show that `add n (Succ m) = Succ (add n m)`, by induction on `n`.

2. Using this property, together with `add n Zero = n`, show that addition is commutative, `add n m = add m n`, by induction on `n`.

3. Using the following definition for the library function that decides if `all` elements of a list satisfy a predicate

   ```
   all p []     = True
   all p (x:xs) = p x && all p xs
   ```

   complete the proof of the correctness of `replicate` by showing that it produces a list with identical elements, `all (== x) (replicate n x)`, by induction on `n ⩾ 0`. Hint: show that the property is always `True`.

4. Using the definition

```
[]      ++ ys = ys
(x:xs) ++ ys = x : (xs ++ ys)
```

verify the following two properties, by induction on `xs`:

```
xs ++ []  = xs

xs ++ (ys ++ zs)  =  (xs ++ ys) ++ zs
```

Hint: the proofs are similar to those for the add function.

5. Using the above definition for `++`, together with

```
take 0 _     = []
take _ []    = []
take n (x:xs) = x : take (n-1) xs

drop 0 xs    = xs
drop _ []    = []
drop n (_:xs) = drop (n-1) xs
```

show that `take n xs ++ drop n xs = xs`, by simultaneous induction on the integer $n \geqslant 0$ and the list `xs`. Hint: there are three cases, one for each pattern of arguments in the definitions of `take` and `drop`.

6. Given the type declaration

```
data Tree = Leaf Int | Node Tree Tree
```

show that the number of leaves in such a tree is always one greater than the number of nodes, by induction on trees. Hint: start by defining functions that count the number of leaves and nodes in a tree.

7. Verify the functor laws for the `Maybe` type. Hint: the proofs proceed by case analysis, and do not require the use of induction.

8. Given the type and instance declarations below, verify the functor laws for the `Tree` type, by induction on trees.

```
data Tree a = Leaf a | Node (Tree a) (Tree a)

instance Functor Tree where
    -- fmap :: (a -> b) -> Tree a -> Tree b
    fmap g (Leaf x)   = Leaf (g x)
    fmap g (Node l r) = Node (fmap g l) (fmap g r)
```

9. Verify the applicative laws for the `Maybe` type.

10. Verify the monad laws for the list type. Hint: the proofs can be completed using simple properties of list comprehensions.

11. Given the equation `comp' e c = comp e ++ c`, show how to construct the recursive definition for `comp'`, by induction on `e`.

Solutions to exercises 1–5 are given in appendix A.

17 Calculating compilers

In this final chapter we show how the reasoning techniques introduced in the previous chapter can be used to calculate compilers. We start by showing how a semantics for a language can be transformed into a compiler in a series of steps, and then show how the steps can be combined to allow a compiler to be calculated directly from a statement of its correctness.

17.1 Introduction

The ability to calculate compilers has been a key objective in the field of program transformation since its earliest days. Starting from a high-level semantics for a source language, the aim is to transform the semantics into a compiler that translates source programs into a lower-level target language, together with a virtual machine that executes the resulting target programs.

There are two main advantages of such an approach. Firstly, the compiler, target language and virtual machine are *systematically derived* during the transformation process, rather than having to be manually defined by the user. And secondly, the resulting compiler and virtual machine do not usually require subsequent proofs of correctness, as they are *correct by construction.*

In chapter 16 we presented a compiler for arithmetic expressions, and proved its correctness. In this chapter we show how the compiler can be calculated directly from a statement of its correctness. We develop our approach in two stages, first introducing the basic ideas using a series of transformation steps, and then showing how the separate steps can be combined into a single step. For simplicity, we restrict our attention to arithmetic expressions, but the same techniques can also be used to calculate compilers for more sophisticated languages.

17.2 Syntax and semantics

We start in the same manner as the compiler correctness example from the previous chapter, with two definitions that respectively capture the syntax (form) and semantics (meaning) of a simple language of arithmetic expressions built up from integer values using an addition operator:

```
data Expr = Val Int | Add Expr Expr

eval :: Expr -> Int
eval (Val n)   = n
eval (Add x y) = eval x + eval y
```

For example, the expression $1 + 2$ can be evaluated as follows:

$$
\begin{array}{ll}
& \texttt{eval (Add (Val 1) (Val 2))} \\
= & \{ \text{applying } \texttt{eval} \} \\
& \texttt{eval (Val 1) + eval (Val 2)} \\
= & \{ \text{applying the first } \texttt{eval} \} \\
& \texttt{1 + eval (Val 2)} \\
= & \{ \text{applying } \texttt{eval} \} \\
& \texttt{1 + 2} \\
= & \{ \text{applying } \texttt{+} \} \\
& \texttt{3}
\end{array}
$$

We now show how to calculate a compiler based on this semantics using a series of three transformation steps. The first two steps generalise the evaluation function, and the final step simplifies the resulting definitions.

17.3   Adding a stack

The first step is to transform the evaluation function `eval` into a version that utilises a stack, in order to make the manipulation of argument values explicit. In particular, rather than returning a single value of type `Int`, we seek to define a more general evaluation function, `eval'`, that takes a stack of integers as an additional argument, and returns a modified stack given by pushing the value of the expression onto the top of the stack. More precisely, if we represent a stack as a list of integers (where the head is the top element)

```
type Stack = [Int]
```

then we seek to define a function

```
eval' :: Expr -> Stack -> Stack
```

with the following property:

```
eval' e s = eval e : s
```

Rather than first defining `eval'` and then proving by induction on the expression `e` that it satisfies the above equation, we use the technique introduced in the previous chapter and calculate a definition for `eval'` that satisfies this equation, using the desire to apply the induction hypotheses as the driving force for the calculation process. In the base case, `Val n`, the calculation is easy:

```
    eval' (Val n) s
=      { specification of eval' }
    eval (Val n) : s
=      { applying eval }
    n : s
=      { define: push n s = n : s }
    push n s
```

Note that in the final step we defined an auxiliary function, push, that captures the idea of pushing a number onto the stack. With the above calculation, we have discovered the definition of eval' for expressions of the form Val n:

```
eval' (Val n) s = push n s
```

In the inductive case, Add x y, we proceed as follows:

```
    eval' (Add x y) s
=      { specification of eval' }
    eval (Add x y) : s
=      { applying eval }
    (eval x + eval y) : s
```

Now we appear to be stuck, as no further definitions can be applied. However, as we are performing an inductive calculation, we can make use of the induction hypotheses for the two argument expressions x and y, namely:

```
eval' x s' = eval x : s'

eval' y s' = eval y : s'
```

In order to use these hypotheses, it is clear that we must push the values eval x and eval y onto the stack, which can readily be achieved by introducing another auxiliary function, add, that captures the idea of adding the top two numbers on the stack. The remainder of the calculation is then straightforward:

```
    (eval x + eval y) : s
=      { define: add (m : n : s) = n+m : s }
    add (eval y : eval x : s)
=      { induction hypothesis for x }
    add (eval y : eval' x s)
=      { induction hypothesis for y }
    add (eval' y (eval' x s))
```

□

Note that pushing eval x onto the stack before eval y above corresponds to addition evaluating its arguments from left-to-right. It would be perfectly valid to push the values in the opposite order, which would correspond to right-to-left evaluation. In conclusion, we have calculated the following definition

```
eval' :: Expr -> Stack -> Stack
eval' (Val n)   s = push n s
eval' (Add x y) s = add (eval' y (eval' x s))
```

where:

```
push :: Int -> Stack -> Stack
push n s = n : s

add :: Stack -> Stack
add (m : n : s) = n+m : s
```

Finally, our original evaluation function `eval` can now be recovered from our new function by substituting the empty stack `s = []` into the equation `eval' e s = eval e : s` from which `eval'` was constructed, and selecting the unique value in the resulting singleton stack using the function `head`:

```
eval :: Expr -> Int
eval e = head (eval' e [])
```

For example, using this new definition evaluation of $1+2$ now proceeds by pushing the two values onto the stack prior adding them together:

```
      eval (Add (Val 1) (Val 2))
=        { applying eval }
      head (eval' (Add (Val 1) (Val 2)) [])
=        { applying eval' }
      head (add (eval' (Val 2) (eval' (Val 1) [])))
=        { applying the inner eval' }
      head (add (eval' (Val 2) (push 1 [])))
=        { applying eval' }
      head (add (push 2 (push 1 [])))
=        { applying push }
      head (add (2 : 1 : []))
=        { applying add }
      head (3 : [])
=        { applying head }
      3
```

17.4   Adding a continuation

The next step is to transform the stack-based evaluation function `eval'` into *continuation-passing style*, in order to make the flow of control explicit. In particular, we seek to define a more general evaluation function, `eval''`, that takes a function from stacks to stacks (the continuation) as an additional argument, which is used to process the stack that results from evaluating the expression. More precisely, if we define a type for continuations

```
type Cont = Stack -> Stack
```

then we seek to define a function

```
eval'' :: Expr -> Cont -> Cont
```

such that:

```
eval'' e c s = c (eval' e s)
```

We calculate the definition for `eval''` directly from this equation by induction on the expression `e`. The base case is once again easy,

```
    eval'' (Val n) c s
=       { specification of eval'' }
    c (eval' (Val n) s)
=       { applying eval' }
    c (push n s)
```

while for the inductive case we calculate as follows:

```
    eval'' (Add x y) c s
=       { specification of eval'' }
    c (eval' (Add x y) s)
=       { applying eval' }
    c (add (eval' y (eval' x s)))
=       { unapplying . }
    (c . add) (eval' y (eval' x s))
=       { induction hypothesis for y }
    eval'' y (c . add) (eval' x s)
=       { induction hypothesis for x }
    eval'' x (eval'' y (c . add)) s
```

$\square$

In conclusion, we have calculated the following definition:

```
eval'' :: Expr -> Cont -> Cont
eval'' (Val n)   c s = c (push n s)
eval'' (Add x y) c s = eval'' x (eval'' y (c . add)) s
```

Our previous evaluation function `eval'` can now be recovered by substituting the identity continuation `c = id` into the equation `eval'' e c s = c (eval' e s)` from which the function `eval''` was constructed:

```
eval' :: Expr -> Cont
eval' e s = eval'' e id s
```

For example, evaluation of $1 + 2$ now proceeds by transferring control to evaluation of the second argument once evaluation of the first has completed:

```
    eval' (Add (Val 1) (Val 2)) []
=      { applying eval' }
    eval'' (Add (Val 1) (Val 2)) id []
=      { applying eval'' }
    eval'' (Val 1) (eval'' (Val 2) (id . add)) []
=      { applying the outer eval'' }
    eval'' (Val 2) (id . add) (push 1 [])
=      { applying eval'' }
    (id . add) (push 2 (push 1 []))
=      { applying . }
    id (add (push 2 (push 1 [])))
=      { applying push }
    id (add (2 : 1 : []))
=      { applying add }
    id [3]
=      { applying id }
    [3]
```

17.5   Defunctionalising

The third and final step is to transform the evaluation function back into first-order style, using *defunctionalisation*. In particular, rather than using functions of type `Cont = Stack -> Stack` for continuations passed as arguments and returned as results, we define a new type that represents the specific forms of continuations that we actually need for our evaluation function.

Within the definitions for `eval'` and `eval''`, there are only three forms of continuations that are used, namely one to halt the evaluation process, one to push a number onto the top of the stack, and one to add the top two numbers on the stack. We begin by separating out these three forms, by giving them names and passing their variables as parameters. That is, we define three *combinators* for constructing the required forms of continuations:

```
haltC :: Cont
haltC = id

pushC :: Int -> Cont -> Cont
pushC n c = c . push n

addC :: Cont -> Cont
addC c = c . add
```

Using these combinators, our evaluators can now be rewritten as follows:

```
eval' :: Expr -> Cont
eval' e = eval'' e haltC

eval'' :: Expr -> Cont -> Cont
eval'' (Val n)   c = pushC n c
eval'' (Add x y) c = eval'' x (eval'' y (addC c))
```

It is easy to check by expanding definitions that these are equivalent to the previous versions. The next stage in applying defunctionalisation is to define a new type, Code, whose constructors represent the three combinators:

```
data Code = HALT | PUSH Int Code | ADD Code
               deriving Show
```

The constructors of this type have the same types as the corresponding combinators, except that the new type Code now plays the role of Cont:

```
HALT :: Code
PUSH :: Int -> Code -> Code
ADD  :: Code -> Code
```

The name Code for the type reflects the fact that its values represent code for a virtual machine that evaluates expressions using a stack. For example, the code PUSH 1 (PUSH 2 (ADD HALT)) corresponds to the expression $1 + 2$. The fact that values of type Code represent continuations of type Cont is formalised by defining a function that maps from one to the other:

```
exec :: Code -> Cont
exec HALT       = haltC
exec (PUSH n c) = pushC n (exec c)
exec (ADD c)    = addC (exec c)
```

In turn, we then simplify the definition for exec by expanding out the definitions for the type Cont and its three combinators.

HALT case:

```
    exec HALT s
=       { applying exec }
    haltC s
=       { applying haltC }
    id s
=       { applying id }
    s
```

PUSH case:

```
    exec (PUSH n c) s
=      { applying exec }
    pushC n (exec c) s
=      { applying pushC }
    (exec c . push n) s
=      { applying . }
    exec c (push n s)
=      { applying push }
    exec c (n : s)
```

ADD case:

```
    exec (ADD c) s
=      { applying exec }
    addC (exec c) s
=      { applying addC }
    (exec c . add) s
=      { applying . }
    exec c (add s)
=      { assume s of the form m : n : s' }
    exec c (add (m : n : s'))
=      { applying add }
    exec c (n+m : s')
```

□

In conclusion, we have calculated the following definition:

```
exec :: Code -> Stack -> Stack
exec HALT       s           = s
exec (PUSH n c) s           = exec c (n : s)
exec (ADD c)    (m : n : s) = exec c (n+m : s)
```

That is, `exec` is a function that executes code using an initial stack to give a final stack. In other words, `exec` is a virtual machine for executing code.

Finally, defunctionalisation itself now proceeds by simply replacing occurrences of the combinations `haltC`, `pushC` and `addC` in the evaluation functions `eval'` and `eval''` by their respective counterparts `HALT`, `PUSH` and `ADD` from the type `Code`, which results in the following two new definitions:

```
comp :: Expr -> Code
comp e = comp' e HALT

comp' :: Expr -> Code -> Code
comp' (Val n)   c = PUSH n c
comp' (Add x y) c = comp' x (comp' y (ADD c))
```

That is, we have now derived a function `comp` that compiles an expression to code, which is itself defined in terms of an auxiliary function `comp'` that takes additional code as an extra argument. This is essentially the same compiler that we developed in the previous chapter, except that all the required compilation machinery — compiler, target language and virtual machine — has now been systematically derived from a semantics for the source language using equational reasoning. The only difference is that rather than representing code as a list, we now have a dedicated recursive type for code. For example, `[PUSH 1, PUSH 2, ADD]` is now written as `PUSH 1 (PUSH 2 (ADD HALT))`.

The correctness of the compilation functions `comp` and `comp'` is captured by the following two equations, which are consequences of defunctionalisation, or can be verified by simple inductive proofs on the expression argument:

```
exec (comp e) s  =  eval' e s

exec (comp' e c) s  =  eval'' e (exec c) s
```

Expanding the right-hand sides of these equations using the original specifications for the functions `eval'` and `eval''`, we obtain the same compiler correctness equations that were used in the previous chapter:

```
exec (comp e) s  =  eval e : s

exec (comp' e c) s  =  exec c (eval e : s)
```

17.6   Combining the steps

We have now shown how an evaluation function for arithmetic expressions can be transformed into a compiler using a systematic three-step process:

1. calculate a generalised evaluation function that uses a stack;
2. calculate a further generalised version that uses a continuation;
3. defunctionalise to produce a compiler and a virtual machine.

However, there appear to be some opportunities for simplifying this process. In particular, steps 1 and 2 both calculate generalised versions of the original evaluation function. Could these steps be combined to avoid the need for separate generalisation steps? In turn, step 2 introduces the use of continuations, which are then immediately removed in step 3. Could these steps be combined the avoid the need for continuations? In fact, it turns out that *all* the transformation steps can be combined together. This section shows how this can be achieved, and explains the benefits that result from doing so.

In order to simplify the above stepwise process, let us first consider the types and functions that are involved in the process in more detail. We started off by defining a type `Expr` that represents the syntax of the source language, together with an evaluation function `eval :: Expr -> Int` that provides a semantics for the language, and a type `Stack` that represents a stack of integer values. Then we derived four additional components:

- a type `Code` that represents code for the virtual machine;
- a function `comp :: Expr -> Code` that compiles expressions to code;
- a function `comp' :: Expr -> Code -> Code` with a code argument;
- a function `exec :: Code -> Stack -> Stack` that executes code.

Moreover, the relationships between the semantics, compilers and virtual machine were captured by the following two correctness equations:

```
exec (comp e) s = eval e : s

exec (comp' e c) s = exec c (eval e : s)
```

The key to combining the transformation steps is to use these two equations directly as a *specification* for the four additional components, from which we then aim to calculate definitions that satisfy the specification. Given that the equations involve three known definitions (`Expr`, `eval` and `Stack`) and four unknown definitions (`Code`, `comp`, `comp'` and `exec`), this may seem like an impossible task. However, with the benefit of the experience gained from our earlier calculations in the previous sections, it turns out to be straightforward.

We begin with the correctness equation for `comp'`, and proceed by induction on the expression e. In each case, we aim to rewrite the left-hand side `exec (comp' e c) s` of the equation into the form `exec c' s` for some code `c'`, from which we can then conclude that the definition `comp' e c = c'` satisfies the specification in this case. In order to do this we will find that we need to introduce new constructors into the `Code` type, along with their interpretation by the function `exec`. In the base case, `Val n`, we proceed as follows:

```
    exec (comp' (Val n) c) s
=      { specification of comp' }
    exec c (eval (Val n) : s)
=      { applying eval }
    exec c (n : s)
```

Now we appear to be stuck, as no further definitions can be applied. However, recall that we are aiming to end up with a term of the form `exec c' s` for some code `c'`. Hence, to complete the calculation we need to solve the equation:

```
exec c' s = exec c (n : s)
```

Note that we can't simply use this equation as a definition for `exec`, because the variables n and c would be unbound in the body of the definition. The solution is to package these two variables up in the code argument `c'` by means of a new constructor in the `Code` type that takes these variables as arguments,

```
PUSH :: Int -> Code -> Code
```

and define a new equation for `exec` as follows:

```
exec (PUSH n c) s = exec c (n : s)
```

That is, executing the code `PUSH n c` proceeds by pushing the value `n` onto the stack and then executing the code `c`, hence the choice of the name for the new constructor. Using these ideas, it is now easy to complete the calculation:

```
    exec c (n : s)
=       { unapplying exec }
    exec (PUSH n c) s
```

The final term now has the form `exec c' s`, where `c'` = `PUSH n c`, from which we conclude that the specification is satisfied in the base case by defining:

```
comp' (Val n) c = PUSH n c
```

For the inductive case, `Add x y`, we begin in the same way as above by first applying the specification and the definition of the evaluation function:

```
    exec (comp' (Add x y) c) s
=       { specification of comp' }
    exec c (eval (Add x y) : s)
=       { applying eval }
    exec c (eval x + eval y : s)
```

Once again we appear to be stuck, as no further definitions can be applied. However, as we are performing an inductive calculation, we can make use of the induction hypotheses for the two argument expressions `x` and `y`, namely

```
exec (comp' x c') s' = exec c' (eval x : s')

exec (comp' y c') s' = exec c' (eval y : s')
```

In order to use these hypotheses, it is clear that we must push the values `eval x` and `eval y` onto the stack, by transforming the term that we are manipulating into the form `exec c' (eval y : eval x : s)` for some code `c'`. That is, we need to solve the following equation:

```
exec c' (eval y : eval x : s) = exec c (eval x + eval y : s)
```

First of all, we generalise from specific values `eval x` and `eval y` to give:

```
exec c' (m : n : s) = exec c (n+m : s)
```

Once again, however, we can't use this equation as a definition for `exec`, this time because the variable `c` is unbound. The solution is to package this variable up in the code argument `c'` by means of a new constructor in the `Code` type

```
ADD :: Code -> Code
```

and define a new equation for `exec` as follows:

```
exec (ADD c) (m : n : s) = exec c (n+m : s)
```

That is, executing the code `ADD c` proceeds by adding the top two values on the stack and then executing the code `c`, hence the choice of the name for the new constructor. Using these ideas, it is now easy to complete the calculation:

```
    exec c (eval x + eval y : s)
=      { unapplying exec }
    exec (ADD c) (eval y : eval x : s)
=      { induction hypothesis for y }
    exec (comp' y (ADD c)) (eval x : s)
=      { induction hypothesis for x }
    exec (comp' x (comp' y (ADD c))) s
```

The final term now has the form `exec c' s`, from which we conclude that the specification is satisfied in the inductive case by defining:

```
comp' (Add x y) c = comp' x (comp' y (ADD c))
```

□

Note that as in our earlier calculation of the stack-based evaluator, we chose to transform the stack into the form `eval y : eval x : s`. We could equally well have chosen the opposite order, `eval x : eval y : s`, which would have resulted in right-to-left evaluation for `Add`. We have this freedom in the calculation because the semantics defined by `eval` does not specify an evaluation order.

Finally, we complete the development of our compiler by considering the function `comp :: Expr -> Code` specified by the equation `exec (comp e) s = eval e : s`. In a similar manner to above, we aim to rewrite the left-hand side `exec (comp e) s` of the equation into the form `exec c s` for some code `c`, from which we can then conclude that the definition `comp e = c` satisfies the specification. In this case there is no need to use induction as simple calculation suffices, during which we introduce a new constructor `HALT :: Code` in order to transform the term being manipulated into the required form:

```
    exec (comp e) s
=      { specification of comp }
    eval e : s
=      { define: exec HALT s = s }
    exec HALT (eval e : s)
=      { specification of comp' }
    exec (comp' e HALT) s
```

□

In conclusion, we have calculated the following definitions:

```
data Code = HALT | PUSH Int Code | ADD Code
```

```
comp :: Expr -> Code
comp e = comp' e HALT

comp' :: Expr -> Code -> Code
comp' (Val n)   c = PUSH n c
comp' (Add x y) c = comp' x (comp' y (ADD c))

exec :: Code -> Stack -> Stack
exec HALT       s           = s
exec (PUSH n c) s           = exec c (n : s)
exec (ADD c)    (m : n : s) = exec c (n+m : s)
```

These are precisely the same definitions as we produced in the previous section, except that they have now been calculated directly from a specification of compiler correctness, rather than indirectly by means of a series of separate transformation steps. Moreover, the combined approach also has the advantage that it only uses simple equational reasoning techniques. In particular, the use of continuations and defunctionalisation is no longer required!

17.7   Chapter remarks

Further details about calculating compilers can be found in [39], upon which this chapter is based. This article shows how the same approach can be used to calculate compilers for a wide range of programming language features and their combination, including arithmetic expressions, exceptions, state and various forms of lambda calculi. A similar approach can also be used to calculate abstract machines [40], such as the example from chapter 8.

17.8   Exercises

1. Suppose that we extend the language of arithmetic expressions with simple primitives for throwing and catching an *exception*, as follows:

```
data Expr = Val Int
          | Add Expr Expr
          | Throw
          | Catch Expr Expr
```

Informally, Catch x h behaves as the expression x unless evaluation of x throws an exception, in which case the catch behaves as the handler expression h. An exception is thrown if evaluation of Throw is attempted. To define a semantics for this extended language, we first recall the Maybe type:

```
data Maybe a = Nothing | Just a
```

That is, a value of type `Maybe a` is either `Nothing`, which we view here as an exceptional value, or has the form `Just x`, which we view as a normal value. Using this type, our original evaluation function for expressions can be rewritten to take account of exceptions as follows:

```
eval :: Expr -> Maybe Int
eval (Val n)     = Just n
eval (Add x y)   = case eval x of
                       Just n -> case eval y of
                           Just m  -> Just (n + m)
                           Nothing -> Nothing
                       Nothing -> Nothing
eval Throw       = Nothing
eval (Catch x h) = case eval x of
                       Just n  -> Just n
                       Nothing -> eval h
```

Using the approach described in this chapter, calculate a compiler for this language. Hint: this is a challenging exercise!

A solution to exercise 1 is given in appendix A.

Appendix A Selected solutions

In this appendix we present model solutions to selected exercises for each chapter. If solutions are being tested out using GHCi, note that some functions may need to be renamed to avoid clashing with built-in functions from the standard prelude. For example, `product` could be renamed to `myproduct`.

A.1   Introduction

Exercise 1

```
      double (double 2)
  =       { applying the inner double }
      double (2 + 2)
  =       { applying double }
      (2 + 2) + (2 + 2)
  =       { applying the first + }
      4 + (2 + 2)
  =       { applying the second + }
      4 + 4
  =       { applying + }
      8
```

or

```
      double (double 2)
  =       { applying the outer double }
      (double 2) + (double 2)
  =       { applying the second double }
      (double 2) + (2 + 2)
  =       { applying the second + }
      (double 2) + 4
  =       { applying double }
      (2 + 2) + 4
  =       { applying the first + }
      4 + 4
  =       { applying + }
```

8

There are a number of other possible answers.

Exercise 2

```
    sum [x]
=       { applying sum }
    x + sum []
=       { applying sum }
    x + 0
=       { applying + }
    x
```

Exercise 3

```
product []      = 1
product (n:ns) = n * product ns
```

For example:

```
    product [2,3,4]
=       { applying product }
    2 * (product [3,4])
=       { applying product }
    2 * (3 * product [4])
=       { applying product }
    2 * (3 * (4 * product []))
=       { applying product }
    2 * (3 * (4 * 1))
=       { applying * }
    24
```

A.2   First steps

Exercise 2

```
(2^3)*4
```

```
(2*3)+(4*5)
```

```
2+(3*(4^5))
```

Exercise 3

```
n = a 'div' length xs
    where
        a = 10
        xs = [1,2,3,4,5]
```

Exercise 4

```
last xs = head (reverse xs)
```

or

```
last xs = xs !! (length xs - 1)
```

A.3   Types and classes

Exercise 1

```
['a','b','c'] :: [Char]

('a','b','c') :: (Char,Char,Char)

[(False,'0'),(True,'1')] :: [(Bool,Char)]

([False,True],['0','1']) :: ([Bool],[Char])

[tail, init, reverse] :: [[a] -> [a]]
```

Exercise 2

```
bools = [False,True]

nums = [[1,2],[3,4],[5,6]]

add x y z = x+y+z

copy x = (x,x)

apply f x = f x
```

There are a number of other possible answers for bools, nums and add.

A.4   Defining functions

Exercise 1

```
halve xs = (take n xs, drop n xs)
           where n = length xs `div` 2
```

or

```
halve xs = splitAt (length xs `div` 2) xs
```

Exercise 2

```
third xs = head (tail (tail xs))

third xs = xs !! 2

third (_:_:x:_) = x
```

Exercise 3

```
safetail xs = if null xs then [] else tail xs

safetail xs | null xs   = []
            | otherwise = tail xs

safetail []     = []
safetail (_:xs) = xs
```

Exercise 4

```
False || False = False
False || True  = True
True  || False = True
True  || True  = True

False || False = False
_     || _     = True

False || b = b
True  || _ = True

b || c | b == c    = b
       | otherwise = True
```

A.5 List comprehensions

Exercise 1

```
sum [x^2 | x <- [1..100]]
```

Exercise 2

```
grid m n = [(x,y) | x <- [0..m], y <- [0..n]]
```

Exercise 3

```
square n = [(x,y) | (x,y) <- grid n n, x /= y]
```

Exercise 4

```
replicate n x = [x | _ <- [1..n]]
```

Exercise 5

```
pyths n = [(x,y,z) | x <- [1..n],
                     y <- [1..n],
                     z <- [1..n],
                     x^2 + y^2 == z^2]
```

A.6 Recursive functions

Exercise 1

The function does not terminate, because each application of `fac` decreases the argument by one, and hence the base case is never reached.

```
fac 0           = 1
fac n | n > 0 = n * fac (n-1)
```

Exercise 2

```
sumdown 0 = 0
sumdown n = n + sumdown (n-1)
```

Exercise 3

```
(^) :: Int -> Int -> Int
m ^ 0 = 1
m ^ n = m * (m ^ (n-1))
```

For example:

```
    2 ^ 3
=      { applying ^ }
    2 * (2 ^ 2)
=      { applying ^ }
    2 * (2 * (2 ^ 1))
=      { applying ^ }
    2 * (2 * (2 * (2 ^ 0)))
=      { applying ^ }
    2 * (2 * (2 * 1))
=      { applying * }
    8
```

Exercise 4

```
euclid x y | x == y = x
           | x < y  = euclid x (y-x)
           | y < x  = euclid (x-y) y
```

A.7   Higher-order functions

Exercise 1

```
map f (filter p xs)
```

Exercise 2

```
all p = and . map p

any p = or . map p

takeWhile _ []                = []
takeWhile p (x:xs) | p x      = x : takeWhile p xs
                   | otherwise = []

dropWhile _ []                = []
dropWhile p (x:xs) | p x      = dropWhile p xs
                   | otherwise = x:xs
```

Exercise 3

```
map f = foldr (\x xs -> f x : xs) []
```

```
filter p = foldr (\x xs -> if p x then x:xs else xs) []
```

Exercise 4

```
dec2int = foldl (\x y -> 10*x + y) 0
```

Exercise 5

```
curry :: ((a,b) -> c) -> (a -> b -> c)
curry f = \x y -> f (x,y)

uncurry :: (a -> b -> c) -> ((a,b) -> c)
uncurry f = \(x,y) -> f x y
```

A.8   Declaring types and classes

Exercise 1

```
mult m Zero     = Zero
mult m (Succ n) = add m (mult m n)
```

Exercise 2

```
occurs x (Leaf y)     = x == y
occurs x (Node l y r) = case compare x y of
                             LT -> occurs x l
                             EQ -> True
                             GT -> occurs x r
```

This version is more efficient because it only requires one comparison between x and y for each node, whereas the previous version may require two.

Exercise 3

```
leaves (Leaf _)   = 1
leaves (Node l r) = leaves l + leaves r

balanced (Leaf _)   = True
balanced (Node l r) = abs (leaves l - leaves r) <= 1
                          && balanced l && balanced r
```

Exercise 4

```
halve xs = splitAt (length xs 'div' 2) xs

balance [x] = Leaf x
balance xs  = Node (balance ys) (balance zs)
              where (ys,zs) = halve xs
```

A.9   The countdown problem

Exercise 1

```
choices xs = [zs | ys <- subs xs, zs <- perms ys]
```

Exercise 2

```
removeone x []                    = []
removeone x (y:ys) | x == y       = ys
                   | otherwise = y : removeone x ys

isChoice []      _  = True
isChoice (x:xs) [] = False
isChoice (x:xs) ys = elem x ys && isChoice xs (removeone x ys)
```

Exercise 3

It would lead to non-termination, because recursive calls to exprs would no
longer be guaranteed to reduce the length of the list.

A.10   Interactive programming

Exercise 1

```
putStr xs = sequence_ [putChar x | x <- xs]
```

Exercise 2

```
putBoard = putBoard' 1

putBoard' r []     = return ()
putBoard' r (n:ns) = do putRow r n
                        putBoard' (r+1) ns
```

Exercise 3

```
putBoard b = sequence_ [putRow r n | (r,n) <- zip [1..] b]
```

A.11   Unbeatable tic-tac-toe

Exercise 1

Using the definitions

```
nodes :: Tree a -> Int
nodes (Node _ ts) = 1 + sum (map nodes ts)

mydepth :: Tree a -> Int
mydepth (Node _ []) = 0
mydepth (Node _ ts) = 1 + maximum (map mydepth ts)
```

we have:

```
> let tree = gametree empty O

> nodes tree
549946

> mydepth tree
9
```

Exercise 2

```
import System.Random hiding (next)

bestmoves :: Grid -> Player -> [Grid]
bestmoves g p = [g' | Node (g',p') _ <- ts, p' == best]
                where
                     tree = prune depth (gametree g p)
                     Node (_,best) ts = minimax tree

play' :: Grid -> Player -> IO ()
play' g p
   | wins O g = putStrLn "Player O wins!\n"
   | wins X g = putStrLn "Player X wins!\n"
   | full g   = putStrLn "It's a draw!\n"
   | p == O   = do i <- getNat (prompt p)
                   case move g i p of
                        [] -> do putStrLn "ERROR: Invalid move"
```

```
                          play' g p
                  [g'] -> play g' (next p)
    | p == X   = do putStr "Player X is thinking... "
                 let gs = bestmoves g p
                 n <- randomRIO (0,length gs - 1)
                 play (gs !! n) (next p)
```

Note that the function **next** from the imported library is hidden to avoid clashing with our **next** function on player values.

A.12   Monads and more

Exercise 1

```
instance Functor Tree where
   -- fmap :: (a -> b) -> Tree a -> Tree b
   fmap g Leaf         = Leaf
   fmap g (Node l x r) = Node (fmap g l) (g x) (fmap g r)
```

Exercise 2

```
instance Functor ((->) a) where
   -- fmap :: (b -> c) -> (a -> b) -> (a -> c)
   fmap = (.)
```

Exercise 3

```
instance Applicative ((->) a) where
   -- pure :: b -> (a -> b)
   pure = const

   -- (<*>) :: (a -> b -> c) -> (a -> b) -> (a -> c)
   g <*> h = \x -> g x (h x)
```

Exercise 4

```
instance Functor ZipList where
   -- fmap :: (a -> b) -> ZipList a -> ZipList b
   fmap g (Z xs) = Z (fmap g xs)

instance Applicative ZipList where
   -- pure :: a -> ZipList a
   pure x = Z (repeat x)
```

```
-- <*> :: ZipList (a -> b) -> ZipList a -> ZipList b
(Z gs) <*> (Z xs) = Z [g x | (g,x) <- zip gs xs]
```

A.13   Monadic parsing

Exercise 1

```
comment = do string "--"
             many (sat (/= '\n'))
             return ()
```

Exercise 2

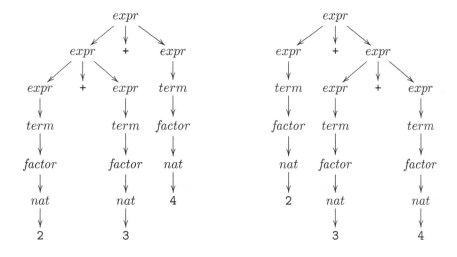

Exercise 3

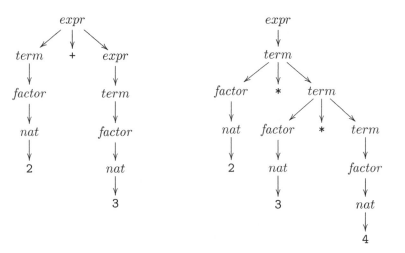

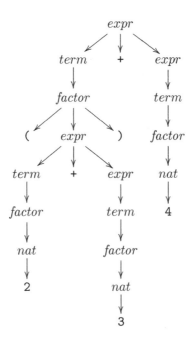

Exercise 4

Without left-factorising, the resulting parser would backtrack excessively and take exponential time in the size of the expression. For example, a number would be parsed four times before being recognised as an expression.

A.14   Foldables and friends

Exercise 1

```
instance (Monoid a, Monoid b) => Monoid (a,b) where
   -- mempty :: (a,b)
   mempty = (mempty, mempty)

   -- mappend :: (a,b) -> (a,b) -> (a,b)
   (x1,y1) `mappend` (x2,y2) =
       (x1 `mappend` x2, y1 `mappend` y2)
```

Exercise 2

```
instance Monoid b => Monoid (a -> b) where
   -- mempty :: a -> b
   mempty = \_ -> mempty
```

```
-- mappend :: (a -> b) -> (a -> b) -> (a -> b)
f 'mappend' g = \x -> f x 'mappend' g x
```

A.15   Lazy evaluation

Exercise 1

The only redex in 1+(2*3) is 2*3, which is both innermost and outermost.

The redexes in (1+2)*(2+3) are 1+2 and 2+3, with the first being innermost.

The redexes in fst (1+2,2+3) are 1+2, 2+3 and fst (1+2,2+3), with the first of these being innermost and the last being outermost.

The redexes in (\x -> 1 + x) (2*3) are 2*3 and (\x -> 1 + x) (2*3), with the first being innermost and the second being outermost.

Exercise 2

Outermost:

```
    fst (1+2, 2+3)
=       { applying fst }
    1+2
=       { applying + }
    3
```

Innermost:

```
    fst (1+2, 2+3)
=       { applying the first + }
    fst (3, 2+3)
=       { applying + }
    fst (3, 5)
=       { applying fst }
    3
```

Outermost evaluation is preferable because it avoids evaluation of the second argument, and hence takes one fewer reduction steps.

Exercise 3

```
    mult 3 4
=       { applying mult }
```

```
      (\x -> (\y -> x * y)) 3 4
=        { applying the outer lambda }
      (\y -> 3 * y) 4
=        { applying the lambda }
      3 * 4
=        { applying * }
      12
```

A.16   Reasoning about programs

Exercise 1

Base case:

```
      add Zero (Succ m)
=        { applying add }
      Succ m
=        { unapplying add }
      Succ (add Zero m)
```

Inductive case:

```
      add (Succ n) (Succ m)
=        { applying add }
      Succ (add n (Succ m))
=        { induction hypothesis }
      Succ (Succ (add n m))
=        { unapplying add }
      Succ (add (Succ n) m)
```

Exercise 2

Base case:

```
      add Zero m
=        { applying add }
      m
=        { property of add }
      add m Zero
```

Inductive case:

```
      add (Succ n) m
=        { applying add }
      Succ (add n m)
=        { induction hypothesis }
```

```
      Succ (add m n)
  =       { property of add }
      add m (Succ n)
```

Exercise 3

Base case:

```
      all (== x) (replicate 0 x)
  =       { applying replicate }
      all (== x) []
  =       { applying all }
      True
```

Inductive case:

```
      all (== x) (replicate (n+1) x)
  =       { applying replicate }
      all (== x) (x : replicate n x)
  =       { applying all }
      x == x && all (== x) (replicate n x)
  =       { applying == }
      True && all (== x) (replicate n x)
  =       { applying && }
      all (== x) (replicate n x)
  =       { induction hypothesis }
      True
```

Exercise 4

Base case:

```
      [] ++ []
  =       { applying ++ }
      []
```

Inductive case:

```
      (x : xs) ++ []
  =       { applying ++ }
      x : (xs ++ [])
  =       { induction hypothesis }
      x : xs
```

Base case:

```
      [] ++ (ys ++ zs)
=        { applying ++ }
      ys ++ zs
=        { unapplying ++ }
      ([] ++ ys) ++ zs
```

Inductive case:

```
      (x : xs) ++ (ys ++ zs)
=        { applying ++ }
      x : (xs ++ (ys ++ zs))
=        { induction hypothesis }
      x : ((xs ++ ys) ++ zs)
=        { unapplying ++ }
      (x : (xs ++ ys)) ++ zs
=        { unapplying ++ }
      ((x : xs) ++ ys) ++ zs
```

Exercise 5

Base case:

```
      take 0 xs ++ drop 0 xs
=        { applying take, drop }
      [] ++ xs
=        { applying ++ }
      xs
```

Base case:

```
      take (n+1) [] ++ drop (n+1) []
=        { applying take, drop }
      [] ++ []
=        { applying ++ }
      []
```

Inductive case:

```
      take (n+1) (x:xs) ++ drop (n+1) (x:xs)
=        { applying take, drop }
      (x : take n xs) ++ (drop n xs)
=        { applying ++ }
      x : (take n xs ++ drop n xs)
=        { induction hypothesis }
      x : xs
```

A.17   Calculating compilers

Exercise 1

A solution is given in [39], on which this chapter is based.

Appendix B Standard prelude

In this appendix we present some of the most commonly used definitions from the Haskell standard prelude. For expository purposes, a number of the definitions are presented in simplified form. The full version of the prelude is available from the Haskell home page, http://www.haskell.org.

B.1   Basic classes

Equality types:

```
class Eq a where
   (==), (/=) :: a -> a -> Bool

   x /= y = not (x == y)
```

Ordered types:

```
class Eq a => Ord a where
   (<), (<=), (>), (>=) :: a -> a -> Bool
   min, max             :: a -> a -> a

   min x y | x <= y    = x
           | otherwise = y

   max x y | x <= y    = y
           | otherwise = x
```

Showable types:

```
class Show a where
   show :: a -> String
```

Readable types:

```
class Read a where
   read :: String -> a
```

Numeric types:

```
class Num a where
   (+), (-), (*)        :: a -> a -> a
   negate, abs, signum :: a -> a
```

Integral types:

```
class Num a => Integral a where
   div, mod :: a -> a -> a
```

Fractional types:

```
class Num a => Fractional a where
   (/)   :: a -> a -> a
   recip :: a -> a

   recip n = 1/n
```

B.2   Booleans

Type declaration:

```
data Bool = False | True
            deriving (Eq, Ord, Show, Read)
```

Logical conjunction:

```
(&&) :: Bool -> Bool -> Bool
False && _ = False
True  && b = b
```

Logical disjunction:

```
(||) :: Bool -> Bool -> Bool
False || b = b
True  || _ = True
```

Logical negation:

```
not :: Bool -> Bool
not False = True
not True  = False
```

Guard that always succeeds:

```
otherwise :: Bool
otherwise = True
```

B.3   Characters

Type declaration:

```
data Char = ...
             deriving (Eq, Ord, Show, Read)
```

The definitions below are provided in the library `Data.Char`, which can be loaded by entering the following in GHCi or at the start of a script:

```
import Data.Char
```

Decide if a character is a lower-case letter:

```
isLower :: Char -> Bool
isLower c = c >= 'a' && c <= 'z'
```

Decide if a character is an upper-case letter:

```
isUpper :: Char -> Bool
isUpper c = c >= 'A' && c <= 'Z'
```

Decide if a character is alphabetic:

```
isAlpha :: Char -> Bool
isAlpha c = isLower c || isUpper c
```

Decide if a character is a digit:

```
isDigit :: Char -> Bool
isDigit c = c >= '0' && c <= '9'
```

Decide if a character is alpha-numeric:

```
isAlphaNum :: Char -> Bool
isAlphaNum c = isAlpha c || isDigit c
```

Decide if a character is spacing:

```
isSpace :: Char -> Bool
isSpace c = elem c " \t\n"
```

Convert a character to a Unicode number:

```
ord :: Char -> Int
ord c = ...
```

Convert a Unicode number to a character:

```
chr :: Int -> Char
chr n = ...
```

Convert a digit to an integer:

```
digitToInt :: Char -> Int
digitToInt c | isDigit c = ord c - ord '0'
```

Convert an integer to a digit:

```
intToDigit :: Int -> Char
intToDigit n | n >= 0 && n <= 9 = chr (ord '0' + n)
```

Convert a letter to lower-case:

```
toLower :: Char -> Char
toLower c | isUpper c = chr (ord c - ord 'A' + ord 'a')
          | otherwise = c
```

Convert a letter to upper-case:

```
toUpper :: Char -> Char
toUpper c | isLower c = chr (ord c - ord 'a' + ord 'A')
          | otherwise = c
```

B.4   Strings

Type declaration:

```
type String = [Char]
```

B.5   Numbers

Type declarations:

```
data Int = ...
            deriving (Eq, Ord, Show, Read, Num, Integral)

data Integer = ...
                deriving (Eq, Ord, Show, Read, Num, Integral)

data Float = ...
            deriving (Eq, Ord, Show, Read, Num, Fractional)

data Double = ...
                deriving (Eq, Ord, Show, Read, Num, Fractional)
```

Decide if an integer is even:

```
even :: Integral a => a -> Bool
even n = n 'mod' 2 == 0
```

Decide if an integer is odd:

```
odd :: Integral a => a -> Bool
odd = not . even
```

Exponentiation:

```
(^) :: (Num a, Integral b) => a -> b -> a
_ ^ 0 = 1
x ^ n = x * (x ^ (n-1))
```

B.6   Tuples

Type declarations:

```
data () = ...
          deriving (Eq, Ord, Show, Read)

data (a,b) = ...
             deriving (Eq, Ord, Show, Read)

data (a,b,c) = ...
               deriving (Eq, Ord, Show, Read)
```

Select the first component of a pair:

```
fst :: (a,b) -> a
fst (x,_) = x
```

Select the second component of a pair:

```
snd :: (a,b) -> b
snd (_,y) = y
```

Convert a function on pairs to a curried function:

```
curry :: ((a,b) -> c) -> (a -> b -> c)
curry f = \x y -> f (x,y)
```

Convert a curried function to a function on pairs:

```
uncurry :: (a -> b -> c) -> ((a,b) -> c)
uncurry f = \(x,y) -> f x y
```

B.7   Maybe

Type declaration:

```
data Maybe a = Nothing | Just a
               deriving (Eq, Ord, Show, Read)
```

B.8   Lists

Type declaration:

```
data [a] = [] | a:[a]
           deriving (Eq, Ord, Show, Read)
```

Select the first element of a non-empty list:

```
head :: [a] -> a
head (x:_) = x
```

Select the last element of a non-empty list:

```
last :: [a] -> a
last [x]    = x
last (_:xs) = last xs
```

Select the nth element of a non-empty list:

```
(!!) :: [a] -> Int -> a
(x:_)  !! 0 = x
(_:xs) !! n = xs !! (n-1)
```

Select the first n elements of a list:

```
take :: Int -> [a] -> [a]
take 0 _      = []
take _ []     = []
take n (x:xs) = x : take (n-1) xs
```

Select all elements of a list that satisfy a predicate:

```
filter :: (a -> Bool) -> [a] -> [a]
filter p xs = [x | x <- xs, p x]
```

Select elements of a list while they satisfy a predicate:

```
takeWhile :: (a -> Bool) -> [a] -> [a]
takeWhile _ []                = []
takeWhile p (x:xs) | p x       = x : takeWhile p xs
                   | otherwise = []
```

Remove the first element from a non-empty list:

```
tail :: [a] -> [a]
tail (_:xs) = xs
```

Remove the last element from a non-empty list:

```
init :: [a] -> [a]
init [_]    = []
init (x:xs) = x : init xs
```

Remove the first n elements from a list:

```
drop :: Int -> [a] -> [a]
drop 0 xs     = xs
drop _ []     = []
drop n (_:xs) = drop (n-1) xs
```

Remove elements from a list while they satisfy a predicate:

```
dropWhile :: (a -> Bool) -> [a] -> [a]
dropWhile _ []                    = []
dropWhile p (x:xs) | p x          = dropWhile p xs
                   | otherwise = x:xs
```

Split a list at the nth element:

```
splitAt :: Int -> [a] -> ([a],[a])
splitAt n xs = (take n xs, drop n xs)
```

Produce an infinite list of identical elements:

```
repeat :: a -> [a]
repeat x = xs where xs = x:xs
```

Produce a list with n identical elements:

```
replicate :: Int -> a -> [a]
replicate n = take n . repeat
```

Produce an infinite list by iterating a function over a value:

```
iterate :: (a -> a) -> a -> [a]
iterate f x = x : iterate f (f x)
```

Produce a list of pairs from a pair of lists:

```
zip :: [a] -> [b] -> [(a,b)]
zip []      _      = []
zip _       []     = []
zip (x:xs) (y:ys) = (x,y) : zip xs ys
```

Append two lists:

```
(++) :: [a] -> [a] -> [a]
[]      ++ ys = ys
(x:xs) ++ ys = x : (xs ++ ys)
```

Reverse a list:

```
reverse :: [a] -> [a]
reverse = foldl (\xs x -> x:xs) []
```

Apply a function to all elements of a list:

```
map :: (a -> b) -> [a] -> [b]
map f xs = [f x | x <- xs]
```

B.9   Functions

Type declaration:

```
data a -> b = ...
```

Identity function:

```
id :: a -> a
id = \x -> x
```

Function composition:

```
(.) :: (b -> c) -> (a -> b) -> (a -> c)
f . g = \x -> f (g x)
```

Constant functions:

```
const :: a -> (b -> a)
const x = \_ -> x
```

Strict application:

```
($!) :: (a -> b) -> a -> b
f $! x = ...
```

Flip the arguments of a curried function:

```
flip :: (a -> b -> c) -> (b -> a -> c)
flip f = \y x -> f x y
```

B.10   Input/output

Type declaration:

```
data IO a = ...
```

Read a character from the keyboard:

```
getChar :: IO Char
getChar = ...
```

Read a string from the keyboard:

```
getLine :: IO String
getLine = do x <- getChar
             if x == '\n' then
                 return ""
             else
                 do xs <- getLine
                    return (x:xs)
```

Read a value from the keyboard:

```
readLn :: Read a => IO a
readLn = do xs <- getLine
            return (read xs)
```

Write a character to the screen:

```
putChar :: Char -> IO ()
putChar c = ...
```

Write a string to the screen:

```
putStr :: String -> IO ()
putStr ""     = return ()
putStr (x:xs) = do putChar x
                   putStr xs
```

Write a string to the screen and move to a new line:

```
putStrLn :: String -> IO ()
putStrLn xs = do putStr xs
                 putChar '\n'
```

Write a value to the screen:

```
print :: Show a => a -> IO ()
print = putStrLn . show
```

Display an error message and terminate the program:

```
error :: String -> a
error xs = ...
```

B.11   Functors

Class declaration:

```
class Functor f where
    fmap :: (a -> b) -> f a -> f b
```

Maybe functor:

```
instance Functor Maybe where
   -- fmap :: (a -> b) -> Maybe a -> Maybe b
   fmap _ Nothing  = Nothing
   fmap g (Just x) = Just (g x)
```

List functor:

```
instance Functor [] where
   -- fmap :: (a -> b) -> [a] -> [b]
   fmap = map
```

IO functor:

```
instance Functor IO where
   -- fmap :: (a -> b) -> IO a -> IO b
   fmap g mx = do {x <- mx; return (g x)}
```

Infix version of `fmap`:

```
(<$>) :: Functor f => (a -> b) -> f a -> f b
g <$> x = fmap g x
```

B.12   Applicatives

Class declaration:

```
class Functor f => Applicative f where
   pure  :: a -> f a
   (<*>) :: f (a -> b) -> f a -> f b
```

Maybe applicative:

```
instance Applicative Maybe where
   -- pure :: a -> Maybe a
   pure = Just

   -- (<*>) :: Maybe (a -> b) -> Maybe a -> Maybe b
   Nothing  <*> _  = Nothing
   (Just g) <*> mx = fmap g mx
```

List applicative:

```
instance Applicative [] where
   -- pure :: a -> [a]
   pure x = [x]

   -- (<*>) :: [a -> b] -> [a] -> [b]
```

```
    gs <*> xs = [g x | g <- gs, x <- xs]
```

IO applicative:

```
instance Applicative IO where
  -- pure :: a -> IO a
  pure = return

  -- (<*>) :: IO (a -> b) -> IO a -> IO b
  mg <*> mx = do {g <- mg; x <- mx; return (g x)}
```

B.13   Monads

Class declaration:

```
class Applicative m => Monad m where
  return :: a -> m a
  (>>=)  :: m a -> (a -> m b) -> m b

  return = pure
```

Maybe monad:

```
instance Monad Maybe where
  -- (>>=) :: Maybe a -> (a -> Maybe b) -> Maybe b
  Nothing  >>= _ = Nothing
  (Just x) >>= f = f x
```

List monad:

```
instance Monad [] where
  -- (>>=) :: [a] -> (a -> [b]) -> [b]
  xs >>= f = [y | x <- xs, y <- f x]
```

IO monad:

```
instance Monad IO where
  -- return :: a -> IO a
  return x = ...

  -- (>>=) :: IO a -> (a -> IO b) -> IO b
  mx >>= f = ...
```

B.14   Alternatives

The declarations below are provided in the library `Control.Applicative`, which can be loaded by entering the following in GHCi or at the start of a script:

```
import Control.Applicative
```

Class declaration:

```
class Applicative f => Alternative f where
   empty :: f a
   (<|>) :: f a -> f a -> f a
   many  :: f a -> f [a]
   some  :: f a -> f [a]

   many x = some x <|> pure []
   some x = pure (:) <*> x <*> many x
```

Maybe alternative:

```
instance Alternative Maybe where
   -- empty :: Maybe a
   empty = Nothing

   -- (<|>) :: Maybe a -> Maybe a -> Maybe a
   Nothing  <|> my = my
   (Just x) <|> _  = Just x
```

List alternative:

```
instance Alternative [] where
   -- empty :: [a]
   empty = []

   -- (<|>) :: [a] -> [a] -> [a]
   (<|>) = (++)
```

B.15   MonadPlus

The declarations below are provided in the library `Control.Monad`, which can
be loaded by entering the following in GHCi or at the start of a script:

```
import Control.Monad
```

Class declaration:

```
class (Alternative m, Monad m) => MonadPlus m where
   mzero :: m a
   mplus :: m a -> m a -> m a

   mzero = empty
   mplus = (<|>)
```

Maybe monadplus:

```
instance MonadPlus Maybe
```

List monadplus:

```
instance MonadPlus []
```

B.16   Monoids

Class declaration:

```
class Monoid a where
   mempty  :: a
   mappend :: a -> a -> a

   mconcat :: [a] -> a
   mconcat = foldr mappend mempty
```

The declarations below are provided in a library `Data.Monoid`, which can be loaded by entering the following in GHCi or at the start of a script:

```
import Data.Monoid
```

Maybe monoid:

```
instance Monoid a => Monoid (Maybe a) where
   -- mempty :: Maybe a
   mempty = Nothing

   -- mappend :: Maybe a -> Maybe a -> Maybe a
   Nothing 'mappend' my       = my
   mx      'mappend' Nothing = mx
   Just x  'mappend' Just y  = Just (x 'mappend' y)
```

List monoid:

```
instance Monoid [a] where
   -- mempty :: [a]
   mempty = []

   -- mappend :: [a] -> [a] -> [a]
   mappend = (++)
```

Numeric monoid for addition:

```
newtype Sum a = Sum a
                 deriving (Eq, Ord, Show, Read)
```

```
getSum :: Sum a -> a
getSum (Sum x) = x

instance Num a => Monoid (Sum a) where
    -- mempty :: Sum a
    mempty = Sum 0

    -- mappend :: Sum a -> Sum a -> Sum a
    Sum x 'mappend' Sum y = Sum (x+y)
```

Numeric monoid for multiplication:

```
newtype Product a = Product a
                        deriving (Eq, Ord, Show, Read)

getProduct :: Product a -> a
getProduct (Product x) = x

instance Num a => Monoid (Product a) where
    -- mempty :: Product a
    mempty = Product 1

    -- mappend :: Product a -> Product a -> Product a
    Product x 'mappend' Product y = Product (x*y)
```

Boolean monoid for conjunction:

```
newtype All = All Bool
                deriving (Eq, Ord, Show, Read)

getAll :: All -> Bool
getAll (All b) = b

instance Monoid All where
    -- mempty :: All
    mempty = All True

    -- mappend :: All -> All -> All
    All b 'mappend' All c = All (b && c)
```

Boolean monoid for disjunction:

```
newtype Any = Any Bool
                deriving (Eq, Ord, Show, Read)

getAny :: Any -> Bool
getAny (Any b) = b
```

```
instance Monoid Any where
   -- mempty :: Any
   mempty = Any False

   -- mappend :: Any -> Any -> Any
   Any b 'mappend' Any c = Any (b || c)
```

Infix version of mappend:

```
(<>) :: Monoid a => a -> a -> a
x <> y = x 'mappend' y
```

B.17   Foldables

The declarations below are provided in the library `Data.Foldable`, which can be loaded by entering the following in GHCi or at the start of a script:

```
import Data.Foldable
```

Class declaration:

```
class Foldable t where
   foldMap :: Monoid b => (a -> b) -> t a -> b
   foldr   :: (a -> b -> b) -> b -> t a -> b

   fold    :: Monoid a => t a -> a
   foldl   :: (a -> b -> a) -> a -> t b -> a
   foldr1  :: (a -> a -> a) -> t a -> a
   foldl1  :: (a -> a -> a) -> t a -> a

   toList  :: t a -> [a]
   null    :: t a -> Bool
   length  :: t a -> Int
   elem    :: Eq a => a -> t a -> Bool
   maximum :: Ord a => t a -> a
   minimum :: Ord a => t a -> a
   sum     :: Num a => t a -> a
   product :: Num a => t a -> a
```

Default definitions:

```
foldMap f = foldr (mappend . f) mempty
foldr f v = foldr f v . toList

fold      = foldMap id
```

```
foldl f v = foldl f v . toList
foldr1 f  = foldr1 f . toList
foldl1 f  = foldl1 f . toList

toList    = foldMap (\x -> [x])
null      = null . toList
length    = length . toList
elem x    = elem x . toList
maximum   = maximum . toList
minimum   = minimum . toList
sum       = sum . toList
product   = product . toList
```

The minimal complete definition for an instance is to define `foldMap` or `foldr`, as all other functions in the class can be derived from either of these two using the above default definitions and the following instance for lists.

List foldable:

```
instance Foldable [] where

    -- foldMap :: Monoid b => (a -> b) -> [a] -> b
    foldMap _ []     = mempty
    foldMap f (x:xs) = f x 'mappend' foldMap f xs

    -- foldr :: (a -> b -> b) -> b -> [a] -> b
    foldr _ v []     = v
    foldr f v (x:xs) = f x (foldr f v xs)

    -- fold :: Monoid a => [a] -> a
    fold = foldMap id

    -- foldl :: (a -> b -> a) -> a -> [b] -> a
    foldl _ v []     = v
    foldl f v (x:xs) = foldl f (f v x) xs

    -- foldr1 :: (a -> a -> a) -> [a] -> a
    foldr1 _ [x]     = x
    foldr1 f (x:xs)  = f x (foldr1 f xs)

    -- foldl1 :: (a -> a -> a) -> [a] -> a
    foldl1 f (x:xs) = foldl f x xs

    -- toList :: [a] -> [a]
    toList = id
```

```
-- null :: [a] -> Bool
null []    = True
null (_:_) = False

-- length :: [a] -> Int
length = foldl (\n _ -> n+1) 0

-- elem :: Eq a => a -> [a] -> Bool
elem x xs = any (==x) xs

-- maximum :: Ord a => [a] -> a
maximum = foldl1 max

-- minimum :: Ord a => [a] -> a
minimum = foldl1 min

-- sum :: Num a => [a] -> a
sum = foldl (+) 0

-- product :: Num a => [a] -> a
product = foldl (*) 1
```

Decide if all logical values in a structure are True:

```
and :: Foldable t => t Bool -> Bool
and = getAll . foldMap All
```

Decide if any logical value in a structure is True:

```
or :: Foldable t => t Bool -> Bool
or = getAny . foldMap Any
```

Decide if all elements in a structure satisfy a predicate:

```
all :: Foldable t => (a -> Bool) -> t a -> Bool
all p = getAll . foldMap (All . p)
```

Decide if any element in a structure satisfies a predicate:

```
any :: Foldable t => (a -> Bool) -> t a -> Bool
any p = getAny . foldMap (Any . p)
```

Concatenate a structure whose elements are lists:

```
concat :: Foldable t => t [a] -> [a]
concat = fold
```

B.18   Traversables

Class declaration:

```
class (Functor t, Foldable t) => Traversable t where
    traverse  :: Applicative f => (a -> f b) -> t a -> f (t b)
    sequenceA :: Applicative f => t (f a) -> f (t a)

    mapM      :: Monad m => (a -> m b) -> t a -> m (t b)
    sequence  :: Monad m => t (m a) -> m (t a)
```

Default definitions:

```
traverse g = sequenceA . fmap g
sequenceA  = traverse id

mapM       = traverse
sequence   = sequenceA
```

The minimal complete definition for an instance of the class is to define **traverse**
or **sequenceA**, as all other functions in the class can be derived from either of
these two using the above default definitions.

Maybe traversable:

```
instance Traversable Maybe where
    -- traverse :: Applicative f =>
    --     (a -> f b) -> Maybe a -> f (Maybe b)
    traverse _ Nothing  = pure Nothing
    traverse g (Just x) = pure Just <*> g x
```

List traversable:

```
instance Traversable [] where
    -- traverse :: Applicative f => (a -> f b) -> [a] -> f [b]
    traverse _ []     = pure []
    traverse g (x:xs) = pure (:) <*> g x <*> traverse g xs
```

Bibliography

[1] P. Hudak, "Conception, Evolution and Application of Functional Programming Languages," *ACM Computing Surveys*, vol. 21, no. 3, 1989.

[2] P. Hudak, J. Hughes, S. Peyton Jones, and P. Wadler, "A History of Haskell: Being Lazy with Class," in *Proceedings of the Conference on History of Programming Languages*. ACM Press, 2007.

[3] P. Wadler, "Theorems for Free!" in *Proceedings of the International Conference on Functional Programming and Computer Architecture*. ACM Press, 1989.

[4] S. Marlow, Ed., *Haskell Language Report*, 2010, available on the web from: https://www.haskell.org/definition/haskell2010.pdf.

[5] M. P. Jones, "Typing Haskell in Haskell," in *Proceedings of the Haskell Workshop*. University of Utrecht, Technical Report UU-CS-1999-28, 1999.

[6] H. Barendregt, *The Lambda Calculus, Its Syntax and Semantics*. North Holland, 1985.

[7] S. Singh, *The Code Book: The Secret History of Codes and Code Breaking*. Fourth Estate, 2002.

[8] H. Glaser, P. Hartel, and P. Garratt, "Programming by Numbers: A Programming Method for Novices," *The Computer Journal*, vol. 43, no. 4, 2000.

[9] J. Gibbons and O. de Moor, Eds., *The Fun of Programming*. Palgrave, 2003.

[10] G. Hutton, "A Tutorial on the Universality and Expressiveness of Fold," *Journal of Functional Programming*, vol. 9, no. 4, 1999.

[11] G. Hutton and J. Wright, "Calculating an Exceptional Machine," in *Trends in Functional Programming Volume 5*. Intellect, 2006.

[12] G. Huet, "The Zipper," *Journal of Functional Programming*, vol. 7, no. 5, 1997.

[13] G. Hutton, "The Countdown Problem," *Journal of Functional Programming*, vol. 12, no. 6, 2002.

[14] R. Bird and S.-C. Mu, "Countdown: A Case Study in Origami Programming," *Journal of Functional Programming*, vol. 15, no. 5, 2005.

[15] S. Peyton Jones, "Tackling the Awkward Squad: Monadic Input/Output, Concurrency, Exceptions, and Foreign-Language Calls in Haskell," in *Engineering Theories of Software Construction*. IOS Press, 2001.

[16] D. E. Knuth and R. W. Moore, "An Analysis of Alpha-Beta Pruning," *Artificial Intelligence*, vol. 6, no. 4, 1975.

[17] S. Awodey, *Category Theory*. Oxford University Press, 2010.

[18] P. Wadler, "Monads for Functional Programming," in *Proceedings of the Marktoberdorf Summer School on Program Design Calculi*. Springer, 1992.

[19] C. McBride and R. Paterson, "Applicative Programming With Effects," *Journal of Functional Programming*, vol. 18, no. 1, 2008.

[20] G. Hutton and D. Fulger, "Reasoning About Effects: Seeing the Wood Through the Trees," in *Proceedings of Trends in Functional Programming*, 2008.

[21] G. Hutton and E. Meijer, "Monadic Parser Combinators," University of Nottingham, Technical Report NOTTCS-TR-96-4, 1996.

[22] ——, "Monadic Parsing in Haskell," *Journal of Functional Programming*, vol. 8, no. 4, 1998.

[23] V. Rayward-Smith, *A First Course in Formal Language Theory*. Blackwell Scientific Publications, 1983.

[24] D. Leijen, "Parsec: A Parsing Library for Haskell," available on the web from: https://hackage.haskell.org/package/parsec.

[25] A. Gill and S. Marlow, "Happy: A Parser Generator for Haskell," available on the web from: https://hackage.haskell.org/package/happy.

[26] D. Piponi, "Haskell Monoids and their Uses," 2009, available on the web from: http://tinyurl.com/piponi-monoids.

[27] E. Meijer, M. Fokkinga, and R. Paterson, "Functional Programming with Bananas, Lenses, Envelopes and Barbed Wire," in *Proceedings of the Conference on Functional Programming and Computer Architecture*. Springer, 1991.

[28] L. Meertens, "Calculate Polytypically!" in *Proceedings of the International Symposium on Programming Languages: Implementations, Logics, and Programs*. Springer, 1996.

[29] J. C. Reynolds, *Theories of Programming Languages*. Cambridge University Press, 1998.

[30] J. Hughes, "Why Functional Programming Matters," *The Computer Journal*, vol. 32, no. 2, 1989.

[31] J. Launchbury, "A Natural Semantics for Lazy Evaluation," in *Proceedings of the Symposium on Principles of Programming Languages*. ACM Press, 1993.

[32] S. Peyton Jones and D. Lester, *Implementing Functional Languages: A Tutorial*. Prentice Hall, 1992.

[33] N. Danielsson and P. Jansson, "Chasing Bottoms: A Case Study in Program Verification in the Presence of Partial and Infinite Values," in *Proceedings of the Conference on Mathematics of Program Construction*. Springer, 2004.

[34] J. Gibbons and G. Hutton, "Proof Methods for Corecursive Programs," *Fundamenta Informaticae*, vol. 66, no. 4, 2005.

[35] K. Claessen and J. Hughes, "QuickCheck: A Lightweight Tool for Random Testing of Haskell Programs," in *Proceedings of the International Conference on Functional Programming*, 2000.

[36] J. Gibbons and R. Hinze, "Just Do It: Simple Monadic Equational Reasoning," in *Proceedings of the International Conference on Functional Programming*, 2011.

[37] G. Hutton and J. Wright, "Compiling Exceptions Correctly," in *Proceedings of the Conference on Mathematics of Program Construction*. Springer, 2004.

[38] P. Wadler, "The Concatenate Vanishes," 1989, University of Glasgow.

[39] P. Bahr and G. Hutton, "Calculating Correct Compilers," *Journal of Functional Programming*, vol. 25, 2015.

[40] G. Hutton and P. Bahr, "Cutting Out Continuations," in *Proceedings of Wadler-Fest, A List of Successes That Can Change the World*. Springer, 2016.

Index